S0-BBM-730

OXFORD THEOLOGICAL MONOGRAPHS

Editorial Committee

H. CHADWICK	F. W. DILLISTONE
F. L. CROSS	S. L. GREENSLADE
V. A. DEMANT	J. MARSH

H. F. D. SPARKS

Oxford Theological Monographs

CANONS OF THE COUNCIL OF SARDICA
A.D. 343
A Landmark in the Early Development of Canon Law
By HAMILTON HESS. 1958

THE LAW AND THE GOSPEL IN LUTHER
A Study of Martin Luther's Confessional Writings
By THOMAS M. MCDONOUGH. 1963

THE NEW TEMPLE

The Church in the New Testament

BY

R. J. McKELVEY

OXFORD UNIVERSITY PRESS

1969

Oxford University Press, Ely House, London W. 1

GLASGOW NEW YORK TORONTO MELBOURNE WELLINGTON
CAPE TOWN SALISBURY IBADAN NAIROBI LUSAKA ADDIS ABABA
BOMBAY CALCUTTA MADRAS KARACHI LAHORE DACCA
KUALA LUMPUR SINGAPORE HONG KONG TOKYO

© OXFORD UNIVERSITY PRESS 1969

PRINTED IN GREAT BRITAIN

BV
597
M3

TO MY
MOTHER AND FATHER

PREFACE

IN recent times attention has been drawn to the number and variety of images used for the church in the New Testament.[1] This is to be welcomed. For too long certain images have dominated thinking on the church to the neglect of others. To think of the church is for many people to think of the body of Christ. But the body is only one of a whole series of images, all of which have to be kept in mind if one is to arrive at anything like a satisfactory understanding of the New Testament doctrine of the church.[2]

This book seeks to draw attention to one of the neglected images of the church in the New Testament, namely, the church as God's new temple. Apart from Père Yves Congar's book, *The Mystery of the Temple* (1961), which is more of a general study, I know of no treatment of the subject.[3] A. Causse showed the importance of the temple in the eschatology of the Old Testament,[4] and Sundkler[5] and Jeremias[6] have found the eschatological role of Jerusalem in the Old Testament helpful for understanding the ministry of Jesus.[7] A study of the subject has been made all the more urgent by the discovery of the Dead Sea Scrolls. Gärtner has shown what valuable light the scrolls have to shed on the teaching of the epistles on the church as a spiritual temple.[8] The reason why the subject should have been neglected is not easy to determine. The temple image in the New

---

[1] P. S. Minear, *Images of the Church in the New Testament* (1960).

[2] Minear writes: 'The church must perennially open its imagination to the wide panorama of New Testament imagery and especially to those images which have temporarily lost their potency' (ibid., p. 25).

[3] The following studies are concerned with the dynamic character of the church as the body of Christ: P. Vielhauer, *Oikodome: Das Bild vom Bau in der christlichen Literatur vom Neuen Testament bis Clemens Alexandrinus* (1939); P. Bonnard, *Jésus-Christ édifiant son Église* (1948); J. Pfammatter, *Die Kirche als Bau. Eine exegetisch-theologische Studie zur Ekklesiologie der Paulusbriefe* (1961).

[4] See the bibliography.

[5] B. Sundkler, 'Jésus et les païens', *RHPR* 16 (1936), 462–99.

[6] J. Jeremias, *Jesus' Promise to the Nations* (1958).

[7] The theme has also been used to explain the missionary strategy of Paul cf. J. Munck, *Paul and the Salvation of Mankind* (1959), pp. 247 ff.

[8] B. Gärtner, *The Temple and the Community in Qumran and the New Testament* (1965).

Testament has a long and significant ancestry. Moreover, the idea of the divine presence is central to the eschatology of the Old Testament and the intertestamental literature. Eschatology could and often did exist without the figure of a Messiah but never without the thought of God's dwelling in the midst of his people.

The new temple of Ezekiel 40–8 is properly speaking our *point de départ*, but I felt it necessary to devote the first chapter to the significance of the temple for the people of the Ancient Near East. The succeeding three chapters examine the different ways in which the conception of the divine presence was developed in Israel. They show how the hope of the new temple arose and persisted and was connected with the doctrine of a heavenly temple on the one hand and a spiritual temple on the other hand. Although eschatology, and not history, is our chief concern attention is paid to the latter inasmuch as history shapes eschatology. The fortunes of the second temple of Jerusalem are therefore traced in these and succeeding chapters. Chapters V–XI seek to show how the hope of a new temple is fulfilled in Jesus and his church.

English quotations from the Bible and the Apocrypha are from the Revised Standard Version but where a different rendering is followed it is, unless otherwise indicated, my own. I have used Charles's edition of the Pseudepigrapha, Danby's translation of the Mishnah, Singer's edition of the Jewish Prayer Book, and the Soncino edition of the Babylonian Talmud. Quotations from Philo and the classical authors are from the Loeb edition.

This book grew out of a thesis for a doctorate in the University of Oxford. My thanks are therefore specially due to my supervisor, the Revd. Dr. A. M. Farrer, who gave me so generously of his time and learning. I take this opportunity to record my debt to my college principals, the late Revd. Dr. Maurice Charles who gave me much encouragement, and to the Revd. Dr. John Marsh for his interest and guidance in many matters. I am also grateful to Professors F. F. Bruce, G. B. Caird, and D. Daube, Dr. E. Best, and the Revd. C. E. B. Cranfield who read parts of the manuscript and made important criticisms, and to Professor Moule and the members of his New Testament seminar at Cambridge who very kindly considered some of the problems I encountered in regard to the Epistle to the Hebrews. In the preparation of the manuscript for publication I received valuable

assistance from my colleagues at the Federal Seminary, Miss
G. M. H. Darroll and the Revd. Fr. M. Tweedy, C.R., which it
would be ungracious of me not to acknowledge. I should also
like to thank the Committee for Advanced Studies and the
Delegates of the Press in the University of Oxford for publishing
this volume. Finally, to my wife and three small children who
patiently bore with me during the years this book was being
written I express appreciation and gratitude.

R. J. McKELVEY

Adams United College
The Federal Theological Seminary of Southern Africa
Cape Province
Alice
Republic of South Africa

ACKNOWLEDGEMENTS

ACKNOWLEDGEMENT is due to the following for permission to quote from copyright material:

Basil Blackwell (A. Dupont-Sommer, *The Essene Writings from Qumran*); E. J. Brill (J. Strugnell, 'The Angelic Liturgy at Qumrân'— *4Q serek šîrôt 'ôlat haššabāt, VT Suppl. VII*; P. Wernberg-Møller, *The Manual of Discipline, Translated and Annotated with an Introduction*); Cambridge University Press (E. E. Ellis, 'II Corinthians 5. 1–10 in Pauline Eschatology', *NTS* 6; R. J. McKelvey, 'Christ the Cornerstone', *NTS* 8); The Clarendon Press (R. H. Charles, ed., *The Pseudepigrapha*; H. Danby, *The Mishnah*); Darton, Longman & Todd and Doubleday & Co. Ltd; Loeb Classical Library: Heinemann Educational Books and Harvard University Press (F. H. Colson and G. H. Whitaker, *Philo*; L. H. Feldman, R. Marcus, H. St. J. Thackeray, *Josephus*; R. M. Gummere, *Seneca*; W. A. Oldfather, *Epictetus*; P. Shorey, *Plato*); National Council of the Churches of Christ in the U.S.A. (*Revised Standard Version* of the Bible and Apocrypha); Martin Secker & Warburg Ltd. (T. H. Gaster, *The Scriptures of the Dead Sea Sect*); Soncino Press Ltd. (I. Epstein, *The Babylonian Talmud Translated into English* (ed.)); S.P.C.K. (A. Corell, *Consummatum Est*); United Synagogue, London (S. Singer, *The Authorized Daily Prayer Book of the United Hebrew Congregation of the British Empire* (ed.)).

CONTENTS

ABBREVIATIONS

I. THE TEMPLE IN THE OLD TESTAMENT   I
     The Significance of the Temple in the Ancient Near East   I
     The Temple of Jerusalem   3
     The Destruction of the Temple of Jerusalem   6
     Summary   7

II. THE NEW TEMPLE IN JEWISH LITERATURE   9
     The Old Testament   9
     The Apocrypha and Pseudepigrapha   15
     The Rabbis   20
     Summary   22

III. THE HEAVENLY TEMPLE IN JEWISH AND GREEK
     LITERATURE   25
     The Transcendentalizing of the Divine Presence   25
     The Pseudepigrapha   28
     The Rabbis   34
     The Dead Sea Scrolls   36
     Plato and Philo   38
     Summary   40

IV. THE SPIRITUAL TEMPLE IN JEWISH AND GREEK
     LITERATURE   42
     The Spiritualizing of the Cultus in Jewish Writings   43
     Community as Temple   46
     Man as Temple   53
     Summary   55

V. JESUS AND THE TEMPLE 58

The Synoptic Gospels 58

Summary 74

VI. FROM OLD TEMPLE TO NEW 75

The Fourth Gospel 75

Summary 83

The Acts of the Apostles 84

Summary 91

VII. THE NEW TEMPLE IN THE EPISTLES OF PAUL 92

2 Corinthians 6. 16–7. 1 93

1 Corinthians 3. 16–17 98

1 Corinthians 6. 19–20 102

Summary 106

VIII. THE NEW TEMPLE IN THE EPISTLES OF PAUL
(*continued*) 108

Ephesians 2. 20–2 108

Summary 123

IX. THE NEW TEMPLE IN I PETER AND MISCEL-
LANEOUS TEXTS 125

1 Peter 125

Miscellaneous Texts 132

Summary 138

X. THE HEAVENLY TEMPLE IN THE NEW TESTAMENT 140

Miscellaneous Texts 140

The Epistle to the Hebrews 147

The Book of Revelation 155

Summary 176

XI. CONCLUSION 179

CONTENTS

APPENDIX A. THE FOUNDATION STONE IN ZION   188

APPENDIX B. UPON THIS ROCK   193

APPENDIX C. CHRIST THE CORNERSTONE   195

APPENDIX D. THE TRUE SANCTUARY OF HEBREWS
    AND THE HEAVENLY CITY OF PLATO   205

BIBLIOGRAPHY   207

INDEXES   217

ABBREVIATIONS

AJSL	*American Journal of Semitic Languages and Literature* (Chicago)
Ang.	*Angelos* (Leipzig)
Ap. Mos.	Apocalypse of Moses
Apoc. Abr.	Apocalypse of Abraham
Arist.	*Letter of Aristeas*
ASHL	*Acta Reg. Societatis Humaniorum Litterarum* (Lund)
Ass. Mos.	Assumption of Moses
B.	The Babylonian version of the Talmud
BA	*Biblical Archeologist* (New Haven)
BASOR	*Bulletin of the American Schools of Oriental Research* (New Haven)
B.B.	Baba Bathra
Ben.	Benediction
Ber.	Berakhoth
Bet. ha-Midr.	Bet. ha-Midrash
BJRL	*Bulletin of the John Rylands Library* (Manchester)
BSNTS	*Bulletin of Studiorum Novi Testamenti Societas* (Cambridge)
BZ	*Biblische Zeitschrift* (Paderborn)
CBQ	*Catholic Biblical Quarterly* (Washington)
CD	Cairo Genizah Document of Damascus
Cic.	Cicero
CN	*Coniectanea Neotestamentica* (Uppsala)
CO	*Joannis Calvini Opera, Corpus Reformatorum*
CR	*Corpus Reformatorum*
CRev.	*The Classical Review* (Oxford)
DCG	*A Dictionary of Christ and the Gospels*, ed. J. Hastings, T. & T. Clark (Edinburgh)
EGT	*Expositor's Greek Testament*
'Er.	'Erubin
ET	*Expository Times* (Edinburgh)
ETL	*Ephremerides Theologicae Lovanienses*
EVV	English versions (Authorized, Revised, Revised Standard versions, New English Bible)
Exp.	*The Expositor* (London)
Gen. R.	Genesis Rabbah
Hag.	Hagigah
HDB	*Hastings's Dictionary of the Bible* (Edinburgh)
HE	*Historia Ecclesiastica*
HTR	*Harvard Theological Review* (Cambridge, Mass.)
HUCA	*Hebrew Union College Annual* (Cincinnati)
IB	*Interpreter's Bible* (New York)

Ign.	Ignatius
Inst.	Institutes
Isoc.	Isocrates
JB	Jerusalem Bible
JBL	*Journal of Biblical Literature* (Philadelphia)
JE	*Jewish Encyclopaedia* (New York and London)
JEH	*Journal of Ecclesiastical History* (London)
Jos.	Josephus
JRS	*Journal of Roman Studies* (London)
JRSR	*Journal de recherches de science religieuse* (Paris)
JSS	*Journal of Semitic Studies* (Manchester)
JTS	*Journal of Theological Studies* (Oxford)
Kel.	Kelim
Keth.	Kethuboth
Ḳid.	Ḳiddushin
Lev. R.	Leviticus Rabbah
M.	Mishnah
Mak.	Makkoth
Meg.	Megillah
Mekl.	Mekilta
Men.	Menaḥoth
MGWJ	*Monatsschrift für Geschichte und Wissenschaft des Judentums* (Breslau)
Mid.	Middoth
Midr.	Midrash
M–M	J. H. Moulton and G. Milligan. See *VGT*
MS	Medieval Studies (Toronto)
NEB	New English Bible
NKZ	*Neue kirchliche Zeitschrift* (Erlangen)
NT	*Novum Testamentum* (Leiden)
NTS	*New Testament Studies* (Cambridge)
Nu. R.	Numbers Rabbah
OS	*Oudtestamentische Studiën* (Leiden)
P.	Palestinian version of the Talmud
par.	parallel
pars.	parallels
PEQ	*Palestine Exploration Quarterly* (London)
Pes.	Pesaḥim
PG	*Patrologia Graeca*
Pl.	Plato
PL	*Patrologia Latina*
PRE	*Pirkê de Rabbi Eliezer*
Pss. Sol.	Psalms of Solomon
QE	*Questions and Answers on Exodus*
1 Q	1st Qumran cave
1 QH	Hymns
1 QHab.	Habakkuk commentary
1 QM	Rule of War

1 QS	Manual of Discipline
1 QSa	Additional two columns of 1 QS
1 QSb	Additional columns of 1 QS (Blessings)
4 Q Flor.	Florilegium
4 Q PB	Patriarchal Blessings
4 QpIsa^d	Commentary on Isaiah, fourth copy
4 Q TLevi	Testament of Levi, copy found at Qumran
RB	*Revue Biblique* (Paris)
REJ	*Revue des études juives* (Paris)
R.H.	Rosh Hashanah
RHPR	*Revue d'histoire et de philosophie religieuses* (Paris)
RSPT	*Revue des sciences philosophiques et théologiques* (Paris)
RSR	*Recherches de science religieuse* (Paris)
RSV	*Revised Standard Version*
RT	*Revue thomiste* (Paris)
Sanh.	Sanhedrin
S–B	Strack, H. L. and Billerbeck, P., *Kommentar zum Neuen Testament aus Talmud und Midrasch*
SH	*Scripta Hierosolymitana* (Jerusalem)
Shab.	Shabbath
Shek.	Shekalim
Sib. Or.	Sibylline Oracles
SJT	*Scottish Journal of Theology* (Edinburgh)
Slav. En.	*Slavonic Enoch*
Sol.	Solomon
ST	*Studia Theologica* (Lund)
Suk.	Sukkah
Ta'an.	Ta'annith
TDNT	*Theological Dictionary of the New Testament*, English translation of *TWNT*
Test. Sol.	Testament of Solomon
Theod.	Theodotion's Greek Old Testament
Tos.	Tosefta
TS	*Theological Studies* (Baltimore)
TWNT	*Theologisches Wörterbuch zum Neuen Testament*
TZ	*Theologische Zeitschrift* (Basle)
VAA	*Verhandelingen der Koninklijke Akademie van Wetenschappen te Amsterdam*
VD	*Verbum Domini* (Rome)
VGT	*Vocabulary of the Greek Testament*
VT	*Vetus Testamentum* (Leiden)
Yeb.	Yebamoth
Zeb.	Zebahim
ZHB	*Zeitschrift für hebraische Bibliographie* (Frankfurt)
ZTK	*Zeitschrift für Theologie und Kirche* (Tübingen)
ZNW	*Zeitschrift für neutestamentliche Wissenschaft* (Berlin)

I

THE TEMPLE IN THE OLD TESTAMENT

The Significance of the Temple in the Ancient Near East

RELIGION has always had its holy places since it is of the essence of religion to express itself in tangible institutions. But where the significance of the sanctuary or temple for the ancients is concerned the modern mind encounters considerable difficulty. The difficulty lies chiefly in the fact that in contrast to our diverse and atomistic society ancient society was homogeneous. The most notable expression of its unity was the temple or holy place. The community in question might be large, as in Egypt or Babylon, or small, as in Palestine or Syria where geographical continuity and cohesion were lacking, but always the sanctuary was the focal point. It was there that the god dwelt in the midst of his people, there that the community realized its unity with the deity and within itself and with its ancestors, there that it centred its covenants, its laws, its organization, its history, its hopes and sentiment, there that it imbibed the holiness and power without which it would disintegrate.

The temple impinged upon the life of the community at practically every point.[1] In addition to providing holiness for the nation, it fostered learning and played an important role in the preservation and transmission of tribal and national traditions. Connected with the temple were innumerable buildings and extensive holdings of land. There were lodgings for the priesthood and servants, stores, kitchens, refectories, kraals, and abattoirs, not to speak of the various offices where the numerous officials administered the business of the cult. Temple estates produced food for the priests and raised flocks and herds to

---

[1] G. E. Wright and others, 'The Significance of the Temple in the Ancient Near East', *BA* 7 (1944), 41–88 (= *The Biblical Archaeologist Reader*, ed. G. E. Wright and D. N. Freedman (1961), pp. 145–84); H. Frankfort, *Kingship and the Gods* (1948), pp. 221 ff.; *Before Philosophy* (ed.) (1949), pp. 200 ff.

ensure an adequate supply of sacrifices. In Egypt and Meso-potamia temples amassed considerable wealth through royal en-dowments and taxation of the people, and frequently temples acted as banks where the nation deposited its wealth and treasures for safe keeping. One can readily imagine how such a thriving and comprehensive institution as the temple dictated the pattern of culture and influenced the whole social and economic struc-ture of the nation. The outstanding example in this respect is Babylon, which was a temple-state.

In the light of the foregoing it is not difficult to understand why the temple was looked upon as the source of life and well-being for the community and, indeed, the universe. The Israelites and their neighbours referred to the temple as the 'navel of the earth'.[1] Since the sanctuary was invariably erected on high ground it was naturally believed to be the first thing to have been created.[2] The royal temple of Marduk was said to be built upon the 'bosom of the earth', and the ziggurat to the famous god of Nippur bore the inscription 'bond of heaven and earth'.[3] The significance of such cosmological designations is obvious. What they are saying in one way or another is that the whole created order owes its existence to the temple. Thus, as we shall see, in the end-time the river of life is depicted as flowing from Jerusalem.

While the temple occupied the same place of central impor-tance for Israel which it occupied for other Near Eastern peoples, it did not do so for the same reason or to the same degree. The distinction, which must always be made, lay in the unique character of Yahwism. The historical and transcendental nature of Israelite religion prevented its holy places from being regarded simply as a means of maintaining a harmonious relation between man and nature. The divine indwelling in Israel was bound up with the covenant, i.e. it had to do with grace. Far from Yah-weh's depending upon the cult, the cult was his gift to Israel, his way of accommodating himself to his people's creaturely capacity, so to speak, in order that they might receive his blessings.

---

[1] See at length Appendix A.

[2] Frankfort, *Kingship and the Gods*, p. 152.

[3] F. Jeremias, 'Das orientalische Heiligtum', *Ang.* 4 (1932), 63; E. Burrows, 'Some Cosmological Patterns in Babylonian Religion', *The Labyrinth*, ed. S. H. Hooke (1935), pp. 47 ff.

The Temple of Jerusalem

The focal and unifying role of the sanctuary in Israel is seen right from the beginning of the nation's history. The ancient ark, whatever its origin, was in truth the ark of the covenant. Popularly regarded as the actual dwelling of the invisible deity who personally headed the sacred amphictyony (Num. 10. 35 f.; 2 Sam. 15. 25), it welded the different tribes together in the service of the one God.[1] The same is true of the tent of meeting. As its name (אהל מועד) implies,[2] it unified the Israelite host (e.g. Exod. 33. 8, 10). Whatever the actual relation of the ark and the tent in the Mosaic period, it is clear that the one or the other, or the one and afterwards the other, constituted the rallying-point of the tribal league (Num. 10. 33–6; 14. 14, 44).[3] The unity of the tribes was based on common worship at a common sanctuary.[4] Whether there were in fact twelve tribes from the beginning need not concern us here. What is important is the undisputed fact that the ancient desert sanctuary united and held together the various tribes which came out of Egypt. The tabernacle of the priestly tradition, which is represented as stationed at the centre of the Israelite host, and made and appointed in such a way that it is the tangible symbol of the unity and cohesion of the people of God, is a development quite in the spirit of history.[5]

The sanctuaries of Palestine which Israel appropriated and put to the service of historic Yahwism greatly influenced the life and worship of the various tribes and families.[6] Shiloh, where the ark eventually found a home (1 Sam. 1–4. 3), was the leading sanctuary of the confederacy (Josh. 18. 1; Judg. 18. 31; 1 Sam. 1. 3). The presence of the ark at the central sanctuary fostered the natural centripetal tendencies of Yahwism and was of decisive importance in moulding Israel's cultic traditions.

The unique role of the sanctuary in the national life was

---

[1] Cf. H. G. May, 'The Ark—A Miniature Temple', *AJSL* 52 (1936), 215–34; and (earlier) W. R. Arnold, *Ephod and Ark* (1917), p. 133.

[2] i.e. tent of reunion, or of meeting (cf. e.g. F. M. Cross, 'The Priestly Tabernacle', *BA* 10 (1947), 65 ff. = *The Biblical Archaeologist Reader*, pp. 223 ff.).

[3] It is noteworthy that while the oldest tradition mentions the tent (Exod. 33. 7–11) and the ark (Num. 10. 33–4; 14. 44) it never connects them. Cf. the discussion by R. E. Clements, *God and Temple* (1965), pp. 35 ff.

[4] M. Noth, *Das System der zwölf Stämme Israels* (1930).

[5] On the sanctuary in the priestly tradition see below.

[6] Cf. e.g. H.-J. Kraus, *Worship in Israel* (1966), pp. 125 ff.

undoubtedly one of the reasons why David had the ark transferred to Jerusalem when he made the city his capital. The action was of incalculable significance.[1] Jerusalem now became the amphictyonic centre and heir of Israel's historic traditions. These traditions were taken over by the temple of Jerusalem when it was built, and when the ark was installed there. Although the temple began as one sanctuary among many others and was to some extent the palace chapel, the presence of the ark soon made it the central sanctuary in Israel.

In time the attempt was made to establish Jerusalem not only as the central sanctuary of the nation but as the one and only sanctuary. Influenced by the teaching of the prophets (Jer. 26. 18 f.), King Hezekiah closed the rural sanctuaries, cleansed the Jerusalem worship, and sought to persuade the people of the now defunct northern state to worship at Jerusalem (2 Kgs. 18. 3–6; 2 Chr. 29–31). The attempt came to little: Manasseh, the successor to Hezekiah, rebuilt the high places (2 Kgs. 21. 1 ff.). Yet the ideal remained. A century later (622 B.C.) a similar and more thoroughgoing reform was undertaken by Josiah (2 Kgs. 22. 3–23. 25). The basis of this reform was 'the book of the law', which was probably some form of the book of Deuteronomy. This document sternly reminded Israel of her obligations to the covenant of Sinai and essayed to revive (in a form suited to the times) the old amphictyonic order under a single sanctuary. Outlying sanctuaries were closed, and the temple was cleansed of idolatrous practices and established by law as the one legitimate place of worship (cf. Deut. 12). But the hope of a united people with Jerusalem as its centre was short lived. Josiah died in 609, and the land was once again overrun by foreign powers, who confined the royal rule to Judah. Nevertheless the religious gains of the reform were not wholly lost. Jerusalem was now firmly established as the centre of true Yahwism for the whole of Israel.

The unique position that the temple of Jerusalem came to enjoy was also due in no small way to its cult. The centralization of worship made it possible to fix the time of assemblies for the nation as a whole, whereas previously festivals had been held according to the harvest-times of the different parts of the country.

---

[1] Cf. M. Noth, 'Jerusalem und die israelitische Tradition', *OS* 8 (1950), 28–46 (= *The Laws in the Pentateuch* (1960), pp. 132–44.)

The result was that the festivals now acquired national significance. They assembled, at any rate representatively, the whole
of the nation.[1] This fact is well illustrated by the practice of
timing synagogue services to coincide with the temple services
(B. Ber 26b; J. Ber 4. i. 7b), the participation of representatives
of the dispersion in the temple worship (M Ta'an 4. 2), and the
custom of sending letters of convocation to the dispersion (2
Macc. 1–2). The temple worship was thus a powerful factor
assisting in the creation of unity in Israel.

The annual pilgrimages to Jerusalem became occasions of
great sentiment. The journey to Zion was the chief joy of life
(Isa. 30. 29; 35. 10; Pss. 42. 1 ff.; 43. 3 f.; 122. 1 ff.; 137. 6).

> How lovely is thy dwelling place,
> O Lord of hosts!
> My soul longs, yea, faints
> for the courts of the Lord;
> my heart and flesh sing for joy
> to the living God (Ps. 84. 1–2).

One must go to Jerusalem because that is where God is. To be
away from the temple is to be away from God (Ps. 137. 4; cf.
1 Sam. 26. 19; Ezek. 11. 15; Jonah 2. 4); to go up to the temple
is to go up to God (Pss. 42. 2; 63. 2; 65. 1 f., etc.). A single day
spent in the sanctuary is worth more than a thousand elsewhere
(Ps. 84. 10).

Jerusalem was never so truly the city of God as at festival time
(Isa. 30. 29; 33. 20; 35. 10; 65. 19; Zech. 8. 19; Pss. 48. 12–14;
122. 3–9). Israel, also, was never so truly the people of God, the
people of the covenant, as at festival time. The mighty acts of
God were told and retold, infusing into the worshippers a consciousness of their unity, and evoking pride in their history and
hope for the future. These assemblies expressed a great deal more
than a sense of natural solidarity of blood and soil. They were
above all occasions when the covenant was recalled and renewed
(Deut. 6. 20–5; 26. 5–11; cf. Josh. 24. 2–13). The cult was a
dynamic expression of the unity of the participants and their
oneness with those who personally covenanted with Yahweh
at Sinai.

---

[1] G. F. Moore, *Judaism* (1927–30), ii. 12; Y. M. J. Congar, *The Mystery of the Temple* (1958), p. 88.

This concentration of worship and sentiment at Jerusalem helped to create a theology of Jerusalem. The city was included within the idea of election: as God had chosen David so he had also chosen Zion (Ps. 132. 11–14; cf. 2 Sam. 7. 12–16). The divine election of Jerusalem took precedence over the political and strategic considerations for David's choice of the city, and it became one of the principal themes of the cult, with earlier history treated as largely ancillary.

All this had the effect of raising Jerusalem and its temple to a level of supra-historical importance. It was not enough that David should have instructed his son to build the temple and provided him with the plans and materials for its erection; the idea came from God himself, who revealed the pattern to Israel as far back as the time of Moses; and the tabernacle, the archetype of the temple, had been Israel's place of worship from the beginning. It was not enough that the temple should have been built upon the rock at which the father of Israel had demonstrated his obedience: its foundation belonged to creation itself, and, lifted high above the vicissitudes of time, would last for ever (Pss. 78. 69; 93. 2 ff.; 125. 1; cf. Isa. 2. 2; Mic. 4. 1).[1] Nor did it suffice to believe that the temple was the place where Yahweh revealed his will to Israel and commanded his blessing to go forth upon Palestine; the destinies of the nations were also decided there (Amos 1. 2 ff.; Pss. 47. 8; 82; 99. 1 f.); the well-being of the whole earth depended upon him who controlled the great deep from his throne in Zion (Pss. 29. 10; 46. 1 ff.; 93. 1 ff.). Thus, as we shall see, Jerusalem became the type of the final and universal salvation of the eschatological age, the symbol of the unity not only of Israel but of mankind (Isa. 2. 2–4; Mic. 4. 1–3; Zech. 14. 16 ff.).[2]

The Destruction of the Temple of Jerusalem

The destruction of the temple of Jerusalem in 587 B.C. by the pagan king Nebuchadnezzar (2 Kgs. 25. 1 ff.; Jer. 39. 1–8; 52. 4 ff.) was in the truest sense a catastrophe of the first order. It is no accident that the literature in question should reveal a preoccupation with the event. The ruin of Jerusalem, the cessation

[1] J. Pedersen, *Israel* (1940), iii–iv. 262 f.
[2] Cf. N. W. Porteous, 'Jerusalem–Zion: The Growth of a Symbol', *Verbannung und Heimkehr*, ed. A. Kuschke, 1961, pp. 235–52.

of statehood, and the deportation of the best of the population were grievous enough; but they were not to be compared with the destruction of the temple. For the latter created a theological problem. The loss of the temple meant nothing less than the loss of God's presence (Ezek. 9. 3; 10. 4–5; 11. 23; cf. 1 Sam. 4. 21 f.). And with God no longer in the midst of his people only further misfortune could be expected. The belief that God had to all intents and purposes cast off his people was the bitter dregs of the cup Israel had to drink (Jer. 14. 19; Lam. 1–2; 5. 22; Isa. 49. 14; 54. 6–8).

However painful it was for the inhabitants of Palestine to look at the ruins of their beloved temple, it was their brethren of the exile who felt the loss most keenly. Scattered throughout Babylonia, Egypt, and other foreign lands, they saw no hope of fulfilling their divinely appointed destiny (Ps. 137. 1–6). Indeed, to some at least it seemed that Israel had no future at all (Isa. 40. 27). Exile in pagan lands intensified the sense of deprivation, and made a burning issue of the meaning of God's presence at Jerusalem and the worship offered to him there. Substitute temples were built at Elephantine and Leontopolis, and synagogues sprang up in many places, but nothing could take the place of the temple. The spiritual desolation felt by the Jews of the dispersion is poignantly expressed in the 137th Psalm:

> How shall we sing the Lord's song
>   in a foreign land?
> If I forget you, O Jerusalem,
>   let my right hand wither!
> Let my tongue cleave to the roof
>   of my mouth,
>   if I do not remember you,
> if I do not set Jerusalem
>   above my highest joy!
>   (vv. 4–6)

It was to such disconsolate spirits that the new temple became the symbol of hope.

Summary

The conclusion of this introductory survey is that the temple of Jerusalem was the focal and unifying point of Israelite life, and that the destruction of the temple meant the break-up of unity in Israel.

In the light of this thesis we proceed to consider the hope of a new temple in the exilic, post-exilic, and intertestamental writings.

II

THE NEW TEMPLE IN JEWISH LITERATURE[1]

The Old Testament

THAT Israel was able to survive the test of faith brought on by the destruction of the temple of Jerusalem and the break-up of the nation was due largely to the fact that the prophets had prepared people in advance. Preaching a message, which to their countrymen seemed not only grossly unpatriotic and defeatist but also irreligious, these men had declared that the nation was not living as it ought and that it would incur the judgement of God. History vindicated their message as the word of God. As the nation reflected upon this and threw itself upon the mercy of God, hope was born. For the word of God through the prophets had not only been a word of judgement but also of forgiveness and restoration. A remnant would be spared, from which the nation would again grow (Isa. 4. 2–4, etc.; Jer. 23. 5 f.), the outcasts of Israel would be gathered home (Isa. 11. 11 ff.; 27. 13; Jer. 31. 6 ff.; Ezek. 20. 40 ff.; 34. 11 ff.), and the temple would be restored and become the centre not only of Israel but of the nations (Isa. 2. 2–4; Mic. 4. 1–3; Jer. 3. 17 f.). These occasional shafts of hope which penetrate the otherwise dark picture of pre-exilic prophecy heralded the bright future predicted by the later prophets.

In Ezekiel 40–8 the hope takes the novel form of an architect's drawing. The plan of the new temple shown to the prophet is revolutionary. Previously the temple was part of the royal complex. Such an arrangement had confused Israel as to her true destiny and resulted in disaster (43. 7–9). The new temple is therefore set apart from the city and made the unmistakable centre of the nation. This is made clear from the geographical and architectural details of the plan.[2]

[1] For the present we use the word 'new' in the sense of 'renewed' rather than 'different' (cf. Pss. 51. 10; 103. 5; 104. 30; Lam. 5. 21).

[2] We use the term 'plan' in a broad sense. It is not easy to say whether the prophet has an actual blue print in mind or simply an ideal.

The temple is situated at the centre of a series of concentric squares or zones. Next to it is the sacred reserve, which is for the priests (45. 3–4), then to the north and south is the land apportioned to the twelve tribes (48. 1 ff.) and to the east and west the land occupied by the prince (48. 21–2; cf. 45. 7–8). The temple itself repeats the idea. It is four-square (42. 15–20), and comprises an outer and an inner court. In the inner court is the holy place and the holy of holies, each perfect in length and breadth (41. 3–4, 13–14). The entire plan is a unit, governed by the sanctuary.[1]

The meaning of the plan is not difficult to discern. The new temple is the symbol of the new people of God. The symmetry and unity of its plan represent the unity and cohesion of the twelve-fold Israel. To this ideal community the *kĕbhôdh-Yahweh* will return and there remain for ever (43. 1 ff.).

A similar plan of a temple-centred community is presented by the priestly writers. There is this difference though: whereas Ezekiel projected his plan into the future, these writers retrojected their ideal into the past. Their ultimate aim, however, is the same. By expressing what to their mind was the essential meaning of Israel's history, the priests of the exile hoped to guide the nation in planning its new temple and community.[2]

For our purpose it is not necessary to attempt to disentangle the various strands in which the description of the tabernacle has come down to us, or to iron out the difficulties long recognized in the details of its construction and appointment. We are concerned simply with the symbolism of the tabernacle in its final form.

The tabernacle is a rectangle of 100 cubits by 50, which forms two squares. The first square is the outer or people's court (Exod. 27. 9–19; cf. 38. 9 ff.). At its centre stands the altar, also a square (27. 1–8; cf. 38. 1–7). The second square houses the

[1] Ezekiel's new city reveals the same symmetrical design. It is a square (48. 15 ff.), and has twelve gates, three on each side with the name of a tribe engraved on each (48. 30–5). The sacred reserve on which both temple and city stand, moreover, shares the same ideal proportions: it is a square of 25,000 cubits. Similarly, the land to the north and south of the sacred reserve is divided equally among the twelve tribes (48. 1 ff.), even if the southerly aspect of Jerusalem made it necessary to station the tribes disproportionately, seven to the north and five to the south.

[2] For the use made of existing traditions and their reinterpretation by the priestly writers see G. von Rad, 'Zelt und Lade', *NKZ* 42 (1931), 476–98.

sanctuary proper, which is positioned in such a way that the ark, its focal point, is at its centre. The sanctuary itself repeats the symmetry, a thick, heavily embroidered veil dividing it into two equal parts: the holy place and the holy of holies (26. 31–5; cf. 36. 35–8). In the holy of holies is the centre-piece of everything, the ark of the covenant (25. 10–22; 37. 1–9).

Like Ezekiel, the priestly architects extend their symbolism beyond the confines of the sanctuary for the purpose of showing that the life of the entire nation is determined by the divine indwelling. Here, however, they are at an advantage over Ezekiel. Bound in no way by the geographical and topographical restraints which obliged Ezekiel to produce a plan which was neither practicable nor tolerable, these writers give full rein to their idea of the twelve-fold Israel 'encamping tribe by tribe' (Num. 24. 2). The tribes are stationed on all four sides of the dwelling (Num. 2). Each tribe is thus within equal distance of the tabernacle, and the tabernacle is at the centre of the nation. The meaning of this symbolism is the same as that of Ezekiel: the sanctuary is the central and unifying factor of Israelite life.

In marked contrast to the architectural symbolism of Ezekiel and the priestly writers we have the hope of a restored people worshipping God at a new and magnificent temple and city expressed in more familiar language in Deutero-Isaiah and the later prophets.[1]

Deutero-Isaiah pictures the exiles streaming home from many lands (40. 11; 41. 17 ff.; 43. 5 f.; etc.). The new Jerusalem, her boundaries greatly extended to accommodate her increased population (49. 19 ff.; 54. 1–3), will be a city of surpassing beauty (54. 11–12; 60. 13–18).[2] Not only so. The new temple will be 'a house of prayer for all peoples' (56. 7). The experience of

---

[1] These writers frequently use 'Zion' and 'Jerusalem' as synonyms, notwithstanding the fact that the Mount was geographically separate from the city (Isa. 1. 26 f.; 60. 14; cf. Ps. 48. 2). The temple is often identified with Zion (Jer. 50. 28; 51. 10 f.), and the biblical writers can easily say that God dwells in Zion (Isa. 8. 18; Jer. 8. 19; Zech. 8. 3; Ps. 2. 6; 9. 11, etc.). The term Zion thereby acquired a strong religious connotation which made it more than simply a synonym for Jerusalem (M. Schmidt, *Prophet und Tempel* (1948), pp. 37 ff.).

[2] The writer only once mentions the rebuilding of the temple (44. 28), and some scholars would delete the reference. But to suggest that the prophet is not greatly interested in the temple would be gratuitous. See his references to 'my house' (56. 5, 7; cf. 60. 7; 66. 20; and 60. 13). The descriptions of the New Zion presuppose a new temple, for no good Israelite could think of one without the other.

living in foreign lands evidently had the effect of making the prophet reflect upon the disunity of mankind at large. He concluded that since Yahweh is the creator God, the one beside whom there is no other, the Gentiles must have their place in the new temple. This conviction is dramatically expressed in the description of the pilgrimage of the nations to Zion:[1]

> Lift up your eyes round about, and see;
>   they all gather together, they come to you;
> your sons shall come from far,
>   and your daughters shall be carried in the arms.

> Then you shall see and be radiant,
>   your heart shall thrill and rejoice;
> because the abundance of the sea
>   shall be turned to you,
>   the wealth of the nations shall come to you.

> All the flocks of Kedar shall be gathered to you,
>   the rams of Nebaioth shall minister to you;
> they shall come up with acceptance
>   on my altar,
>   and I will glorify my glorious house.

(60. 4–5, 7; cf. 56. 6–8; 66. 18–21)

Although the imagery used by Isaiah 40–66 differs strikingly from that of Ezekiel and the priestly writers, the meaning is the same. Eschatology has as its central idea the regathering and reunion of Israel at the divine dwelling. The extension of the new temple concept to include the Gentiles marks an important new development, and will be with us to the end of our study.

The same kind of presentation is found in the writings of Haggai and Zechariah. Numbers of exiles had by this time returned to their homeland, and the hardships they encountered made the hope for the fulfilment of earlier prophecies more intense. Thus Haggai promises that 'the latter splendour of this house shall be greater than the former' (2. 9).[2] Zechariah, similarly, gives point to his assurance that the long-awaited age is

---

[1] Cf. A. Causse, 'La vision de l'humanité dans la prophétie deutéro-ésaïque', *RHPR* 2 (1922), 465–98; 'Le mythe de la nouvelle Jérusalem du deutéro-ésaïa à la IIIᵉ Sibylle', *RHPR* 18 (1938), 377–414.

[2] Haggai's reference to the magnificence of the new temple is usually taken to mean that the older inhabitants of Jerusalem who remembered Solomon's temple were not impressed by what was to take its place (cf. Ezra 3. 12–13; 1 Esd. 5. 63–5).

now about to be ushered in by having Zerubbabel symbolically anointed (along with Joshua the high priest, 4. 11–14) and crowned in readiness.[1] In the person of Zerubbabel, of the royal line of David, the undivided house (kingdom) of David would be restored[2] and the temple rebuilt (1. 16; 4. 9 f.; 6. 12, 15). Zechariah's description of the spiritual and material glories of the new Jerusalem (8. 3–8) closely follows that of Second Isaiah, and the Gentiles continue to occupy an important place in the vision (8. 20–3). The later chapters of the book (9–14) repeat the theme: the Jews will be regathered (10. 8 ff.), and Jerusalem will be rebuilt to her former dimensions and miraculously elevated above the earth (14. 10), with the nations going up every year to keep the feast of Tabernacles (14. 16 ff.).

The remonstrances of Haggai and the reassurances of Zechariah had their effect. The rebuilding of the temple was taken in hand, and it was completed in the sixth year of Darius's reign, i.e. 515 B.C. (Ezra 6. 15). The priesthood was restored and what cultic arrangements existed were reorganized. So one may infer from the book of Malachi. But although a brave attempt was made to invest the new temple with all possible significance (1–2 Chr.)[3] the hard facts of the post-exilic period belied any suggestion that the restored temple was the temple of the great prophecies concerning the eschatological age. The nation, far from becoming great, was again subjected to foreign rule, this time by the Persians (Mal. 1. 8), and the temple was the worshipping-place of the Jews alone. The prevailing sense of anticlimax took its toll on the spirit of the nation. A feeling of heartlessness settled over the people (3. 14), resulting in negligence and open disregard for the requirements of worship. Blemished and worthless sacrifices dishonoured the altar, and a sceptical priesthood cared little about the proper conduct of worship (1. 6–2. 9).

Malachi therefore summons Israel to repentance, declaring that the great day of the Lord will surely arrive. God will suddenly come to his temple, and he will cleanse it of its abuses and establish a pure worship (3. 1–4). In other words, attention is

---

[1] It is interesting to note that although the king is to share the government with the high priest, he alone will build the temple (4. 9 f.; 6. 12).

[2] The language of 3. 10 also indicates that the restoration was thought of in terms of the united kingdom before the rupture of north and south (cf. 9. 10).

[3] Cf. W. Rudolph, 'Problems of the Books of Chronicles', *VT* (1954), pp. 401–9; T. Hannay, 'The Temple', *SJT* 3 (1950), 278–87.

once again directed towards the future. It is then, in the eschatological age, that the temple will be glorified and its worship be
acceptable to God.

The foregoing pages have attempted to show the important
place which the new temple occupied in the eschatology of the
Old Testament. The restoration of Israel means the restoration of
the temple, and the restoration of the temple means the ingathering and reunion of Israel. There is no suggestion as yet
that the new temple is materially different from the old temple.
It is still the old temple restored, albeit on more magnificent
lines. Development of the subject is, however, present within the
Old Testament.

In the first place we note that, whereas Ezekiel severed royalty
from the temple and downgraded it to the point of virtual extinction, Haggai and Zechariah evidently felt that the connection of
royalty and divine presence was too firmly established a pattern
of Israel's cultic tradition not to be provided for in the new age.
The king, of course, must be a new David, not simply because
David was the ideal king but because he was the spiritual builder
of the temple of Jerusalem. Hence the task of rebuilding the
temple, which is not mentioned in the earliest expressions of the
hope, is now assigned to a particular individual, a son of David.
This connection of the new David with the eschatological temple
prepares the way for what is an important and interesting aspect
of our study, viz. the Messiah as the builder of the new temple.
The point at which the connection between the Messiah and the
temple was made is not clear,[1] but it seems fairly certain that the
prophecy of Zechariah contributed to it, because the Targum
on Zech. 6. 12 makes Zerubbabel the messianic builder of the
new temple.[2]

Similarly we should note, in the second place, that the complementary idea of the ingathering of the people to their own land
which is frequently thought of as the work of God himself is on
occasion attributed to a representative of his. Deutero-Isaiah
attributes it to the Servant of the Lord (49. 6). We shall find that

---

[1] Cf. S–B i. 1003–5; *TDNT* iii. 239 f.
[2] S–B i. 94. It is worth noting in this connection that in the Targum on Isa. 53. 5
the Servant (understood by the writer as the Messiah) is the builder of the temple.
Cf. S–B i. 482.

the ingathering and reunion of Israel is one of the tasks assigned to the Messiah in connection with his work in regard to the temple by intertestamental authors.

Thirdly, a development of considerable importance is the pilgrimage of the nations to the eschatological temple. Most, if not all, of the Old Testament expressions of universalism are linked to the temple. Non-Jews are envisaged as being converted not in the place where they live but at Jerusalem. That is to say, the eschatological movement is always centripetal.[1] To attribute this simply to ethnocentrism would be superficial. Jerusalem is the centre of the earth; it is where God is; Jew and Gentile alike must go there for salvation. The belief that Jerusalem would one day become the worshipping place of the whole of mankind was, as we have seen, something of a theological necessity, arising from the doctrine of Yahweh as creator. The new temple thus becomes the symbol not only of the unity of Israel but of mankind.

Apocrypha and Pseudepigrapha

The bulk of the Apocrypha and Pseudepigrapha was written during the Hasmonean dynasty. The prosperity of this period led some at least to think that the messianic time had come.[2] The temple in particular benefited from the prevailing peaceful conditions. Its physical appearance was greatly enhanced by the building programme undertaken by the Maccabees (1 Macc. 10. 11 f.; 12. 36 f.; 13. 10; 14. 37), and to all intents and purposes it was the accepted centre of Jewish life and religion (Ecclus. 50; Arist. 83–104). In such circumstances it is something of a surprise to find that the idea of a new temple still held its appeal. The reasons for this will become clear as we proceed.

We begin with two works, similar in outlook, from the earlier part of the intertestamental period: Tobit (c. 200 B.C.)[3] and Ecclesiasticus (180 B.C.). Tobit describes Jerusalem as 'chosen from among all the tribes of Israel, where all the tribes should sacrifice and where the temple of the dwelling of the Most High was consecrated and established for all generations for ever'

---

[1] Cf. Causse, RHPR 2. 465–98; B. Sundkler, 'Jésus et les païens', RHPR 16 (1936), 462–99.

[2] 1 Macc. 14. 4–15 reads like a paraphrase of Old Testament prophecy on the new age.

[3] Fragments found at Qumran suggest an earlier date.

(1. 4). Even so it is quite clear that the writer did not regard the existing Jerusalem as the city of the eschatological time. The future temple, he says, 'will not be like the former one until the times of the age are completed', but will be rebuilt 'with a glorious building for all generations for ever, *just as the prophets said of it*' (14. 5). To the new centre of worship the exiles will return and the Gentiles also come to praise God (13. 5, 11; 14. 4 ff.).

The expectation of the reunion of the people of God at a glorified temple is again present in Ben-Sira's famous prayer of hope (Ecclus. 36. 11–14). Its significance is all the greater when it is considered with chapter 50 in mind. The latter is a glowing account of Israel at worship in the temple of Jerusalem, and taken on its own might easily give one the impression that the author believed that Israel had entered upon the final stage of her religious inheritance. As it is, the sense of fulfilment is wanting here also, and the chapter closes with a backward look to the good old days and the prayer that God in his mercy will 'deliver us in our days' (50. 22–4). The hope of the return of the dispersed reappears, and as usual takes the form of an eschatological event. Elijah, we are told, will appear[1] and gather in the tribes of Jacob (48. 10).

A further illustration of how the expectation of a new temple persisted alongside a flourishing cultus is 2 Maccabees. The prologue contains a beautiful prayer for the reunion of God's people (1. 24–9). Reunion, as we have come to expect, is at the temple. 'God . . . will gather us from everywhere under heaven into his holy place' (2. 18). It is then, when 'God gathers his people together again' (2. 7), and not until then, that the whereabouts of the ark, the tabernacle, and the altar of incense, the vital contents of the sanctuary which were missing since the destruction of the old temple, will be disclosed (2. 4–8).

An important new stage in the development of our subject is marked by the Psalms of Solomon (c. 70–40 B.C.). By the time these were written the Hasmonean era had ended and Israel was again at the mercy of foreign powers.[2] The ancient hope

---

[1] Probably understood as the forerunner of the Messiah (S. Mowinckel, *He that Cometh* (1956), p. 298).

[2] On the historical background see R. H. Charles, *The Apocrypha and Pseudepigrapha* (1913), ii. 629 f.

took on a new significance and a new form. The author of the 17th Psalm prays fervently for a king, a new David,[1] who will recover the ancient glories of Israel.

The task assigned to the expected leader unites in an interesting fashion various tendencies we have noted in different contexts. Firstly, the Messiah will throw off the hard (Roman?) yoke from the Jews (17. 24). Secondly, and of greater interest to us, he will gather in the tribes to Palestine and settle them in the land, as Ezekiel predicted:

And he shall gather together a holy people, whom he shall lead in righteousness, and he shall judge the tribes of the people that has been sanctified by the Lord his God. . . . And he shall divide them according to their tribes upon the land (17. 28, 29; cf. v. 48).

Thirdly, he will have cultic functions. In language reminiscent of Malachi 3. 1–4 the author writes of him, 'He shall glorify the Lord in a place to be seen of all the earth;[2] and he shall purge Jerusalem, making it holy as of old' (17. 32 f.).[3] To this cleansed temple and city the nations of the earth will come, bringing with them, as gifts for the king, Jews of the dispersion (17. 33 f.).

These Psalms, while thus representing a reworking of old material, introduce a number of interesting new features. The theological problems created by the continued disunity of Israel have become more serious. It is recognized that disunity can lead only to the extinction of Israel (8. 36). Restoration of the temple is therefore made one of the chief offices of the Messiah. The fact that it is again the already existing temple, i.e. the temple of Zerubbabel, which is to be cleansed is noteworthy; we shall return to this in due course. A further point to be noted is the author's use of the crucial Old Testament passage 2 Sam. 7 in his description of the future king. Apparently the Messiah's work in respect of the temple is thought of as in some sense fulfilling the

---

[1] He is called 'the anointed of the Lord' (17. 36; 18. 8). Cf. the allusion to 2 Sam. 7 at 17. 5, 23.

[2] So Gray renders ἐν ἐπισήμῳ (Charles, *Apocrypha and Pseudepigrapha*, ii. 650), following H. E. Ryle and M. R. James, Ψαλμοὶ Σολομῶντος, *Psalms of the Pharisees* (1891), pp. 140 f., who find here a reference to the miraculous elevation of the temple in the eschatological age (cf. Isa. 2. 2; Mic. 4. 1; Zech. 14. 10).

[3] The cleansing in mind here, as distinct from that at 17. 24, must refer to the temple. See 2. 3; 8. 13; cf. Mal. 3. 1–4.

prediction of Nathan's prophecy concerning the son of David and the temple.

The inclusion of non-Jews in the new temple concept which we noted in earlier writings is a very pronounced feature of the last example we shall cite from the Pseudepigrapha, namely, the Sibylline Oracles (*c.* 140 B.C.–A.D. 70). These writings have the additional value of being a witness of Hellenistic Judaism to our thesis.

Assuming the role of the great pagan prophetess Sibyl, this Jew of the dispersion delivers her message to Jew and Gentile alike. It is an attempt on the one hand to keep alive in Hellenistic Jewry the ancient hope of reunion in the fatherland and on the other hand to demonstrate to interested Greeks that Zion can easily vie with Hellas for the heart and mind of mankind. After exposing the sins of the pagan races and warning of the judgement to come, the Sibyl proceeds to describe the golden age that is in store for all who worship the one true God. The whole world, we are told, will be transformed into a veritable Eden (Sib. Or. iii. 616–23; cf. 367–80, 744–58, 788–808). Gathering up ideas from all the prophets and apocalyptists before her the Sibyl delivers her remarkable prophecy concerning the new temple:

> Then again all the sons of the great God shall live quietly around the temple, rejoicing in those gifts which He shall give who is the Creator and sovereign and righteous Judge. For He by Himself shall shield them, standing beside them alone in His might, encircling them, as it were, with a wall of flaming fire.[1] Free from war shall they be in city and country . . . . And then all the isles and the cities shall say, How doth the Eternal love those men![2] . . . Come, let us all fall upon the earth and supplicate the Eternal King, the mighty, everlasting God. Let us make procession to His temple, for He is the sole Potentate (iii. 702–7, 710 f., 716–18).

Similarly later in the same Oracle we read that 'there shall be no other house for men in future generations to know but only that which He has given to faithful men to honour. For mortals shall call that alone the temple[3] of the great God' (773–6).

The fifth Oracle adds to the account by stating that the new temple will be erected by the Messiah and have a giant tower

---

[1] Cf. Zech. 2. 5.   [2] Cf. Zech. 8. 20–3.

[3] Reading ναός instead of υἱός, after W. Bousset, *Die Religion des Judentums im späthellenistichen Zeitalter*, 3rd. edn. ed. by H. Gressmann (1926), p. 239.

reaching to the clouds, around which the nations will gather together. The idea of the tower is interesting, for it looks back to the third Oracle (iii. 98–104), which describes the unity of mankind at the time of the tower of Babel (regarded by the ancients as a temple).[1] What the author appears to be saying is that the unity of mankind which was lost at Babel will be recovered at the temple which the Messiah will build in the new age. His thought is clearly seen if the texts in question are set out in parallel fashion.

They made a tower . . . and they desired to ascend into the starry heaven (iii. 98, 100).	(he, i.e. the Messiah, made) a giant tower touching the very clouds and seen of all (v. 424 f.).
the Eternal . . . dashed down the great tower from on high, and incited mortal men to mutual strife (iii. 101–3).	there shall be a great peace throughout all the earth, and king shall be friendly with king till the end of the age (iii. 755 f.).
when the tower was fallen and men's tongues divided off with divers kinds of sounds, then the whole earth began to be filled with separate kingdoms (iii. 105–7).	East and West have hymned forth the glory of God: for no longer are wretched mortals beset with deeds of shame . . . (v. 428 f.). Then again all the sons of the great God shall live quietly around the temple . . . free from war shall they be in city and country (iii. 702, 707).

The description of the temple as the symbol of the eschatological unity of mankind in the *Oracula Sibyllina* is interesting for its explicit statement of a corollary which was accepted by many Israelites from at least the time of the Deuteronomists, and which has been in the background throughout our study of those authors who sought to work out the implications of monotheism. We refer to the belief that since there is only one God there can be only one temple in which he can dwell, and since he dwells in the temple of Jerusalem that is where he must be worshipped.[2]

---

[1] Cf. J. Skinner, *Genesis* (1910), pp. 223–6; H. Gressmann, *The Tower of Babel* (1928), pp. 1–19.

[2] The thought is formulated by Philo as follows: 'Since God is one there should be also only one temple' (ἱερὸν ἓν εἶναι μόνον) (*Spec.* i. 67). Cf. Jos. *Ap.* 2. 193.

This Jew of the diaspora understood the sentiments not only of his countrymen but of humanity, and rethought the faith of Israel in terms of a grand *rapprochement* comparable to that of the Isaiah of the exile. That he succeeded in offering a hope which answered the aspirations of many is undoubted. The great Roman poet Virgil (70–19 B.C.) paints his notable picture of the 'age of gold' in his Fourth Eclogue (*c.* 40 B.C.) with colours which are very likely taken from the Jewish Sybil; as indeed did the authors of Baruch, Fourth Ezra, and Revelation.

The Rabbis

Although the various collections of rabbinic traditions were not written down until after the New Testament had appeared, they are important for our purpose. Many sayings were in circulation long before they were committed to writing, and take us back to the New Testament period. Particularly relevant in this respect are the Mishnah and *Shᵉmôneh 'Esrēh* or the Eighteen Benedictions.

Hope of a new temple is feelingly expressed in one of the prayers of R. Akiba (died *c.* A.D. 135), which is used by orthodox Jews to this day in the liturgy for the eve of Passover:

> Therefore, O Lord our God and the God of our fathers, bring us in peace to the other set feasts and festivals which are coming to meet us, while we rejoice in the building-up of thy city and are joyful in thy worship; and may we eat there of the sacrifices and of the Passover-offerings whose blood has reached with acceptance the wall of thy Altar, and let us praise thee for our redemption and for the ransoming of our soul. Blessed art thou, O Lord, who hast redeemed Israel (M. Pes. 10. 6).

Prayers for the restoration of the dispersed at a new temple are offered repeatedly in *Shᵉmôneh 'Esrēh*, especially in the 10th, 14th, and 17th Benedictions. Thus the 14th Benediction, which dates from well before the fall of Jerusalem in A.D. 70:

> And to Jerusalem, thy city, return in mercy, and dwell therein as though hast spoken; rebuild it soon in our days as an everlasting building, and speedily set up therein the throne of David. Blessed art thou, O Lord, who rebuildest Jerusalem.[1]

---

[1] S. Singer (ed.), *The Authorized Daily Prayer Book of the United Hebrew Congregations of the British Empire*, 26th edn. (1960), p. 49.

That the new temple is understood as the fulfilment of Ezekiel's prophecy can be seen from the following comment upon one of the rites at Tabernacles:

And why was it called the Water Gate? Because through it they brought in the flagon of water for the libation at the Feast. R. Eliezer b. Jacob (*c.* 90) says: Through it *the waters trickle forth*[1] and hereafter they will *issue out from under the threshold of the house* (M. Shek. 6. 3).[2]

The restoration of the temple of course means the restoration of Israel to Palestine, and the latter idea is equally strongly expressed by the rabbis. The 10th Benediction is an early example:

Blow the great trumpet for our liberation, and lift a banner to gather our exiles, and gather us into one body from the four corners of the earth; blessed be Thou, O Lord, who gatherest the dispersed of Thy (His) people.[3]

From the abundance of Talmudic material on the subject we select one example. It is a *baraitha* on the Benedictions just quoted, and its importance lies in its fusion of various aspects of the eschatological hope in the person of the Messiah:

And when Jerusalem is built (i.e. 14th Ben.), David will come (i.e. 15th Ben.), as it says, *Afterwards shall the children of Israel return and seek the Lord their God, and David their king* (Hos. 3. 5). And when David comes, prayer will come (i.e. 16th Ben.), as it says, *Even them will I bring to my holy mountain, and make them joyful in my house of prayer* (Isa. 56. 7). And when prayer has come, the temple service will come (i.e. 17th Ben.), as it says, *Their burnt offerings and their sacrifices shall be acceptable upon mine altar* (Isa. 56. 7) (B. Meg. 17b–18a).

The earlier rabbis generally think of God as the builder of the temple, although one repeatedly finds the name of David in texts dealing with the eschatological temple.[4] The *baraitha* just quoted is probably the earliest rabbinic text in which the Messiah is directly connected with the return and the new temple.[5]

---

[1] Unless otherwise stated the italics here and elsewhere are the translator's and are intended to indicate citation of the Old Testament.

[2] Cf. M. Mid. 2. 6; Tos. Suk. 3. 3; J. Bonsirven, *Textes rabbiniques* (1955), p. 252.

[3] Translation given by *JE* xi. 271. Although occasionally it is stated that the ten tribes will not return (M. Sanh. 10. 3; B. Sanh. 110b), the general view is that all twelve tribes will return (e.g. B. B. B. 122a).

[4] Cf. S–B i. 1003–5; P. Volz, *Die Eschatologie der jüdischen Gemeinde im neutestamentlichen Zeitalter* (1934), p. 217.

[5] Cf. B. Pes. 5a (R. Ishmael, died *c.* 135), where the rebuilding of the temple and the name of the Messiah are said to be rewards to Israel for keeping the festivals (mentioned in Lev. 23. 7, 35, 40).

Finally, we note the eschatological pilgrimage of the nations to Zion, as, for example, in the following:

R. Simeon b. Gamaliel (*c.* 140) said: it (the centre of the world) will one day be Jerusalem; in it all the nations and kingdoms will gather, as it is written: *all the nations will be gathered unto it in the name of the Lord* (Jer. 3. 17) (Aboth of R. Nathan 35).[1]

So great indeed will the concourse of worshippers be that it is doubted whether Jerusalem will hold them all.[2] Rabbinic eschatology,[3] like Jewish eschatology generally, is seen at its most generous expression in relation to the new temple.[4]

Summary

This chapter has sought to show that the new temple is the central idea of Jewish eschatology from its very beginning. It has also indicated how the temple concept drew to itself other eschatological ideas. The Messiah is a figure who stands not in his own right but in relation to the divine dwelling, and the universalist tendencies that appear in the exilic period gravitate towards and become inseparable from the eschatological temple. The literature surveyed is important not only for what it says about the new temple but also for what it says or implies about the existing temple, i.e. it explains why the hope of a new temple persisted after the temple of Jerusalem was restored.

In a sense the temple which was built after the return from the exile was the fulfilment of the prophecies of Deutero-Isaiah, Ezekiel, and others, but in another sense it was not. The restored temple did help to unify the restored community and act as

---

[1] S–B iii. 853.

[2] S–B iii. 849.

[3] For a useful collection of rabbinic texts on Jerusalem in the end-time see F. Weber, *Jüdische Theologie auf Grund des Talmud und verwandter Schriften* (1897), pp. 374–9.

[4] As often, liturgy is a good guide, and Dr. D. Daube kindly draws my attention to a passage in the liturgy prescribed for the New Year Festival which finely expresses the conception of the unity of Israel and the nations in the worship of the new age: 'Now, therefore, O Lord our God, impose thine awe upon all thy works, and thy dread upon all that thou hast created, that all thy works may fear thee and all creatures prostrate themselves before thee, that they may all form a single band to do thy will with a perfect heart . . .' (Singer, op. cit., p. 239a). The *terminus technicus* 'a single band' (כלם אגדה, i.e. one band), which is used in the Old Testament for the united Israel (e.g. 2 Sam. 2. 25), here denotes the whole of mankind ('all thy creatures').

a beacon of hope for the many Jews who did not return, and the little nation became relatively strong and influential. But when the actual was put alongside the ideal the disparity was too great and too painful to bear any comparison. Neither people nor temple came anywhere near to realizing the ancient prophecies concerning them. Moreover, the temple was never able to overcome the prejudice that marked its inception.

The Chronicler states that the leaders and older inhabitants of Jerusalem who remembered the first temple were disappointed in the one that took its place (Ezra 3. 12; cf. 1 Esd. 5. 63–5; Jos. *Ant.* 11. 80–1). Along with the psychological handicap of a pedestrian beginning, the temple also suffered as a result of the economic hardships of the early years of the restoration. An impoverished cult and poorly maintained priesthood brought the temple into disrepute (Mal. 1. 7 ff.; 3. 3 f., 8 f.). Time did not erase these impressions. If anything it served to strengthen them. The desecration of the temple by the heathen Antiochus Epiphanes, notwithstanding the valiant attempt of Judas Maccabaeus to cleanse it, appears to have lingered on in the form of a secret suspicion that the temple was not fully restored to holiness. At all events, we find I Enoch asserting that the worship is polluted (89. 73); before the new temple of the eschatological age is erected, the existing temple will have to be broken up and taken away (90. 28 f.). Similarly, the Apocalypse of Baruch states that Zion will be destroyed in order that a new and more glorious city may take its place (32. 2 ff.). The tractate Yoma attributes the blame to the priests, stating that they have made the second temple far worse than the first (B. Yoma 9b; cf. B. Pes. 57a).

The fact that the second temple was not complete did not help matters either. It lacked the ark, the tabernacle, the altar of incense, and the other furniture, and had to make do with copies. Hence there arose the belief that the temple was inferior to its predecessor as it did not have the originals. But speculation did not end there. Certain Targumists and rabbis went so far as to say that the divine presence had not in fact returned to the temple (Targ. Hag. 1. 8; P. Ta'an 65a; cf. B. Yoma 53b). The pejorative effect which such a suggestion would have upon the popular mind once it gained currency is easily imagined; one has only to recall the importance which Ezekiel, Deutero-Isaiah, and their successors attached to the return of the *kĕbhôdh-Yahweh* to understand the kind of conclusion that would be drawn.

The contrast which developed between the empirical temple and its counterpart of the new age appears to have begun quite early. Malachi declares that in the eschatological era 'the offering of Judah and Jerusalem will be pleasing to the Lord as in the days of old and as in former years' (3. 4). Tobit says that the new temple is 'not like the former' (14. 5), 1 Enoch promises 'a new house greater and loftier than that first' (90. 29), and the Testament of Benjamin says that 'the last temple shall be more glorious than the first' (9. 2). The tendency reaches its conclusion in the categorical assertion of the Apocalypse of Baruch that the eschatological Jerusalem will bear no relation to the present city (4. 2–4).

Thus the ancient prophecies of a new and glorious temple were not regarded as having been realized in the temple built after the exile and continued to exercise a powerful appeal to Jewry, which still looked for their consummation in a temple which would be filled with the glory of God and compel the admiration and devotion of Jew and non-Jew alike. Not is it surprising, as we are now to see, that the temple of the future should come to be thought of as entirely new in character and supernatural in origin.

III

THE HEAVENLY TEMPLE IN JEWISH AND GREEK LITERATURE

The Transcendentalizing of the Divine Presence

THE tendency to think of the new temple in supernatural terms which we met in the last chapter introduces us to an ancient and widespread tradition. R. H. Charles gave it as his opinion that a heavenly temple and worship is implied by the statement in Exod. 25. 9, 40 that Moses had a pattern of the tabernacle revealed to him on Mount Sinai,[1] though he afterwards retracted it, suggesting that the conception arose sometime between 300 and 150 B.C.[2] Most scholars follow this view.[3] A much earlier date seems, however, to be required. The doctrine of correspondence between the heavenly and the earthly world, according to which the earthly is a copy of the heavenly, was a well-established feature of Ancient Near Eastern mythology.[4] Although the Old Testament does not indicate that Yahwism appropriated and converted the idea it does show familiarity with it. The dwelling of the divine being forms the setting for the council of Yahweh (1 Kgs. 22. 19 ff.; Isa. 6. 1 ff.; Zech. 3. 1–7;

---

[1] *Apocrypha and Pseudepigrapha*, ii. 306, 482.

[2] *Studies in the Apocalypse* (1913), p. 166. Cf. *The Apocalypse of Baruch* (1896), pp. 6 f. Exod. 25. 9, 40 does not of itself imply the existence of an archetype in heaven. Wisd. 9. 8 is less easy to interpret. It may point to the conception of the heavenly sanctuary, which, as we shall see, is present in other Jewish writings of the period. On the other hand, it may say no more than Jer. 17. 12. However, the language used (μίμημα) has such Greek philosophical associations (the Neopythagoreans thought of the sensible world as a μίμησις of the heavenly) that one inclines to see in the text an allusion to the heavenly sanctuary. Later Jewish exegesis, as we shall see, took the pattern of the tabernacle to imply the existence of a heavenly archetype. Ezek. 40. 1 ff. has so many features in common with the Babylonian inscription of King Gudea (c. 3000 B.C.) (A. Jeremias, *Das Alte Testament im Lichte des alten Orients* (1904), p. 353) that one might easily conclude that Ezekiel, like Gudea, saw a heavenly model of the temple he is instructed to build, but this is not at all certain.

[3] Cf. G. B. Gray, *Sacrifice in the Old Testament* (1925), pp. 148 ff.

[4] B. Meissner, *Babylonien und Assyrien* (1925), i. 110; M. Eliade, *Der Mythos der ewigen Wiederkehr* (1953), pp. 16 ff.

Dan. 7. 9 ff.; cf. Rev. 4 ff.). The dwelling in question is clearly regarded as a temple at Isa. 6, but even in those texts where a court-room seems to be in mind a temple is undoubtedly implied since for the ancients the temple is the place where the god delivers his judgements (e.g. Amos. 1. 2; Jer. 25. 30).[1]

It remains true, however, that although there is evidence of the conception of the heavenly temple in the Old Testament we find nothing in the way of a systematic attempt to give it a distinct Yahwistic stamp, beyond the assertion that the God who rules the heavenly court is Yahweh. But with the passage of time the conception did become an article of faith and assume fairly considerable importance.

The reasons for the transcendentalizing of the temple idea in Israelite tradition require us to go back to earlier formulations of the doctrine of the divine indwelling. In the period represented by the Old Testament we witness a developing theology of the divine presence. The early narratives represent Yahweh as dwelling in the tent or the sanctuaries of Palestine as a man dwells in his house. Before long the teaching of the pre-exilic prophets on the sovereignty and holiness of God caused people to ask in what sense God might be said to dwell in the temple (1 Kgs. 8. 27). The Deuteronomists sought to provide the answer by stating that it was the name of God which dwelt in the temple. It was a good answer, and it met Israel's needs for a time, but only for a time. The experience of the exile raised the question in still sharper focus. For life in foreign lands served not only to enhance the importance of the temple but also to show that the temple was not indispensable to the worship of Yahweh. The assurance of the prophets that God could and would come to his people and bless them wherever they were, without temple and cult (Ezek. 11. 16), was happily realized (Ps. 139. 7–12). Clearly the traditional doctrine of the divine presence needed restatement. The priestly writers took up the challenge and redesigned Israel's cultic institutions in such a way as to make provision for the new

---

[1] With the idea of the heavenly dwelling one should compare the more general idea of God dwelling in heaven (e.g. 1 Kgs. 8. 30; 39; 43, al.; Pss. 11. 4; 103. 19; 123. 1; Hab. 2. 20; Isa. 66. 1) and also God's dwelling on Sinai (Deut. 5. 4; 33. 2; Judg. 5. 4 f.; Hab. 3. 3; Ps. 68. 7 f., 17 f.), since in primitive cosmology mountain-peaks are connected to heaven. On the ancient myth of the mountain in the far north, the home of the gods, which reached to heaven, see H. Gunkel, *Schöpfung und Chaos in Urzeit und Endzeit* (1922), pp. 133 f.

understanding of God immanent and transcendent. But their solution too served only for a time, and it was left to the apocalyptic writers, on the one hand, to develop the doctrine of the heavenly temple, and to the rabbis, on the other hand, to develop the idea of intermediaries.[1]

The transcendentalizing of the divine presence in Israel is also part and parcel of the interest of late post-exilic Judaism in the supernatural order that followed the transfer of eschatology from prophet to apocalyptist. Apocalyptic with its emphasis on the heavenly world provided a convenient frame of reference for the growing interest in the heavenly temple. Thus belief in a heavenly temple which Israel in common with her Near Eastern neighbours had held from early times became an object of faith and was invested with all the authority of the divine dwelling on earth. The process was developed still further when the heavenly temple came to be understood in terms of the new temple.

It is difficult to say to what extent Jewish thinking on the heavenly temple was affected by Platonic ideas. Philo and the New Testament writers were influenced by it.[2] One may suppose that belief in the heavenly world as the real world and things on earth as merely copies served to strengthen the idea of the heavenly temple,[3] even though the literature of Palestinian Judaism bears little if any trace of Platonism.

It is important to note in regard to the foregoing that the fact that Judaism committed itself to belief in the heavenly temple does not mean that it abandoned the idea of the divine presence on earth. The intertestamental writers are as definite on this point as the Deuteronomists and the priestly writers. There is a heavenly temple and there is an earthly temple, and the one is a companion of the other.[4] As late as the third century A.D. one comes across a saying like the following, 'I (God) will not enter the heavenly Jerusalem until I can enter the earthly Jerusalem' (B. Ta'an 5a). Jewish thinking on the heavenly temple owed most to the oriental doctrine of correspondence. By designating the earthly as the microcosm of the heavenly macrocosm the ancients

[1] For Jewish teaching on the sh^{e}khînâh, mêmrâ, etc., see J. Abelson, *The Immanence of God in Rabbinical Literature* (1912); G. F. Moore, 'Intermediaries in Jewish Theology', *HTR* 15 (1922), 41–85.
[2] See below, pp. 38 ff., 149, 205 f.
[3] Clements, op. cit, p. 127.
[4] S–B iii. 573.

were paying the earthly a tribute, not the reverse. In other words, Jewish writers work from presuppositions quite different from those of Plato. When eventually these writers do say that the heavenly temple is superior to the earthly and will one day replace it there is no suggestion that the earthly temple, for all its shortcomings, has ceased to be God's dwelling-place.

Pseudepigrapha

The fullest description of the heavenly temple in Jewish literature appears in 1 Enoch. The writer describes how Enoch is transported in a vision to heaven and sees the heavenly temple. It is a magnificent building made of crystal and contains an inner house, i.e. the holy of holies, in which God is enthroned in great majesty:

In every respect it so excelled in splendour and magnificence and extent that I cannot describe to you its splendour and its extent. And its floor was of fire, and above it were lightnings and the path of the stars, and its ceiling also was flaming fire. And I looked and saw therein a lofty throne: its appearance was as crystal .... And the Great Glory sat thereon, and His raiment shone more brightly than the sun and was whiter than any snow (14. 16–18, 20).

Chapter 26 is best explained as another picture of the same scene. Here we have the interesting idea of the river flowing from the heavenly temple:

And I went from thence to the middle of the earth (i.e. to the temple), and I saw a blessed place in which there were trees with branches abiding and blooming (of a dismembered tree). And there I saw a holy mountain, and underneath the mountain to the east there was a stream and it flowed towards the south (26. 1–2).

The symbolism of these chapters is novel but not unintelligible. It is best understood by assuming that what the writer has done is to take the familiar Semitic world-picture and project it into heaven. Ideas traditionally associated with the new temple are now used of the temple in heaven. It is the heavenly temple that is the navel or source of life and blessing for the universe. The question one naturally wishes to ask is whether the writer thought of the temple of the eschatological time as the heavenly temple descended to earth. An answer in the affirmative would seem to be suggested by the language of 25. 3; 'This high mountain (the heavenly Mount Zion) . . . is His throne, where the Holy Great One, the Lord of Glory, the Eternal King, will sit, when He shall come down to visit the earth with goodness.'[1] For how could a Jew think of the descent of the heavenly Mount Zion without also having in mind the descent of the heavenly temple? It is, of course, possible that the author is writing figuratively and is wishing to convey the idea of God's sovereignty, but there is no indication that he is, and in fact the language of the context is against such a possibility. One is therefore disposed to think that the heavenly temple of these chapters of Enoch is envisaged as descending to earth, along with the tree of life, in the last times. In other words, the heavenly temple is the new temple.

We proceed to Enoch 85–90. This is a rather different presentation. Here Enoch sees the whole panorama of earthly history unrolled before him in a series of symbols extending from Adam to the Hasmonean period, in the midst of which he himself stands. The narrative abounds with ideas and images which are of interest and help to us. Thus Israel is depicted as a flock of sheep, which in the time of Solomon is represented as grazing peacefully around the temple, 'a tower lofty and great . . .(which) was built on the house[2] for the Lord of the sheep' (89. 50). The disruption of the kingdom and the destruction of the 'house' resulted in the scattering and confusion of the flock and its exposure to attacks by wild beasts (the Gentiles) (89. 51–90. 5). By and by the Lord of the sheep, angered at the pitiless slaughter of his flock, comes to their rescue (90. 15). A throne of judgement is set up in Palestine and justice is re-established (90. 24 ff.). The scene is thus prepared for the new temple and the age of bliss. The old temple is torn down and in its place a magnificent new one is erected.

And I stood up to see till they folded up that old house; and carried off all the pillars, and all the beams and ornaments of the house were at the same time folded up with it, and they carried it off and laid it in a place in the south of the land. And I saw till the Lord of the sheep brought a new house greater and loftier than that first, and set it up in

---

[1] One should also note how easily the writer in the context thinks of the transfer of the tree of life from heaven to earth (25. 4 f.).

[2] The 'tower' represents the temple, and the 'house' very likely stands for Jerusalem.

the place of the first which had been folded up: all its pillars were new, and its ornaments were new and larger than those of the first, the old one which He had taken away, and all the sheep were within it (90. 28–9).[1]

The advent of the new temple will mark great happenings. The ancient hostility between the Jews and the Gentiles will come to an end, and the latter will worship in the temple (90. 33). As a token of their reconciliation the sword which had been given to the Jews to destroy their enemies is put away in the temple (90. 33 ff.). 'And I saw', concludes the author, 'that that house was large and broad and very full' (90. 36).

Charles is not in any doubt that the temple of these chapters (90. 28–36; 91. 13) is the heavenly temple descended to earth.[2] Billerbeck thinks that it is not.[3] Wenschkewitz is uncertain.[4] It ought to be said at the outset that the fact that the earlier chapters of the book probably have in mind the descent of the heavenly temple is not necessarily evidence that will help in determining the origin of the temple in the section now before us. The subject-matter of chapters 1–36 is not the same as that of 85–90. The former is concerned with the heavenly world, the latter with a glorified earth, and caution is essential in proceeding from the one to the other. On the other hand, the fact that the author of chapters 85–90 is not directly interested in celestial matters is no guarantee that such things were not in his mind. Apocalyptic is notoriously fond of alternating its focus between terrestrial and celestial planes, and even fusing them. As far as general considerations go, therefore, the origin of the new temple described in these chapters is not easily determined. The context does perhaps offer us more light. The temple is said to be erected by God himself. Its newness, size, magnificence, and difference from the former temple are emphasized. We also note that the old temple has to be broken up and completely removed before the new one can be erected. Even so, although it would appear that it is the heavenly temple descended to earth that is in mind, certainty is not possible.

---

[1] A variant reading has, 'And the Lord of the sheep was within it'.
[2] *A Critical History of the Doctrine of a Future Life* (= *Eschatology*) (1899), pp. 179, 199.
[3] S–B iii. 796. Cf. Bousset, op. cit., p. 285.
[4] H. Wenschkewitz, 'Die Spiritualisierung der Kultusbegriffe Tempel, Priester und Opfer im Neuen Testament', *Ang.* 4 (1932), 216.

The heavenly temple and the new temple reappear in those later chapters of 1 Enoch which remain to be considered, viz. 37–71, or the *Parables*. It is not necessary to quote the section on the heavenly temple which appears in these chapters (71. 5–7) because it adds nothing to that of chapter 14. What we have to ask is whether this temple is the temple that is described at 53. 6:

And after this (the judgement) the Righteous and Elect One (i.e. the heavenly Son of Man) shall cause the house of his congregation to appear: henceforth they shall no more be hindered in the name of the Lord of Spirits.

Beer and Charles,[1] it is true, take the 'house of his congregation' to refer to the synagogue,[2] but this is seriously to be doubted. It cannot be said that the author has departed so far from the traditional hope as to make the building of synagogues the concern of the Messiah. More conclusively, the context shows that the writer is following the familiar eschatological pattern. He describes the judgement, the reign of peace, the appearance of the Messiah, the erection of the new temple, and (57. 1 f.) the conversion of the Gentiles. That being the case, one wishes to know whether the new temple is the heavenly temple set up on earth. It is very difficult to answer this question. The dramatic appearance of the temple would suggest that it is the heavenly temple come down to earth, but in the absence of other corroborative evidence it seems wisest to leave the question open.

The heavenly temple and cult is also described in the Testament of Levi. The author tells how Levi travels through the heavens to the 'highest of them all' (the seventh?),[3] where he sees the temple and its priesthood and cult:

For in the Highest of all dwelleth the Great Glory, in the holy of holies, far above all holiness. And in (the heaven next to) it are the angels of the presence of the Lord, who minister (λειτουργοῦντες) and make propitiation (ἐξιλασκόμενοι) to the Lord for all the sins of

---

[1] G. Beer, *Apokryphen und Pseudepigraphen des Alten Testaments*, ed. E. Kautzsch (1900), ii. 266; Charles, *Apocrypha and Pseudepigrapha*, ii. 220.

[2] Cf. 46. 8, where, however, the text does not justify Charles's use of the plural 'congregations'. Note the parallel expression 'the congregation of the righteous' in 38. 1 and 'the congregation of the elect and holy' at 62. 8.

[3] So 2 En. 20–1. According to the rabbis the temple is in the fourth heaven (cf. e.g. B. Hag. 12b).

ignorance of the righteous. And they offer to the Lord a sweet-smelling savour, a reasonable and bloodless offering (λογικὴν καὶ ἀναίμακτον προσφοράν[1]) (3. 4–6).[2]

Levi is shown into the temple, and has his consecration explained to him:

And thereupon the angel opened to me the gates of heaven, and I saw the holy temple, and upon a throne of glory the Most High. And He said to me: Levi, I have given thee the blessings of the priest-hood until I come and sojourn in the midst of Israel (5. 1–2).

The use of the priestly nomenclature (God dwelling in the midst of Israel) is interesting. Nothing is said, however, about the nature of the divine dwelling in the new age.

The evidence of 2 Baruch and 4 Ezra may be added to the foregoing pseudepigrapha. Although these writings come from after the beginning of the Christian period they are of value to us inasmuch as they show how Judaism committed itself to the belief that the new temple is the heavenly temple set up on earth.

2 Baruch consoles Jews over the loss of the temple in A.D. 70. The magnitude of the catastrophe and the sorrow it caused is reflected throughout the book, especially in those parts where the author wistfully questions whether the temple will ever be restored (10. 10; 11; 20; 85). He cannot believe, however, that God will forsake his people. If they repent, the dispersed will be brought back and Jerusalem will be rebuilt (4. 1; 6. 8 f.; 32. 4; 44. 7; 77. 6 f.; cf. 5. 1–3). The city of the future will be completely new and bear no material connection with the old Jerusalem. The new Jerusalem is the heavenly city which God made at the creation of the world, the city which Adam had shown to him before he was expelled from Eden and which Abraham saw when the covenant was instituted, the city too which was revealed to Moses on the mount:

Dost thou think that this is that city of which I said: 'On the palm of My hands have I graven thee?' This building now built in your midst is not that which is revealed with me, that which was prepared before-hand here from the time when I took counsel to make Paradise, and

---

[1] Cf. Ap. Mos. 33. 1 ff., where in a similar translation to heaven Eve witnesses the bloodless sacrifice. Cf. also Jub. 6. 18. On the sacrificial service of heaven see Gray, op. cit., pp. 148 ff.; Wenschkewitz, op. cit., p. 110.

[2] MSS. Greek B, Armenian B, and Slavonic (first recension). Cf. M. de Jonge, *Testamenta XII Patriarcharum* (1964), p. 12.

showed it to Adam before he sinned, but when he transgressed the commandment it was removed from him, as also Paradise. And after these things I showed it to My servant Abraham by night among the portions of the victims. And again also I showed it to Moses on Mount Sinai when I showed to him the likeness of the tabernacle and all its vessels.[1] And now, behold, it is preserved with Me, as also Paradise (2 Bar. 4. 2–6).

This interpretation assumes that the author envisaged the descent of the heavenly Jerusalem and temple to earth, though this is nowhere stated. That it is implied, however, is clear from the context, which is concerned with the destruction and restoration of Jerusalem (4. 1; 6. 1–10), and it would appear that the section on the heavenly city is added to make it plain that the city in question will not be made by the hand of man and thus will not suffer the fate of its predecessor.[2] Further support for this conclusion is found in 4 Ezra.

In 4 Ezra the conception of the new Jerusalem is more fully expounded. The writer tells how Ezra is taken to an open field to receive his vision of the city of God (9. 26–10. 57). First he sees the figure of a woman, a widow mourning the death of her son (9. 38–10. 4). Ezra immediately rebukes her, protesting that her sorrow is nothing in comparison with the grief of those who mourn over the loss of Zion, 'the mother of us all' (10. 7). Suddenly the vision changes. The woman becomes a city, great and beautiful, and Ezra is told:

This woman, whom thou sawest, is Sion, whom thou now beholdest as a builded City.... And whereas she said unto thee: 'My son entering into his marriage-chamber died', and that misfortune befell her—this was the fall of Jerusalem that hath come to pass. And lo! thou hast seen the (heavenly) pattern of her, how she mourned her son, and thou didst begin to comfort her for what had befallen. Now, the Most High, seeing that thou art grieved deeply and art distressed wholeheartedly on account of her; hath showed thee the brilliance of her glory, and her majestic beauty (10. 44, 48–50).

Thereupon the seer is invited to enter the city and see its beauty.

[1] Cf. 59. 4, where the idea of the heavenly Zion (i.e. the dwelling of God) as the pattern of the earthly sanctuary is clearer. The Old Testament texts which state that the tabernacle and the temple of Jerusalem were built according to a pattern are now taken to imply the existence of a heavenly archetype.

[2] Cf. 32. 2 ff., which states that the old temple was destroyed to make room for one which would endure for all time. Also cf. 4 Ezra 7. 26 (Eth.).

The interpretation of the vision is not at all straightforward. At first sight it would appear that the writer is thinking of the earthly Jerusalem: he uses the Isaianic image of Jerusalem as a widow and the application of the title 'mother of us all' to the earthly Zion at 10. 7, and describes the city as a widow in mourning. But this creates a difficulty. If the woman is the earthly dwelling-place of God, to whom does her deceased son refer? The problems of interpretation raised by this question lead Box to take the woman to stand for the heavenly city and the son as the earthly counterpart, although he recognizes that this runs counter to the usual biblical image of Jerusalem as a daughter.[1]

Several facts weigh in favour of Box's interpretation. (i) In the context the author (like 2 Baruch) goes out of his way to dissociate the new city from its predecessor: 'I bade thee come into the field where no foundation of any building is, for in the place where the City of the Most High was about to be revealed no building-work of man could endure' (10. 54; cf. 9. 24). (ii) Later in the book the city is said to be already erected; though at present invisible, it 'shall be made manifest to all men, prepared and builded' (13. 36; cf. 7. 26). (iii) In Gal. 4. 26 the heavenly Jerusalem is called 'our mother'. (iv) The notion of the heavenly Zion mourning harmonizes well with the biblical belief that God shares in the afflictions of his people (Isa. 63. 9). (v) The figure of the heavenly city as the mother and the earthly city as her off-spring is very similar to the familiar oriental conception of the heavenly sanctuary and its ectype. It seems fairly conclusive therefore that the city in question is the heavenly Jerusalem of current Jewish thought. But having established the nature of the city we are left with the question of its descent to earth. Although this is not stated in so many words it is undoubtedly presupposed throughout the narrative. One need only refer to the beginning of the vision where Ezra is shown the field which has been re-served as the site of the divinely created city (10. 54; cf. 9. 24).

The Rabbis

Although the conception of the heavenly city and temple does not appear in the Mishnah there is no doubt that it was the sub-

[1] G. H. Box, *The Ezra-Apocalypse* (1912), p. 239; *Apocrypha and Pseudepigrapha*, ed. Charles, ii. 607.

ject of much rabbinical speculation.[1] The rabbis were particularly fond of drawing a correspondence between the earthly Jerusalem and its heavenly counterpart (e.g. B. Ta'an 5a; Gen. R. 55. 7). We are told that the upper and lower temples are directly opposite one another (Mekl. Ex. 15. 17), separated by only eighteen miles (Gen. R. 69. 7). The heavenly temple is in the fourth heaven and Michael the great prince stands offering at the altar (B. Hag. 12b). The heavenly offering is the souls of the righteous (Nu. R. 12. 7). None of the earlier texts suggests that the heavenly temple and city will one day descend to earth. This is probably due in part to the fact that rabbinic thinking was not greatly influenced by apocalyptic and in part to the strong belief of the rabbis that the temple of Jerusalem would be speedily restored again.

Nevertheless, although there appears to have been some reluctance on the part of rabbinic Judaism to follow the apocalyptists in substituting the heavenly Jerusalem for the earthly one, this in fact was what was eventually done. Strack–Billerbeck give a number of Midrashim which show that some rabbis at least believed that the new Jerusalem would be the heavenly Jerusalem come down to earth:

When Moses saw the love which God had for Israel he said to Him: Lord of the universe, bring her (Israel) and plant her there in the holy land and let it be a plantation which shall never be uprooted. Let Jerusalem come down from heaven and never destroy it. Gather there the dispersed of Israel that they may live there in safety (Bet. ha-Midrash 1. 55, 23).

Elijah said: I saw a beautiful and large city coming down from heaven, perfectly built (3. 67. 29).[2]

These Midrashim are late, but they may justly be regarded as the expression of ideas which were current from at least the period represented by the Book of Revelation. Our study of the Pseudepigrapha showed that by the turn of the Christian era Jewish eschatology had committed itself to the belief that the new

---

[1] One finds grandiose descriptions of a city which is equal in length and breadth and of fantastic dimensions, with twelve gates and streets made of gold (S–B iii. 848–52; J. Bonsirven, *Le judaïsme palestinien au temps de Jésus-Christ* (1935), pp. 60 f.; Weber, op. cit., pp. 374–6). It is not always very clear whether it is a heavenly or earthly city that is in mind.

[2] S–B iii. 796.

temple and city would be supernatural in origin. The development was a natural one, even though it was accelerated by factors like the increasing dissatisfaction of people with the historical temple and their misgivings as to whether they could ever hope to build a temple worthy of the God whose holiness and transcendence were being increasingly emphasized. From the contrast between 'the Jerusalem of this world' and 'the Jerusalem of the world to come' (B. B. B. 75b) it was only a short step to the idea of the supersession of the former by the latter, once that contrast was sharpened by the events of A.D. 70 and afterwards. And what could have been more natural than the expectation that the Jerusalem of the new age—perfect in length and breadth, raised high above the earth and emitting the effulgence of the glory of God to such a degree that sun and moon are no more necessary—should be the *civitas Dei* from heaven?

The Dead Sea Scrolls

The idea of heavenly worship and therefore of the heavenly temple is present in the writings of the Dead Sea sect of Jews. This source is of chief interest because of the very close connection it makes between the worship offered in heaven and that offered upon earth. We quote first from the scroll describing the heavenly liturgy.

The servants of the presence of the Glory (כבוד) (are) in the tabernacle (משכן) of the *godly ones* of knowledge. *Before Him* fall the cherubim and they bless as the still voice of *the godly ones* lifts itself up *on high*, and there is a tumult of chanting as their wings lift up the still voice of the *godly ones*. The *structure* of the chariot throne do the cherubim bless from above the firmament and the majesty of the luminous firmament do they chant from beneath the seat of His glory. And as the *wheels* move so do the holy angels of the sanctuary return and there come forth from amid His glorious *hubs* as it were an appearance of fire, the appearance of the Holy of Holies (קודש קדשים). Round about there are Spirits of *rivers* of fire in the likeness of Ḥašmal and shining creatures, in gloriously variegated and wondrously dyed garments *salted* and pure, the Spirits of the Living God walking continually beside the glory of the wondrous chariot (4 Q Sl 40. 2–18).[1]

---

[1] J. Strugnell, 'The Angelic Liturgy at Qumrân—*4Q serek šîrôt ʿôlat haššabāt*', *VT Suppl.* 7 (1960), 337.

This passage is so clearly modelled on Ezekiel's imagery that one is tempted to look for a connection between it and the temple described in the 'New Jerusalem' material found at Qumran, since the latter is directly based upon the vision of the new temple and city in Ezek. 40–8.[1] But probably it is wisest to refer the 'New Jerusalem' texts to the restored temple of Jerusalem.

The presence of the heavenly temple and worship in the Qumran writings reflects the widespread interest of Jews in the subject, though its particular attraction for these Jews probably had to do with their dislike of the temple of Jerusalem and their claim to be the true people of God and the recipients of a superior revelation.[2] How much the sectarians were interested in the heavenly temple and cult *per se* may become clearer with the publication of new material. Yet, even if the conception was largely compensatory and the real interest of Qumran lay with the earthly temple, what the scrolls have to say about the heavenly temple and worship is still significant for the study of the New Testament.

Of particular relevance in this connection is the sect's lively sense of oneness with the angels.[3] Thus, 'He (God) has granted them a share in the lot of the Saints (i.e. the angels), and has united their assembly, the Council of the Community, with the Sons of Heaven' (1 QS 11. 7 f.).[4] Similarly, 'Thou hast cleansed the perverse spirit from great sin that he might watch with the army of the Saints and enter into communion with the congregation of the Sons of Heaven' (1 QH 3. 21 f.; cf. 4. 24 f.).[5] In company with the angels the sect participates in the worship of the heavenly temple, 'Thou hast caused (them) to enter Thy (glo)rious (Covenant) with all the men of Thy council and into a common lot with the Angels of the Face' (1 QH 6. 12 f.).[6] Whether 1 QSb 4 belongs to the same category or refers to the temple of Jerusalem of the messianic time is not very clear. In any case, it is further evidence of the vivid awareness of participation in the

[1] T. J. Milik, 'Description de la Jérusalem Nouvelle', *Discoveries in the Judaean Desert*, ed. D. Barthélemy and T. J. Milik (1955), i. 134 f.; M. Baillet, 'Fragments araméens de Qumrân 2: Description de la Jérusalem Nouvelle', *RB* 62 (1955), 222–45.

[2] Strugnell, op. cit., p. 335.

[3] B. Gärtner, *The Temple and the Community in Qumran and the New Testament* (1965), pp. 94 ff.

[4] A. Dupont-Sommer, *The Essene Writings from Qumran* (1961), p. 102.

[5] Ibid., p. 209.

[6] Ibid., p. 219.

heavenly cult. The priest (? the leader of the community or the high priest of the restored temple of Jerusalem) is 'like an angel of the Presence in the holy dwelling (מעון) (to serve) the glory of the God of hosts (for ever. And thou) shalt be a faithful servant in the temple of the kingdom (היכל מלכות), sharing the lot of the angels of the Presence, and in the council of the community (with the holy ones) for ever and for all eternity' (4. 25 ff.).[1] The same is true of 4 Q Flor. 1. 4. The War Scroll also has the same idea of the angels joining with the faithful, though there the reference is to the eschatological battle.

All this indicates that by the beginning of the Christian era the ideas of the heavenly temple and worship, access to the heavenly world, and union with it were familiar to Palestinian Judaism.

Plato and Philo

The doctrine of the heavenly temple and city in Jewish theology has its parallel in Plato's conception of the archetypal city and Philo's conception of the archetypal tabernacle.

Towards the end of *The Republic* Plato writes:

'I understand,' he said, 'you mean the city ($\pi\delta\lambda\iota s$) whose establishment we have described, the city whose home is in the ideal ($\tau\hat{\eta}$ $\grave{\epsilon}\nu$ $\lambda\delta\gamma o\iota s$ $\kappa\epsilon\iota\mu\epsilon\nu\eta$); for I think that it can be found nowhere on earth.' 'Well,' said I, 'perhaps there is a pattern ($\pi\alpha\rho\delta\delta\epsilon\iota\gamma\mu\alpha$) of it laid up in heaven ($\grave{\epsilon}\nu$ $o\grave{\upsilon}\rho\alpha\nu\hat{\omega}$) for him who wishes to contemplate it and so beholding to constitute himself its citizen' (ix. 592 a, b).

Behind Plato's thinking is his doctrine of ideas ($\iota\delta\epsilon\alpha$). Ideas constitute reality. They are eternal, intangible, and immutable, present always and everywhere, self-existent and self-identical (*Tim.* 28 a–9 a, 52 a). Above all, they are true ($\grave{\alpha}\lambda\eta\theta\eta s$, *Rep.* vii. 515 c, 516 a; *Polit.* 300 d). These ideas form a pattern or model ($\pi\alpha\rho\delta\delta\epsilon\iota\gamma\mu\alpha$) of which all earthly phenomena are a copy ($\epsilon\iota\kappa\omega\nu$ or $\mu\iota\mu\eta\mu\alpha$) or shadow ($\sigma\kappa\iota\delta$) (*Tim.* 29 b, 48 e–49 a; *Rep.* vii. 515 a, c, 516 a, 517 d). Thus the creator made the world by fashioning it after the form of the model. The model, since it is eternal, was there all the time, and all the creator had to do was to look at it and mould a world in its likeness (*Tim.* 28 a–29 a). The phenomenal world is good inasmuch as it is a copy of an

---

[1] Barthélemy and Milik, op. cit., p. 126.

eternal and enduring reality, but it is transient and imperfect
inasmuch as it is only a copy and nothing more (*Rep.* vii. 514 ff.).
Although Plato assigns the ideas to the heavenly world (οὐρανός
or ὑπερουράνιος τόπος) he does not think of them as existing in
a particular place. It is because of our finite understanding that
we assume that they exist 'in some place' (ἔν τινι τόπῳ), occupying
a certain space (*Tim.* 52 b, c).

That Judaism was familiar with this tradition is clear from the
writings of Philo (and, as we shall see, the Epistle to the Hebrews).
Philo employs Platonic idealism to explain the origin of Israel's
cultic system.[1] Starting from the view that God made the
universe (of sense-perception) according to a heavenly pattern
(κόσμος νοητός, so called because it exists in the mind, νοῦς),
which he fashioned first (*Opif.* 15 ff.), Philo writes concerning the
tabernacle:

> It was determined, therefore, to fashion a tabernacle, a work of the
> highest sanctity, the construction of which was set forth to Moses on
> the mount by divine pronouncements. He saw with the soul's eye the
> immaterial forms of the material objects about to be made, and these
> forms had to be reproduced in copies (μιμήματα) perceived by the
> senses, taken from the original draught (ἀρχέτυπος), so to speak, and
> from patterns conceived in the mind . . . . So the shape of the model
> (παράδειγμα) was stamped upon the mind of the prophet, a secretly
> painted or moulded prototype, produced by immaterial and invisible
> forms; and then the resulting work was built in accordance with that
> shape by the artist impressing the stampings upon the material sub-
> stances required in each case (*Mos.* ii. 74–6; see also i. 158; *QE*
> ii. 52, 82).[2]

The archetypal sanctuary, we note, is created by God. More
than that Philo does not tell us, but the absence of other informa-
tion is to be attributed to the nature of the task in hand rather
than to Philo's well-known dislike for traditional Jewish cultic
media. He is describing the tabernacle of Moses and could not
easily embark upon an account of the furnishings or worship of
the heavenly holy place. It is worth noting in this connection,
however, that in his use of the Stoic conception of the cosmic
temple Philo says that the heavenly (or uppermost) part (the
νεώς) of this temple is inhabited by immortal beings (*Som.* i. 34)

---

[1] For Philo's use of the ideas of Plato see H. A. Wolfson, *Philo* (1948), i. 200 ff.
[2] Translation from the Loeb Classical Library edition.

and has angels as priests (*Spec.* i. 66) and the Logos for its high priest (*Som.* i. 215).[1] This interpretation of the heavenly temple and priesthood is of course quite different from the idea of the heavenly temple in the Jewish apocalyptic and rabbinic traditions.[2]

The one point at which Philo reinterprets the Platonic doctrine of archetypes in terms of his Jewish heritage is his statement that the archetypes are created.[3] Here he departs radically from Plato, who, as we have seen, regarded the heavenly ideas or patterns as eternal and uncreated (*Tim.* 28 a–9 b).

We shall find Platonic ideas used to interpret the heavenly sanctuary in the Epistle to the Hebrews.

Summary

The findings of this chapter concerning the heavenly temple indicate one of the ways in which the idea of the new temple developed. They show how from very obscure beginnings the idea of the heavenly dwelling of God took a firm hold in the mind of Judaism and drew to itself the traditional hope of the eschatological or new temple. Since the heavenly temple is the new temple it follows that it must one day descend to earth, and the foregoing chapter shows how the fusion of the concept of the heavenly temple and the new temple found its logical outcome in the conviction that in the eschatological age when God dwelt with his people in a new and unprecedented way he would bring his temple with him from heaven.

The transcendentalizing of the divine presence was in many ways a theological necessity, serving to compensate on the one hand for the non-fulfilment of Old Testament prophecy concerning the earthly temple and on the other hand for the shortcomings of the earthly temple. What if the temple of Jerusalem did not become great, or if men might never build a temple worthy of the presence of God or inviolate by the profanities of men? God had his own temple. 'Dost thou think that this is the city of which I said: "On the palms of my hands have I graven

---

[1] On Philo's reinterpretation of the high priest as the Logos see also *Som.* ii. 188 f.; *Quis Rer.* 205–6.

[2] Cf. Wenschkewitz, op. cit., p. 137.

[3] Usually Philo says that God created the archetypes, but he can say that Moses created them (*Alleg.* iii. 102).

thee"? ' (2 Bar. 4. 2). No indeed. The new temple would not be made by the hand of man. It was the temple which had been with God since before the creation of the world, and it would come down from heaven with him when he once again returned to tabernacle in the midst of his people.

IV

THE SPIRITUAL TEMPLE IN JEWISH AND GREEK LITERATURE[1]

THE period which we are studying in these early chapters also witnessed a further tendency which is important for our understanding of the New Testament doctrine of the church as the new temple, namely, the spiritualizing of temple and cult.

Once again we touch upon a phenomenon of ancient religion which was not peculiar to the Jews alone. The Greeks also spiritualized their religious institutions. Although the theological presuppositions of the Jews and their Hellenistic neighbours were quite different, there was agreement on the view that the cult is the symbol of the disposition of the worshipper (and the deity's acknowledgement of it), and apart from the correct disposition the act itself is valueless. The ramifications of this common outlook were also shared by Jews and non-Jews alike. Throughout the Mediterranean world at the beginning of the Christian period it was a widely accepted belief that the correct disposition of heart and will was acceptable to God whether accompanied by sacrifice or not.

In his valuable study of the subject of the spiritualization of the cultus, Hans Wenschkewitz distinguishes between what he calls a naïve and a reflective form of spiritualization.[2] The former he finds beginning in the prophets and the Psalms of the Old Testament and continuing in the Apocrypha and Pseudepigrapha and the New Testament, where it merges with the reflective

[1] The word 'spiritual' is not altogether satisfactory for our purpose. The opposition in character and in quality to what is bodily, material, and earthly which the term normally implies does not apply to the Biblical and ancient tradition, which never divorced the material and the spiritual. Spiritualization of worship means its interiorization, inasmuch as the emphasis is on the intention, disposition, and motivation of the worshipper, but it means more than this, for the ancients were not only concerned with *why* a certain thing was done but *that* it was done. Perhaps 'integrity' is the word we should have in mind when we think of spiritualization at least in regard to the Old Testament.

[2] 'Die Spiritualisierung der Kultusbegriffe Tempel, Priester und Opfer im Neuen Testament', *Ang.* 4 (1932), 77–230.

type. The reflective type, he says, is represented by the Stoics and Philo. This is a helpful distinction, for there is obviously a difference between the occasional and tentative instances of spiritualization which one finds in the Old Testament and later Jewish writings, and the systematic reinterpretation of the cultus undertaken by Philo and the Stoics; but one would not wish to draw the lines so sharply. The spiritualization in the prophets, such as it is, surely warrants inclusion in the reflective type, while the systematic type which Wenschkewitz believed was confined to Hellenism and Hellenistic Judaism (Philo) is now seen to include Palestinian Judaism (Dead Sea Scrolls).

The Spiritualization of the Cultus in Jewish Writings

The trenchant criticism of sacrifice by the pre-exilic prophets (Amos 5. 21–7; Isa. 1. 11–17; Mic. 6. 6–8; Hos. 6. 6; Jer. 6. 20; 7. 21–2) does not imply a spiritualization of the cult but it prepared the way for it. It did this by distinguishing between the cultic act and the motive of the offerer. The cult was shown to have importance only in so far as it symbolized one's commitment to the covenant; it was the spirit of the worshipper expressing itself in righteousness that gave it value. The effect of the prophetic criticism was thus to make righteous living the touchstone of the cultus.

The Psalms developed this tendency. Ps. 40 recalls the prophetic criticism of sacrifice, but it questions the offering of sacrifice at all as an adequate response to the goodness of God. God is so great and his doings so incomparable (vv. 4–5) that sacrifice is really out of place; the only possible response is a ready and joyful obedience to the will of God (vv. 6–8). Very similar is Ps. 50; cf. Isa. 66. 1–2. The inner disposition of heart and will is now itself regarded as a sacrifice (Ps. 51. 15–17; Hos. 14. 2), though there is no suggestion, however, that this does away with burnt offerings (cf. Ps. 51. 18 f.; 69. 9). Since sacrifice in Israel was essentially the expression of one's response to God in praise and thanksgiving, it was natural that these things should themselves have come to be looked upon as sacrifices (Pss. 50. 23; 69. 30 f.; cf. Hos. 14. 2). The same is true of prayer, which always accompanied sacrifice; it is now considered to be a sacrifice (Ps. 141. 2).

This trend found fruitful soil in diaspora Judaism, since it was very largely cut off from worship at Jerusalem. 'Every sacrifice as a fragrant offering is a small thing, and all fat for burnt offerings to thee is a very little thing, but he who fears the Lord shall be great for ever' (Judith 16. 16). Again, 'When the Lord demands bread, or candles, or flesh, or any other sacrifice, then that is nothing; but God demands pure hearts . . .' (Slav. En. 45. 3). 'What is the highest form of glory? And he said, "To honour God, and this is done not with gifts and sacrifices but with purity of soul and holy conviction"' (*Arist.* 234).[1] The emphasis on the inner motivation is here expressed in terms drawn from a markedly Hellenistic milieu: 'He who offers a sacrifice, makes an offering also of his own soul in all its moods' (ibid. 170). All these witnesses are authors who held the temple of Jerusalem in the highest regard and who evidently practised a non-sacrificial form of religion alongside the conventional mode of worship. But that it represents a tendency which ultimately was able to exist quite apart from the traditional cultus is clear from a passage like the LXX supplement to Dan. 3:

> We have at this time no leader, no prophet, no prince,
> no holocaust, no sacrifice, no oblation, no incense,
> no place where we can offer you the first-fruits
> and win your favour.
> But may the contrite soul, the humbled spirit be as acceptable to you
> as holocausts of rams and bullocks,
> as thousands of fatted lambs:
> such let our sacrifice be to you today,
> and may it be your will that we follow you wholeheartedly,
> since those who put their trust in you will not be disappointed.
>
> (vv. 38–40) (JB)

The one thing more than any other, perhaps, which contributed to the spiritualization of the cultus was the transformation of Israelite religion into a religion of law. Let us recall that in ancient Israel the cult was pre-eminently the symbol of the grace of God (Lev. 17. 11). With the ascendancy of the law the cultus underwent a radical change.[2] The change was a subtle one and

---

[1] Cf. *Arist.* 19, 37 (release of slaves is a sacrifice). Cf. ibid. 169.

[2] Wenschkewitz, op. cit., pp. 88 f.; W. Eichrodt, *Theology of the Old Testament* (1961), i. 169 ff.; J. Behm, *TDNT* iii. 186 f. M. Noth, *The Laws in the Pentateuch and Other Studies* (1966), pp. 1–107.

very likely unnoticed at first. It doubtless appeared to many that
the new importance accorded to the law enhanced the cult. Did
the law not guarantee the regular offering of sacrifice? In actual
fact what it really meant was the reversal of the traditional order
of things. The cult was maintained in order to fulfil the law. The
effect was far reaching. Sacrifice was no longer the sacrament of
the presence of God and communion with him, a source of blessing in its own right, but an *opus operatum* for hastening the
coming of the eschatological age. As the cult thus lost its unique
position as the centre of the sacramental life of Israel and became
integrated into a series of similar meritorious forms of legal ob-
servances, any one of which atoned for sins and merited forgiveness, the way was wide open for interpreting obedience to the
law in a cultic sense.

The mood of the period we are now studying is well illustrated
by Ben-Sira: 'He who keeps the law makes many offerings; he
who heeds the commandments sacrifices a peace offering' (Ecclus.
35. 1). Even in an author so favourably disposed to the temple as
the author of Jubilees one finds the same thing: 'He caused His
commands to ascend as a sweet savour (ὀσμὴ εὐωδίας) acceptable
before Him all the days' (2. 22).[1] The spiritualizing of the cultus
in the Dead Sea Scrolls will be considered in detail below; here
we would note the fact that the founding of the community at
Qumran is entirely bound up with the belief that atonement for
sins is achieved through obedience to the law without any reference
whatever to the temple of Jerusalem. Thus 'He (God) has commanded that a Sanctuary of men be built for Himself, that there
they may send up, like the smoke of incense, the works of the
Law' (4 Q Flor. 1. 6 f; cf. 1 QS 9. 3–5).[2] The worship of the
temple is now replaced by obedience to the law. Similarly
the following is typical of much rabbinic writing on the subject:
'*Even pure oblations* (of Mal. 1. 11)—this refers to one who studies
the Torah in purity . . . whosoever occupies himself with the
Torah is as though he were offering a burnt offering, a meal
offering, a sin offering, and a guilt offering' (B. Men. 110a).

As might be expected this trend was greatly accelerated by the
destruction of the temple of Jerusalem in A.D. 70. All kinds of

---

[1] Cf. Gen. 8. 21. ὀσμὴ εὐωδίας is the expression used at Jub. 3. 27; 4. 26; 6. 3;
16. 23; 21. 7, 9 for the temple sacrifices.
[2] G. Vermes, *The Dead Sea Scrolls in English* (1962), pp. 243 f.

equivalents for sacrifice now appear: prayer, fasting, almsgiving, and suffering patiently borne.[1] In place of the worship of the temple (עבודה) we have the worship of the heart (עבודה שבלב).[2] The rabbis proceeded on the principle 'as if'; the temple no longer existed, but the devout bowed in worship in its direction and learnt and recited the ritual formulae as if it did. But this was done because the law commanded it, and all the while the other principle we noted above was at work: that which said in effect not, do this, and it will be *as if* you had offered sacrifice, but, do this and you do not need to offer sacrifice.[3] Thus we have in the Mishnah the following reinterpretation of the temple: 'If two (persons) sit together and words of the Law (are spoken) between them, the Divine Presence (i.e. the *sh^ekhînâh*) rests between them' (Aboth 3. 2; cf. 3. 6). The important conception of the community of the faithful as a spiritual temple which the rabbis were reaching after is definitively expressed in the Dead Sea Scrolls.

Community as Temple[4]

That the Jews of Qumran were affected by the spiritualizing influences that affected Judaism generally may safely be taken for granted. Their immediate motive for spiritualizing the cultus, however, was their dissatisfaction with the temple of Jerusalem and their belief that they were called by God to provide an alternative means of atonement for both themselves and Israel at large.[5]

The scroll of greatest interest to us is the Manual of Discipline (5. 5–6; 8. 4–10; 9. 3–6). We shall examine each of the passages in turn:

[1] See at length Wenschkewitz, op. cit., pp. 88 ff.; S–B i. 246; iii. 26, 152, 607; iv. 541, 555; Moore, *Judaism*, i. 504 ff.; J. R. Brown, *Temple and Sacrifice in Rabbinic Judaism* (1963); R. A. Stewart, *Rabbinic Theology* (1961), pp. 124 ff. The death of the Maccabean martyrs is already given a sacrificial interpretation at 2 Macc. 7. 37 f. Cf. 4 Macc. 6. 27 ff.; 17. 22. See G. Vermes, *Scripture and Tradition in Judaism* (1961), pp. 193 ff.

[2] Moore, *Judaism*, ii. 217 ff.

[3] Brown, op. cit., p. 28.

[4] Cf. the important study of B. Gärtner, *The Temple and the Community in Qumran and the New Testament* (1965).

[5] On the sect's quarrel with the Jerusalem priesthood and calendar see e.g. J. T. Milik, *Ten Years of Discovery in the Wilderness of Judaea* (1959), pp. 66 ff., 77 ff.

They shall lay a foundation of truth for Israel, for the community of an eternal covenant. They shall atone for all those who devote themselves, for a sanctuary (קודש)[1] in Aaron and for a house of truth (בית האמת) in Israel, and (for) those who join them for a community (5. 5–6).[2]

The text is based on Isa. 28. 16. The original sense of Isaiah's words can hardly be said to apply to a community,[3] but the Qumran exegete gives it this interpretation.[4] The reference is to the founding of the community. Although it is not explicitly stated, one may, on the basis of the use of Isa. 28. 16 at 1 QS 8. 7 ff., take the 'foundation of truth' as a parallel to 'house of truth', and understand the writer to mean that the founding of the community represents the founding of a new and better temple. The community by adhering to God's will as laid down in the law is itself a temple. It is called 'true' in contradistinction to the temple of Jerusalem, which it displaces, because the latter has forfeited its right to be regarded as the representative of the revelation and truth of God.[5] Since the new temple supersedes the old, it takes over its cultic function, and this in turn is spiritualized. The nature of the new cult is not mentioned in this text, but other texts make it clear that it is observance of the law (9. 3 ff.; 4 Q Flor. 1. 6 f.).

The next passage to be considered is 1 QS 8. 4–10. This is the fullest expression of the spiritual temple concept in the Qumran literature. Dupont-Sommer translates as follows:

When these things come to pass in Israel, the Council of the Community shall be established in truth as an everlasting planting.[6] It is the House of holiness for Israel and the Company of infinite holiness for Aaron[7] (בית קודש לישראל וסוד קודש קודשים לאהרון); they

---

[1] Dupont-Sommer and Burrows translate qwdsh as 'holiness'. Wernberg-Møller, following Milik, argues more convincingly that qwdsh parallels byt and should be translated 'sanctuary'.

[2] Translation by P. Wernberg-Møller, *The Manual of Discipline, Translated and Annotated with an Introduction* (1957), p. 28.

[3] Cf., however, S. H. Hooke, *The Siege Perilous* (1956), p. 241.

[4] So also at 1 QS 8. 4 ff. on which see below. At 1 QH 6. 26 the stone of Isa. 28. 16 is alluded to as the basis of God's house of truth.

[5] Gärtner, op. cit., p. 23.

[6] For the description of the community as a plant see also 1 QS 11. 8; CD 1. 7; cf. 1 QH 6. 15 ff. We shall find a similar fusion of architectural and physiological images in the New Testament presentation of the church as the temple (Eph. 2. 19 ff.).

[7] Wernberg-Møller thinks that the preposition ל (לאהרון and לישראל) is used

are the witnesses of truth unto Judgment and the chosen of Loving-kindness appointed to offer expiation for the earth and to bring down punishment upon the wicked. It is the tried wall, the precious corner-stone (פנת יקר); its foundations shall not tremble[1] nor flee from their place. It is the Dwelling of infinite holiness (מעון קודש קודשים) for Aaron in (eternal) Knowledge unto the Covenant of justice and to make offerings of sweet savour; it is the House (בית) of perfection and truth in Israel to establish the Covenant according to the ever-lasting precepts. And they shall be accepted as expiation for the earth and to decree the judgment of wickedness with no perversity re-maining (8. 4–10).[2]

The importance of this passage is evident at once from the fact that it forms the central part of that section of the Manual which is generally regarded as being the charter of the community, 8. 1–10. 16. However, since the section opens with a reference to the 'council of the twelve', the question is immediately raised as to whether what follows (including the doctrine of the spiritual temple) applies to this smaller group within the community. Scholars are divided on this point, but the majority believe that it is the community at large that is in view. In any event, if the 'twelve' symbolize the twelve tribes, as seems likely, the problem is more apparent than real.

to avoid a series of construct states, and accordingly translates the text thus: 'a holy house consisting of Israel, and a most holy congregation consisting of Aaron' (op. cit., p. 33). This, in his opinion, retains what he considers is the essential meaning of the passage, viz. the community as the true temple and the true Israel. On grammatical grounds it is possible, though not usual, to render this use of the preposition by 'of'. What we would question, however, is the interpretation which this rendering gives to the context. The meaning of Plate 8 appears to be that the sectarian exodus to the desert was undertaken in order to atone for the sins of the whole nation (8. 6; 9. 3–5; cf. 1 QSa 1. 3; 1 QM 2. 5–6). In other words the com-munity covenanted to be a sanctuary in which the faithful priesthood (the sons of Zadok, otherwise 'Aaron') could effect atonement not merely for themselves (as Wernberg-Møller implies) but for the whole degenerate nation. That this is the correct interpretation is strongly suggested by the use that the sect made of the Servant motif, which, in fact, is present in the context of our passage (8. 6b). T. H. Gaster's translation of the companion piece 9. 5b–6 preserves what, it seems to me, is the sense of the passage: 'At that time, the men of the community will constitute a true and distinctive temple—a veritable holy of holies—wherein the priesthood may fitly forgather' (*The Scriptures of the Dead Sea Sect* (1957), p. 67).
    [1] According to the textual insertion. Both the author and his editor alter the text of Isa. 28. 16 (note the use of the plurals) to make the reference to their community explicit. Cf. 1 QH. 6. 26 where we have the plural, 'tested stones'. The Targumist saw a reference to the Messiah in Isa. 28. 16. It is obvious that we are not far from the thought of the New Testament (cf. 1 Pet. 2. 4 ff.).
    [2] Op. cit., p. 91.

The thought of this text is similar to that of 5. 5–6, particularly in its use of Isa. 28. 16. This Old Testament text is now employed in an interesting way. The community at Qumran is the righteous remnant which God has laid as a foundation, a tested cornerstone in Israel, in order to confute the falsehood at Jerusalem (cf. Isa. 28. 17 ff.). That the figure of the stone is related to that of the temple (*báyith*) in the preceding lines is highly probable since the author deliberately changes Isaiah's thought to make it apply to the body of believers, whom he has just designated as a temple.[1] The use of the cornerstone idea is very likely an epexegesis on the temple motif, intended, one may assume, to emphasize the divinely authoritative and eschatological character of the sect. The mention of the wall is a new thought and anticipates an interesting fusion of the temple and building figures which we shall find in the New Testament.[2] For this author, however, the 'tried wall' alludes not to the superstructure or process of building, but (as with the foundation-stone) to the stability of the edifice (cf. 1 QH 6. 25 f.; 7. 8 f.).

According to the present text the temple of Qumran has two parts, a holy place and a holy of holies. Unfortunately this detail does not come out very well in the translation used above, but it is quite clear in the original, both here and at 9. 6. One does not have to ask where the author found his inspiration for this interesting elaboration of the image; his fondness for the book of Numbers makes that plain enough. His purpose in designating the priesthood a holy of holies is to show the important place in the community occupied by the priesthood.[3] Thus the description of the community as a temple at 1 QS 9. 5b–7 is immediately followed by directives concerning the prerogatives and authority of the priests at Qumran.

The final text from the Manual of Discipline for our consideration is 9. 3–6. It may be translated as follows:

---

[1] But it does not seem permissible to explain the relation between the cornerstone and the house in this text by saying that the council of the twelve represents the foundation upon which the community is erected (*contra* B. Reicke, *The Scrolls and the New Testament*, ed. K. Stendahl (1958), p. 152).

[2] Gärtner unjustifiably argues that in 1 QS 8. 7 'wall' is a substitute for 'stone' (op. cit., pp. 27, 77 f., 134). It is true that the word 'stone' is missing, but 'corner' (פנה) does service for it. Cf. the use of *pinnāh* alone at Isa. 19. 13; Ps. 118. 22.

[3] Cf. e.g. J. M. Baumgarten, 'Sacrifice and Worship among the Jewish Sectarians of the Dead Sea (Qumrân) Scrolls', *HTR* 46 (1953), 154.

When these (things) come to pass in Israel according to all these regulations, it is to found the spirit of holiness for eternal truth. They shall make atonement for culpable rebellion and wicked wrongdoing, and secure blessing for the land without the flesh of burnt offering and the fat of sacrifice; but the offering of the lips in accordance with the law shall be as an acceptable odour of righteousness, and a perfect way of life as a free-will pleasing sacrifice. At that time the members of the community shall be set apart as a holy place (קודש בית) for Aaron, in order to be united as the holy of holies and a house of community for Israel (קודש קודשים ובית יחד לישראל להוחד) for those who walk in faithfulness.

The text and sense of this passage are much less straightforward than is the case with 5. 5–6 and 8. 4–10. The word we have translated as 'to be united' (להוחד) presents particular difficulty,[1] and, although the two parts of the temple are mentioned, it is not certain whether they are applied to the personnel with the precision of 8. 4–10. However, the general sense is reasonably clear: the community is a cohesive unit and functions as God's temple. For the rest we shall probably be best guided if we adopt the meaning suggested by Gaster's rendering. He paraphrases it thus: 'At that time, the men of the community will constitute a true and distinctive temple—a veritable holy of holies—wherein the priesthood may fitly forgather.'[2] In other words, the laity act as a temple so as to enable the faithful priests to carry on with their duties. This should not be taken to mean, however, that the lay members of the community do not themselves have sacrifices to offer. They do; the whole of the community's life, as it adheres to the law, is sacrificial. At the same time it is clear that those acts performed by the priests within the group were considered to have special importance.

The nature of the cult now receives extended treatment. More than ever its spiritual character is emphasized. The 'offering of lips' takes the place of the material sacrifices of Jerusalem.[3]

Another Qumran text which some scholars take as a reference to the spiritual temple and cult is 4 Q Florilegium. This fragment is a midrash on 2 Sam. 7. 10–14, Nathan's prophecy to David concerning the temple, which is here given an eschatological

---

[1] What justification Wernberg-Møller (op. cit., p. 35) has for treating it as a gloss and rendering it as a substantive is not clear.

[2] Op. cit., p. 67.

[3] See further Gärtner, op. cit., pp. 44–6, 124.

interpretation. But whether or not one finds the doctrine of the spiritual temple in this text depends on how one renders the original. Gärtner translates it as follows: 'And he proposed to build him a temple of (among) men (מקדש אדם), in which should be offered sacrifices before him, the works of the law' (1. 6 f.).[1] This translation gives the temple and cult a spiritual interpretation. Gärtner thus classifies the text along with those considered above from 1 QS. The same interpretation is adopted by Vermes.[2] Other scholars, however, are of the opinion that it is the material temple and cult that is intended. Allegro renders the text thus: 'a man-made sanctuary in which sacrifices might be made for him.'[3] Dupont-Sommer renders it: 'a sanctuary (made by the hands) of man to be built for Himself, that there may be some in this sanctuary to send up the smoke of sacrifice in his honour before Him among those who observe the Law.'[4] The reference is thus to the temple of Jerusalem of the end-time. The latter interpretation should probably be adopted for the following reasons. (a) The general futuristic orientation of 4 Q Flor. suggests that what is in mind is the temple and cult of Jerusalem when it has been restored to the rightful priesthood (cf. 1 QM). (b) The statement in the context that 'strangers shall not again make it desolate, as they desolated once the sanctuary of Israel' (1. 5) rather indicates that the temple which is contrasted with the defiled temple of Jerusalem is the restored temple of Jerusalem of the messianic age.

The fragment 4 Q pIsa[d] is also taken by Gärtner to contain a reference to the spiritual temple.[5] It is a *pesher* on Isa. 54. 11 f.: 'I will set your stones in antimony, and lay your foundations with sapphires.' Gärtner thinks that the 'stones' were taken by the sect to refer to the lay members of the order and the 'sapphires' to the priests, who together form the temple of Qumran. But apart from the fact that the very fragmentary state of the scroll makes such identification uncertain, the sense is much more likely to be eschatological, as in Deutero-Isaiah, and refer to the glorification of Zion.

---

[1] Op. cit., p. 34.
[2] Op. cit., pp. 243 f.
[3] J. Allegro, 'Fragments of a Qumran Scroll of Eschatological Midrāšim', *JBL* 77 (1958), 352.
[4] Op. cit., p. 312.
[5] Op. cit., pp. 42, 78 f.

With the spiritual temple in the foregoing texts one should compare the figurative use of the building image in the *Hodayot*:[1]

> I was like a man who entered a fortified city and sought refuge in a steep wall awaiting deliverance. And I lea(ned on) Thy truth, O my God. For it is Thou who wilt set the foundation upon rock and the frame-work on the cord of righteousness and the plumb-line (of truth) to (tes)t the tried stones in order to (build) a stout bui(ld)i(ng) such as will not shake, and that none who enter there shall stagger (1 QH 6. 25–7).

> Thou hast set me up as a stout tower, as a steep rampart, and hast established my fabric upon rock; and everlasting foundations serve me for my ground and all my walls are a tried rampart which nothing can shake (7. 8–9).[2]

These texts introduce us to a different realm of ideas from that of the temple image; the thought is architectural and not cultic. There is some evidence, however, that the sect fused the two conceptions (1 QS 8. 4 ff.). The dominant idea in the *Hodayot* texts is that of the stability and permanence of the building rather than that of the actual construction or superstructure, even though the foundation and wall are mentioned.[3] In this connection Isa. 28. 16 is the chief source of inspiration, as at 1 QS 8. 4 ff., but here the emphasis is more on the individual and his membership of the community than on the community as in the 1 QS texts (cf. 1 QH 7. 4). To belong to the community is like being part of a building that is erected upon rock. The rock symbolizes God's truth as revealed to the community.

The presence of spiritual temple and spiritual sacrifice in the scrolls encourages one to ask whether the sect also reinterpreted the idea of the priesthood. At times it almost seems that these Jews taught something like the doctrine of the priesthood of all believers (CD 4. 1–2), but in fact they held to traditional ideas in this regard. The priestly caste was preserved, and the community was ruled by priests.[4]

---

[1] Cf. O. Betz, 'Felsenmann und Felsengemeinde', *ZNW* 48 (1957), 49–77.

[2] Dupont-Sommer, op, cit., pp. 220, 222. Similar is the thought of 1 QH 7. 4. Cf. also the Qumran commentary on Ps. 37, where the Teacher of Righteousness is described as the one 'whom (God) established to build for Himself the Congregation' (Dupont-Sommer, op. cit., p. 272).

[3] Gärtner, op. cit., p. 77.

[4] Gärtner, op. cit., p. 9.

This concludes our examination of the scrolls. The novel character of their teaching on the temple is obvious. That there were Jews of Palestine who believed that atonement for sin outside Jerusalem was possible and regarded a spiritual temple and cult as a satisfactory alternative for the traditional temple and cult was of the greatest significance not only for the rise of Christianity but for the future of Judaism. At the same time, it is plain that the spiritualizing undertaken by Qumran, for all its radical and thoroughgoing character, does not mean that the material temple and cult were rejected for good. All the evidence goes to show that the hope of a new or restored temple at Jerusalem was cherished just as ardently by these Jews as by other Jews (CD 4. 1 ff.; 1 QM 2. 1 ff.; 12. 12 ff.; 19. 5 ff.).[1] It would appear that here as elsewhere in late post-exilic Judaism the new temple concept acted as an inhibiting influence, preventing Jewry from regarding the spiritualized cultus as a satisfactory permanent substitute for the material cultus.

Man as Temple

The spiritualization of the cultus is also to be found in Hellenism.[2] It has its roots in a critical attitude towards the material cult which can be traced back to the classical period (cf. e.g. Pl. *Leg.* iv. 716 d; Xenoph. *Mem.* i. iii. 3; *Ana.* v. vii. 32; Isoc. *Orat.* 2. 20; Eur. *Fr.* 329). Sacrifice which does not issue in moral behaviour comes in for particularly severe criticism by the Stoics, even to the point of complete rejection. 'Would you propitiate the gods?' asks Seneca: 'Then be a good man. Whoever imitates them is worshipping them sufficiently' (*Ep.* xcv. 50). The worship most acceptable to the gods is that offered in purity, sincerity, and innocence of thought and speech (Cic. *Nat.* ii. 71).

It is against such a background that we have to consider the Stoic and Philonic idea of man as the temple of God. The Stoics do not actually call man a temple, but the idea is clearly implied. Seneca has most to say on the subject. Every human being, he declares, houses a part of the divine spirit (*Helv.* xi. 7). Divine seeds (*semina divina*) are implanted in human bodies (*Ep.* lxxiii. 16).

---

[1] See also the 'New Jerusalem' texts cited above p. 37, n. 1.
[2] Cf. Wenschkewitz, pp. 113 ff.; Behm, *TDNT* iii. 187 f.; W. Barclay, 'Hellenistic Thought in New Testament Times', *ET* 72 (1961), 258–61.

We do not need to uplift out hands towards heaven, or beg the keeper of a temple to let us approach his idol's ear, as if in this way our prayers were more likely to be heard. God is near you, he is with you, he is within you (*Ep.* xli. 1).

No good man indeed is without God (*Ep.* xli. 2).

The same ideas are also found in the more conservative Epictetus:

Wherefore, when you close your doors and make darkness within, remember never to say that you are alone, for you are not alone; nay, God (θεός) is within you, and your own genius (δαίμων) is within (*Disc.* I. xiv. 13 f.).

Man is a part (ἀπόσπασμα) of God and he should conduct himself accordingly (*Disc.* II. viii. 11 f.). God is in him (ὁ ἐν σοὶ θεός) as guide and counsellor (Marcus Aur. iii. 5). Although there is a certain lack of consistency as to who or what it is that indwells man (sometimes it is God or the δαίμων or ἀπόσπασμα θεοῦ, sometimes the mind, νοῦς or *animus*, or the divine seed(s)), the essential idea is clear: man is the dwelling or temple of a supernatural being or entity.

Philo stands firmly in this tradition. He begins by telling us that there are two temples: the sky, which is the dwelling-place of immortal beings; and the mind or soul of man, which is the temple of God (*Som.* i. 21–34, 215; *Opif.* 145 f.). Philo proceeds to extol the latter:

For what more worthy house could be found for God throughout the whole world of creation, than a soul (ψυχή) that is perfectly purified? (*Sobr.* 62.)

Be zealous therefore, O soul, to become a house of God, a holy temple, a most beauteous abiding-place; for perchance, the Master of the whole world's household shall be thine too and keep thee under His care as His special house, to preserve thee evermore strongly guarded and unharmed (*Som.* i. 149).[1]

The latter is from Philo's commentary on Jacob's dream at Bethel (Gen. 28. 10 ff.). He explains that the ladder at Bethel is the soul. The bottom of the ladder is sense-perception; the top is the purified mind. The descending and ascending angels are the words of God (λόγοι), which cleanse the soul and lead it up to

---

[1] See also *Som.* ii. 251; *Cher.* 100; *Virt.* 188.

God. Thus completely purified, the soul becomes the dwelling-place of the Lord of the universe, who inhabits it in a silent and invisible fashion (*Som.* i. 146–8).

There is this significant difference between Philo and the Stoics: whereas the Stoics regarded the divine indwelling as a natural endowment, Philo regarded it as the result of deliberate moral effort. In other words Philo rejected the pantheistic pre-suppositions of Stoic anthropology.

It is important to note in regard to the teaching of both the Stoics and Philo that the spiritual temple is an essentially in-dividualistic concept. Even where the Stoics deduce the thought of the fatherhood of God and the brotherhood of men from the doctrine of the divine indwelling (Epic. *Disc.* i. xiii), there is nothing comparable to the Qumran and New Testament con-ception of the community forming a spiritual temple. Secondly, in these writers there is a studied reluctance to suggest that the body (σῶμα) is the dwelling-place of the deity. Seneca, who per-haps of all the Stoics comes closest to the idea,[1] makes it clear that the thought of deity indwelling the body is intolerable. The body, he asserts, is essentially useless and perishable flesh (*Ep.* xcii. 10); it is the inconsequential prison-house, or at best the hospice of the soul (*Helv.* xi. 7; *Marc.* xxiv. 5; *Ep.* cxx. 14), in which the soul is never at home, but exists as in a strange place (*Otio* v. 5 f.).[2] The same is true of Philo. Only in the case of Adam, the perfect man, does he suggest that the body is the temple of God (*Opif.* 137). The body for him, as for his Greek mentors, is the prison of the soul (*Migr. Abr.* 9; *Alleg.* i. 108; *Immut.* 150; *Ebr.* 101).

Summary

This chapter has attempted to show how in the ancient world there developed, alongside the traditional cultus, a cultus with-out temples and sacrifices, and that in some quarters the ten-dency was for the latter to supplant the former. The motives of the movement varied greatly. In Palestinian Judaism they had to do mainly with the supersession of traditional cultic media by

[1] Cf. *Ep.* xxxi. 11: 'What else could you call such a (righteous and good) soul than a god dwelling as a guest in a human body (*in corpore humano*)?'

[2] Cf. the body–prison (σῶμα–σῆμα) idea in Pl. *Gorg.* 493 a. The idea is of Orphic origin (cf. *Crat.* 400 c).

the law. In Hellenistic Judaism the same is true but here extra-
neous influences of a mystical and philosophical kind were also
present. There is, moreover, the simple fact that diaspora Judaism,
like Judaism generally of the post A.D. 70 period, learned to
worship God without temple or sacrifice. In Greek circles the
movement away from the material cultus may be said to stem
from the ethicizing of religion. From the point where it was
accepted that the worship of the gods should issue in justice,
love, and mercy in human relationships, it was a short step to the
position where acts of justice, love, and mercy were themselves
considered to be acceptable sacrifices. Where the spiritualization
of the temple is particularly concerned, philosophical tendencies
also played their part; divinity was believed to inhabit man
because it was believed to inhabit everything.

The conception of the community of the faithful as a spiritual
temple is specially significant for students of the New Testament.
Wenschkewitz in his important work gave it as his opinion that
the New Testament doctrine of the church as a spiritual
temple was nowhere anticipated in Palestinian Judaism, and its
origin should be sought in the Stoic and Philonic notion of man
as a temple.[1] This has been a widely held view, as any scholarly
commentary on the epistles of Paul will testify.[2] It must now be
revised. The discovery of the Qumran scrolls has demonstrated
that the idea of the community as a temple did indeed exist
before New Testament times and that it is not necessary to go
outside Palestinian Judaism to look for it.

The findings of this chapter serve to qualify those of preceding
chapters. The new understanding of atonement that followed the
elevation of the law could not but have serious consequences for
the dogma of the new temple, since the latter could exist only
as the traditional cultus was seen to be indispensable. There were
thus opposing tendencies in the Judaism of Jesus' time: the
spiritualizing of the cultus, and the belief in a restored or new
cultus, with the latter acting as a kind of brake on the former.
The transcendentalizing of the divine presence and the identification of the heavenly temple as the new temple did nothing to

---

[1] Wenschkewitz, pp. 164, 178, 180.
[2] It was questioned by M. Fraeyman, 'La Spiritualisation de l'Idée du Temple
dans les Épîtres pauliniennes', *ETL* 23 (1947) 411, but the criticism was of a
general nature because the evidence from the scrolls was not then available.

solve this problem. Robbed of the unique role it had traditionally held, and to all intents and purposes pushed out of the vital centre of Judaism, the temple had for the great majority of Jews become a cipher. The new temple doctrine therefore rested upon a fiction. Only as it was spiritualized could it hope to survive. This never happened in Judaism, and the period closes without this bifurcation of the cultus being overcome. It was left to Christianity to solve the problem in terms of a temple which was at once new and spiritual.

V

JESUS AND THE TEMPLE

The Synoptic Gospels

THE synoptic tradition concentrates Jesus' relations with the temple of Jerusalem into the brief period of the Jerusalem ministry. The crucial importance which his relations with the temple have for the outcome of the ministry is thereby illuminated. Earlier visits to Jerusalem and the temple, which Jesus undoubtedly made during his ministry, are ignored in order to accord the greatest possible significance to this historic visit. But the evangelists have not made all their facts conform to their scheme, or so it would appear. The narratives of the entry into Jerusalem contain certain features which are difficult to explain if the season was Passover as it purports to be. The acclamation *hosanna*, the use of Ps. 118, and more especially the Marcan remark that it was not the time for figs suggest that the visit took place not at Passover but at Tabernacles.[1] It is possible, as Goguel suggested,[2] that Jesus left Galilee shortly before Tabernacles (cf. John 7. 2) in September or October and continued teaching in Jerusalem till the feast of Dedication in December (cf. John 10. 22), and then went to Perea (cf. John 10. 40; 11. 54). His final and all-important visit to the city would then have been at Passover (cf. John 12. 1), when the cleansing of the temple took place. On this showing the difficulties present in the synoptic account arise from fusing the earlier visit at Tabernacles with the one at Passover. Support for this hypothesis does not depend entirely upon the fourth gospel; the synoptics contain hints that the Jerusalem ministry was not as brief as might at first sight appear (Mark 12. 35; 14. 49; Matt. 23. 37; Luke 13. 34; 19. 47; 21. 37; 22. 53).[3]

[1] Cf. T. W. Manson, 'The Cleansing of the Temple', *BJRL* 33 (1951), 271–82; P. Carrington, *The Primitive Christian Catechism* (1957), p. 27; C. W. F. Smith, 'No Time for Figs', *JBL* 79 (1960), 315–27; 'Tabernacles in the Fourth Gospel and Mark', *NTS* 9 (1963), 130–46.

[2] M. Goguel, *The Life of Jesus* (1933), pp. 238 ff., 401 ff.

[3] T. W. Manson, 'The Cleansing of the Temple', op. cit., offers a slightly modified

Whatever the actual circumstances, the synoptic writers succeed eminently in making their point. There is only one journey to Jerusalem, one visit that matters, the royal visitation to Zion that is of supreme importance both for Judaism and Jesus.

The journey to Jerusalem is thus marked by an air of mystery and anticipation on the part of Jesus' followers (Mark 10. 32). Intuitively they know that the kingdom of God is imminent (Luke 19. 11), and speculation naturally begins as to who will be the Messiah's second in command (Mark 9. 33 ff. pars.). For the same reason James and John request to be considered for posts of responsibility in the kingdom (10. 45 pars.).[1] What the disciples have still not learned is that the kingdom proclaimed by Jesus is not what they have their hearts set on. They are expecting the re-establishment of the old Davidic kingdom and the triumph of the Jews over their enemies. Hence Jesus tells them that they need to be converted (Matt. 18. 2 f. pars.), and directs their thoughts to something quite different, to suffering, humility, and service. 'The Son of man also came not to be served but to serve, and to give his life as a ransom for many' (Mark 10. 45 par.). The real issue is not Israel's position in respect of the great powers but her position before God.

The entry of Jesus into Jerusalem is interpreted by all four evangelists as the fulfilment of the eschatological hope of the coming of the Messiah to Zion. Matthew and John actually quote Zech. 9. 9; Luke uses the title 'king'.[2] Mark, who is more restrained, also brings out the messianic character of the event. This is clear from the greeting 'Son of David' in his preceding narrative (10. 47 f.), the reference to the Mount of Olives,[3] the prescience of Jesus concerning the whereabouts and borrowing of the colt,[4] the note that the animal was unridden (i.e. new and

---

reconstruction in which the entry and the cleansing take place at Tabernacles, but this creates the difficulty of allowing for an interval of six months between the cleansing and the trial.

[1] Thus Mark's 'in your glory' (10. 37) becomes in Matthew 'in your kingdom' (20. 21).

[2] In similar vein John states that the foliage used for the homage was palm (12. 13). Cf. 1 Macc. 13. 51; 2 Macc. 10. 6 f.; E. D. Freed, 'The Entry into Jerusalem in the Gospel of John', *JBL* 80 (1961), 329–38.

[3] On the eschatological associations of the Mount of Olives see Zech. 14. 4; Jos. *Wars* ii. 261–3; *Ant.* xx. 169–72.

[4] The acquiring of the colt may itself have messianic significance if the messianically interpreted oracle of Judah at Gen. 49. 11 is in mind. Cf. J. Blenkinsopp,

therefore particularly suited for a special purpose),[1] the act of homage in strewing the garments (cf. 2 Kgs. 9. 13), and the designation 'he who comes' (ὁ ἐρχόμενος), if not also the salutation *hosanna*.[2] Indeed, it is the second evangelist who accords the entry its fullest possible significance inasmuch as he treats it as an event in its own right and not (like Matthew and Luke) as the prelude to the cleansing. He states that Jesus entered Jerusalem, went into the temple, looked around, and then returned to Bethany from which the procession had set out; the temple is not cleansed till the following day. Matthew for his part emphasizes the eschatological nature of the entry by prefacing the words of Zech. 9. 9 with a prophecy from Isa. 62. 11 concerning the vindication of Jerusalem (21. 5) and noting that all Jerusalem was stirred by the event (21. 10; cf. 2. 3). John, similarly, states that the festival crowds from Jerusalem welcomed Jesus (12. 12 ff.).[3]

How the entry was understood by Jesus himself is less easily determined. Some scholars think that our Lord viewed it in the same way as the evangelists, namely, as a declaration of Messiahship, while others, noting that the action did not lead to a direct confrontation with the authorities, maintain that he did not attach any particular significance to it and the messianic character it has in the gospels is due to the church's overlaying (under the influence of Zech. 9. 9) what was originally nothing more than a spontaneous outburst of excitement on the part of the disciples at the sight of Jerusalem.[4] Neither view is satisfactory. The former says too much and the latter does not say enough. If the entry was an open declaration of Messiahship it is difficult to explain why Jesus was not charged either at the time or later with disturbing the peace. On the other hand, the fact that Jesus took the trouble to arrange for the loan of the donkey and used it to enter

'The Oracle of Judah and the Messianic Entry', *JBL* 80 (1961), 55–65; B. Lindars, *New Testament Apologetic* (1961), p. 115. But this is uncertain.

[1] Cf. Num. 19. 2; Deut. 21. 3; 1 Sam. 6. 7.

[2] Cf. E. Werner, ' "Hosanna" in the Gospels', *JBL* 65 (1946), 97–122.

[3] Jeremias sees further messianic significance in the fact that enthronement followed by cultic reform was a common feature of ancient culture (*Jesus als Weltvollender* (1930), pp. 35 ff.). Volz criticizes this suggestion on the ground that this connection is not found in contemporary writings (op. cit., p. 217). Jeremias's thesis is, however, well supported (1 Kgs. 15. 9 ff.; 2 Kgs. 11; 18. 1 ff.; also Judg. 6. 25 f.; Ps. Sol. 17. 33 ff.).

[4] For authorities see V. Taylor, *The Gospel According to St. Mark* (1957), pp. 451 f.

the city when he could easily have walked the short distance in the company of his disciples is against the suggestion that he did not intend any significance to be read into the action. Other scholars therefore think that Jesus was making a veiled assertion of Messiahship.[1] The entry is messianic for those who have eyes to see. Thus in using the colt Jesus deliberately identified himself with Zech. 9. 9, particularly as this was understood by the rabbis,[2] and at the same time dissociated himself from the popular conception of Messiahship, which expected the Messiah to enter Jerusalem as a war lord.[3] The same ambivalence, it is argued, is provided for in the designation 'he who comes' since it could refer to the Messiah or simply to any pilgrim arriving at the feast.[4] But this interpretation also is dubious. It requires one to believe that Jesus, who habitually concealed his identity, now discloses it, even in a partial way.

We shall probably be closest to the mind of Jesus if we say that he meant the entry to be a dramatic affirmation, an acted parable, of the coming of the kingdom of God. Jesus' ministry in Jerusalem is all of a piece with his ministry in Galilee. He is doing now what he has been doing all along; proclaiming the coming of the kingdom and calling upon Israel to repent (Mark 1. 14 f.; Matt. 11. 20–4 par.). The response he evokes is the same as he has already experienced. The disciples half grasp the significance of the sign; Israel at large does not. The nation does not know the time of its visitation (Luke 19. 44). Still it refuses to repent; but still Jesus proclaims his message.

According to the Marcan narrative, Jesus on arriving at the city went into the temple, looked around, and, as the day was ending, retired and spent the night at Bethany (11. 11). The comment that Jesus left the temple because of the lateness of the hour causes the reader to wonder whether Mark is suggesting

---

[1] A. E. J. Rawlinson, *St. Mark* (1925), pp. 151 f.; Taylor, op. cit., pp. 451 f.; C. E. B. Cranfield, *The Gospel According to Saint Mark* (1959), pp. 352 ff.

[2] S–B i. 842 ff.

[3] There is a rabbinic tradition to the effect that if Israel was unworthy the Messiah would come 'lowly, and riding upon an ass' (B. Sanh. 98a), but since this is probably an attempt to harmonize Zech. 9. 9 with the more general expectation of a military leader (cf. Moore, *Judaism*, ii. 334 f.) it is wisest not to interpret Jesus' particular mode of entry as a judgement upon Israel (W. G. Kümmel, *Promise and Fulfilment* (1957), p. 117 n.).

[4] Cf. Taylor, op. cit., p. 457. On the ambiguous character of *hosanna* see Werner, op. cit.

that Jesus would have proceeded with the cleansing had it been earlier in the day. In view of the fact, however, that the evangelist regarded the entry and the cleansing as separate (though related) events it is probably wisest to treat the comment as a simple statement of fact. Compared with the other synoptic accounts, where Jesus cleanses the temple immediately on entering it, the Marcan version has appeared to some commentators as an anti-climax. Accordingly they transform Jesus' presence in the temple at this juncture into a formal inspection,[1] or explain the suspension of the cleansing to the next day as the evangelist's attempt to heighten its importance as a premeditated action.[2] All this is seriously to be doubted. The importance of the cleansing for Mark is obvious enough without resorting to such expedients. Jesus' presence in the temple at this point is the sequel to the entry, not the prelude to the cleansing. By separating the entry from the cleansing Mark is not only able to present the former as an event in its own right but also to preface the latter with an incident which is crucial for his interpretation of it: the cursing or judgement of the useless fig-tree. The evangelist reports that when Jesus was on his way into Jerusalem the next day he cursed a figtree on which he hoped to find fruit but did not.

In their narrative on the cleansing the evangelists tell us that Jesus justified his action by citing Isa. 56. 7 and Jer. 7. 11 (Mark 11. 17 pars.). The Isaiah text reads, 'My house shall be called a house of prayer for all the nations.' Matthew and Luke do not have the words 'for all the nations'. The omission is significant, for it is these words that give point to the universal thrust of the prophecy; but it is not easy to determine what weight to give it. The reason may be deliberate, Matthew and Luke wishing to preclude the possibility of the words being literally identified with the temple (now no longer standing), or due simply to the fact that they were using a copy of Mark that did not have the longer text. The latter is supported by the difficulty of supposing that the third evangelist would have missed such a good illustration of universalism. At any rate, as the texts now stand, the cleansing in Mark is more a question of particularism versus

[1] E. Lohmeyer, *Lord of the Temple* (1961), p. 34. Cf. Rawlinson, op. cit., p. 153. In this connection attention is drawn to the statement that Jesus 'looked round at everything' (περιβλεψάμενος πάντα, 11. 11). But περιβλεψάμενος is too common a word in Mark (3. 5, 34; 5. 32; 10. 23) to have the sense of inspection.

[2] E. F. Scott, *The Crisis in the Life of Jesus* (1952), pp. 22 ff.

universalism, whereas in the others it is insincere worship as against sincere worship.

After narrating the cleansing Mark returns, obviously by way of explanation, to the incident of the fig-tree, noting that it had withered to its very roots (11. 20 ff.). Finally, he records the question of authority (11. 27–33; cf. pars.). Coming after the story of the fig-tree, which goes along with the cleansing, the question can refer only to what Jesus did in the temple (so Mark and Matt.). The parable of the disinheritance and destruction of the unfaithful and wicked husbandmen is probably to be included in the Marcan interpretation of the cleansing since it immediately follows the question on authority,[1] and continues the judgement theme implied by the use of Jer. 7. 11 at the cleansing.

The differences between the Marcan and the other synoptic accounts of the cleansing are probably to be explained by the altered circumstances under which the latter wrote. History had confirmed Jesus' judgement upon Israel and the cleansing lost its value as a sign of the imminent destruction of the temple. The inclusion of non-Jews in the church was no longer in need of justification. Other tasks awaited the gospel writers, and emphases were changed to meet new needs. We are now shown that the temple, like Judaism generally, had a part to play in the inauguration of the new age. Thus Jesus is depicted as cleansing the temple and consecrating it anew, as it were, so that he, the Lord of the temple, may use it. Matthew describes the purged court as the scene of such eschatological actions as the opening of the eyes of the blind and the making of the lame to walk (21. 14 ff.),[2] while Luke states that it is used for the proclamation of the good news of the gospel (19. 47 f.; 20. 1, etc.; cf. Acts 5. 20).[3] The fourth evangelist, for his part, follows Mark in his radical interpretation of the cleansing (2. 13–22). By depicting Jesus as driving out of the temple not only the offending vendors but also the sacrificial beasts, and adding the logion on the destruction and

---

[1] Cf. J. W. Doeve, 'Purification du Temple et Desséchement du Figuier', *NTS*, 1 (1955), 297–308.

[2] Lohmeyer, op. cit., p. 34.

[3] H. Conzelmann, *The Theology of Saint Luke* (1960), pp. 77 f., 164 f., 189; cf. 198. To say that Luke spares the temple is to fail to appreciate the subtlety of his thought. (*See below on Acts.*) For the temple in Luke as the place of eschatological fulfilment see 2. 27 ff.; Acts 1. 4 ff., etc.

replacement of the temple, which in the synoptics belongs to the trial, John, as we shall see, emphasizes the discontinuity between the old order and the new.

The court that Jesus cleansed was the outer court, commonly known as the court of the Gentiles, because it was there that those non-Jews who were so disposed might pray (cf. 1 Kgs. 8. 41 ff.). This court was separated from the inner courts by a barrier which warned non-Jews, on pain of death, not to proceed further (Jos. *Ant.* 15. 417; *Wars* 5. 194). For a Gentile to enter the more sacred parts of the temple he had first to become a Jew, and, as we have seen, Jewish eschatology looked forward to the day when converted Gentiles in great numbers would worship alongside native-born Jews. The size of the court in question helps us to appreciate the significance of Jesus' action. It compared not with a courtyard, as we commonly suppose, but with a small estate. Obviously the action of Jesus could not fail to arouse attention, which it apparently did (Mark 11. 18). Furthermore, it was the occasion, according to Mark, of extended preaching by Jesus (ἐδίδασκεν καὶ ἔλεγεν, 11. 17). Although this court belonged to the outer part of the temple it was regarded as holy, like the rest of the temple (M. Kel. 1. 8 f.; Jos. *Ap.* 2. 103–9; Acts 21. 28 f.).[1] The presence of the money-changers and the booths for the sale of animals and birds for sacrifice in this part of the temple was a necessary convenience for worshippers,[2] and care was taken that the inner and holier parts of the temple were not affected by it. So while it is quite possible that Jesus took exception to the haggling, extortion, and swindling that apparently went on at the stalls,[3] and to the inconvenience that may have been caused to the Gentile worshippers, it does not seem likely that he was attacking the institution as such. Mark's note that he forbade the use of the court as a public thoroughfare rather suggests that the cleansing was an attack on abuses that had come to be tolerated. For one reason or other, the temple

[1] Thus the Mishnah preserves a prohibition against the use of the court as a short cut to the city (Ber. 9. 5).

[2] Only the ancient or Tyrian (Phoenician) coinage was acceptable as payment of the temple tax and for the purchase of sacrifices. Worshippers who availed themselves of the facilities provided in the temple were saved not only the practical difficulty of bringing their offerings with them but also the possible embarrassment of having them rejected as unfit.

[3] S–B ii. 570 f.; P. Gaechter, 'The Hatred of the House of Annas', *TS* 8 (1947), 3–34.

was no longer the place where the Gentiles could worship God. By implication the Gentiles were of no real consequence; God was concerned only with the Jews, whose security the temple guaranteed (Jer. 7). The eschatological destiny of Israel was thus surrendered to racism. In taking it upon himself to interfere in the affairs of the temple Jesus cannot have been unaware of the consequences. The reader is not surprised to find the chief priests and scribes planning to kill him (Mark 11. 18).

The account of the actual cleansing which is given in the second gospel is the most instructive. On a first reading it seems to present Jesus as a religious reformer. Mark alone of the gospel writers notes that Jesus put an end to the practice of using the temple court as a public thoroughfare (11. 16). When, however, the narrative is read in the light of the setting which the evangelist provides for it, something much more radical than a reform of the cult is seen to emerge. By embedding the cleansing in the story of the cursing and withering of the fruitless fig-tree Mark shows that he understands the action of Jesus to mean nothing less than the abrogation of the temple and cult. The unprofitable fig-tree[1] and the secularized temple are symbols of Israel's unfaithfulness and wretchedness before God. The Jews were not simply robbing one another; they were robbing God. Failing to worship God as he desired and (thereby) preventing others from doing so, they were withholding from God what was his due.[2] The order represented by the temple was not merely obsolete; it had become a stumbling-block to the true worship of God. To the mind of Mark there is only one remedy. He therefore takes up the hint of the destruction of the temple, implied in the use of Jer. 7 at the cleansing, by noting that the deceptive fig-tree which Jesus condemned had perished.[3] In similar vein, the evangelist

---

[1] A fig-tree in leaf is a fig-tree that should have fruit (cf. Mark 13. 28). For the view that Mark conflates the entry at Passover with an earlier entry at Tabernacles (the season for figs) and the remark that it was not the time for figs as an explanatory gloss see above, p. 58. It seems over-subtle to interpret the words 'it was not the season for figs' symbolically in the sense that it was as pointless to look for faithfulness and righteousness in Jerusalem at this time as to look for figs in Nisan (so A. M. Farrer, St. Matthew and St. Mark (1954), p. 140 n.).

[2] Lindars, op. cit., pp. 107 f.

[3] The reference to 'this mountain' at 11. 23 refers more naturally to Mount Zion than to the Mount of Olives as is suggested by W. Manson, Jesus the Messiah (1943), pp. 29 f. The mountain of the Lord's house is not elevated as expected (Isa. 2. 2 = Mic. 4. 1), but cast down (C. H. Dodd, The Parables of the Kingdom (1935), p. 63 n.; R. H. Lightfoot, The Gospel Message of St. Mark (1963), p. 78).

adds the parable of the disinheritance and destruction of the unfaithful husbandmen (12. 1–11). Israel had entered upon the final and decisive crisis of her history. In rejecting God's kingly rule as proclaimed by Jesus she sealed her disaster and forfeited her right as a nation to be the people of God. The inheritance goes to others, the stone spurned by the builders becomes the cornerstone of God's new people. The interpretation of the cleansing offered by Mark is thus similar to that given by the fourth gospel (2. 13–22).[1]

To some, Mark's *post eventum* interpretation of the cleansing may seem to breathe more of early Christian polemics than the mind of Christ. Certain commentators believe that the intention of Jesus was simply to rid the temple of an offensive abuse.[2] Appeal is made to Zech. 14. 21 ('in that day there shall be no more the Canaanite (trader) in the house of the Lord of hosts' (AV)) or Mal. 3. 1–4 and Ps. Sol. 17. 30 f. There is truth in this view. Jesus' prohibition of the use of the temple as a short cut implies, as Taylor observes, a respect for the sanctity of the temple and is thoroughly Jewish in spirit.[3] Similarly, the counterquestion of Jesus to the Jewish leaders when he was asked concerning his authority for interfering in the temple indicates that he regarded his action as in some sense fulfilling the ancient prophecies and hopes relating to the Messiah and the temple in the eschatological age. But the truth of this interpretation is at best a half-truth. Jesus could not have hoped to control the temple more than momentarily.

The cleansing of the temple is a prophetic act, like the entry into Jerusalem. It points to the coming of the kingdom of God. The kingdom is correlative to Israel's destiny as the people of God. Jesus' action compels the Jews to face afresh the fundamental question of what it means to be the people of God. To accept his answer will mean (among other things) the inclusion of the Gentiles; to reject it will mean (among other things) the destruction of the temple. The fate of the temple, as in the Old Testament, is contingent upon the fate of the nation. In

---

[1] On the cleansing of the temple in John see below.

[2] F. C. Burkitt, 'Notes and Studies, Hosanna', *JTS* 17 (1916), 142–5; Scott, op. cit., pp. 66 ff.; G. Schrenk, *TDNT* iii. 243 f.; Taylor, op. cit., pp. 463 f.; R. N. Flew, *Jesus and His Church* (1938), pp. 39 f.

[3] Taylor, op. cit., p. 463. Cf. C. Roth, 'The Cleansing of the Temple and Zechariah 14. 21', *NT* 4 (1960), 174–81.

other words, the meaning Jesus attached to the cleansing will thus have been the same as that attached to it by Mark, except that the contingency present in the case of Jesus is absent in Mark, since he was writing at a time when it was clear to all which alternative the Jews had chosen and what it was going to lead to.[1]

It remains to be said that for all its suggestiveness Jesus' action bore that veiledness which marked his works generally. Possessing the character of a traditional cultic action and performed within the existing cult, it was capable of being interpreted simply as a cultic reform. Thus the narrative concludes with the Jewish hierarchy questioning Jesus concerning his authority (11. 27 ff.).

Israel having rejected the will of God, Jesus proceeded to constitute the new people of God (Mark 14. 22–5 pars.). The twelve are united in a covenant, which Jesus will presently seal by the shedding of his blood. The eschatological reunion at Zion predicted by the prophets thus takes place (Luke 22. 28–30), heralding the salvation of the nations, the 'many' for whom Jesus is dying (Mark 10. 45 pars.), who will be gathered in from the four corners of the earth (13. 27 par.). The statement that the new covenant is to be founded through the shedding of Christ's blood points to the sacrificial character of his death. That the early church saw Christ's death as profoundly affecting the traditional cultus is clear, as we shall see, from the circumstances which the evangelists connect with the death.

At the trial of Jesus numerous witnesses gave evidence, but the corroboration necessary to formulate the charge was not secured (Mark 14. 56 par.). One particular accusation is singled out as worthy of mention:

And some stood up and bore false witness against him, saying 'We heard him say, "I will destroy this temple that is made with hands (ἐγὼ καταλύσω τὸν ναὸν τοῦτον τὸν χειροποίητον), and in three days I will build another, not made with hands (καὶ διὰ τριῶν ἡμερῶν ἄλλον ἀχειροποίητον οἰκοδομήσω)"' (Mark 14. 58 par.).

Now the claim to destroy the temple and build another one, or at least the idea of replacing the temple with a better one, was a

---

[1] The universalistic implications of the cleansing are demonstrated by B. Sundkler in another way. Working from the conception of the temple as the centre of the earth, he argues that what happens there has significance for mankind at large ('Jésus et les païens', *RHPR* 16 (1935), 462–99).

messianic claim.[1] Thus the high priest is reported as pressing Jesus for an answer ('What is it that these men testify against you?').[2] Failing to secure this, he went directly to the point by asking Jesus if indeed he was the Messiah.[3] Jesus acknowledged that he was, and there was no further need for witnesses (14. 63 pars.). Now if the high priest's question followed directly upon the accusation regarding the temple, and Jesus by answering it in the affirmative in effect admitted that the accusation was essentially true the question that immediately arises is why it is attributed to false witness.

Various explanations have been offered. It is suggested that Matthew and Mark are defending Jesus against possible criticism that might arise from the fact that their readers knew very well that the temple was still standing. But this is not an adequate explanation. Any difficulty there may have been on that score is fully met elsewhere (Mark 13 pars.). That the evangelists did not consider the accusation false in the sense that it was wholly untrue is suggested by the fact that they attribute to Jesus a prediction of the destruction of the temple (13. 1 f. pars.). A more widely held view is that which sees in the mention of false witness the uneasiness which, it is said, an allegation of this kind would cause for the early Christians who continued to worship at the temple. Support for this is sought in the Matthean form of the accusation ('I am able to destroy the temple . . .' (26. 61)), the Johannine interpretation ('But he spoke of the temple of his body' (2. 21)), and the Lukan omission. This explanation might suffice if Jesus had been accused of saying simply that he would destroy the temple, but he is reported as also predicting the erection of a new temple. Such a thought was too congenial to the Jews to create embarrassment for the church.[4]

---

[1] As Goguel saw clearly (op. cit., p. 510). So also A. H. McNeile, *The Gospel According to St. Matthew* (1915), pp. 339f.; Taylor, op. cit., pp. 563, 567.

[2] S. Kennard suggests that the high priest was informed by Judas that Jesus had said he would destroy and replace the temple (*Jesus in the Temple*, diss. Strassburg, 1935, p. 45).

[3] The word 'again' in Mark 14. 61 (πάλιν ὁ ἀρχιερεὺς ἐπηρώτα . . .) suggests that the evangelist understood the earlier question of the high priest in regard to the accusation concerning the temple (v. 60) as a question regarding Jesus' messiahship.

[4] If Matthew's words 'I am able' represents an attenuation, what is one to make of Matt. 12. 6; 23. 38; 24. 2? It could be argued equally cogently that the Matthean form alludes to Jesus' power or authority over the temple (cf. 12. 6). Again, the

More plausible is the suggestion that the witness is false because it misrepresents what Jesus said. He had spoken about his body, not the temple of Jerusalem (cf. Mark 8. 31 etc., pars.).[1] This interpretation is supported by the fourth gospel (2. 19 ff.); but its weakness lies in its dependence upon the dominical character of the words 'made with hands . . . not made with hands', which few scholars would be prepared to defend.

In asserting that the witness was false the evangelists must mean one of two things: either that Jesus never said any such thing, or that the witnesses produced a garbled version of what he did in fact say. The wisest procedure is to examine the evidence and ascertain which possibility is the more likely. There are two lines of evidence: extant data and intrinsic probability. In the case of the former we have, firstly, the taunt of the bystanders at the cross, 'Aha! You who would destroy the temple and build it in three days, save yourself, and come down from the cross!' (Mark 15. 29–30 par.). This has point only if it represents an actual claim made by Jesus.[2] Secondly, there is the accusation made against Stephen: 'We have heard him say that this Jesus of Nazareth will destroy this place (the temple)' (Acts 6. 14). It is true that the charge is attributed to false witnesses, but it is significant that Stephen in his defence nowhere refutes it. On the contrary, the fault he finds with Jewish worship from beginning to end suggests that he had it on the tip of his tongue to say that Jesus put an end to the whole idolatrous business. Further evidence could be drawn from John 2. 19 and the reading found in certain manuscripts of Mark 13. 2 ('and after three days another (temple) will arise (made) without hands'), if it could be shown that these texts are independent of Mark 14. 58 and 15. 29, but this does not seem possible. In the case of intrinsic probability, it may be said that the allegation represents the kind of thing one would expect Jesus to have said. By cleansing the temple Jesus gave a hint of what would happen to Israel if

omission from Luke means very little because the thought is present at Acts 6. 14 (cf. below p. 86). Since the first and third gospels were written after the fall of the temple, when it was clear to all concerned that it was not Jesus who was responsible, there would be little need to spare Jesus in the way suggested.

[1] A. Cole, *The New Temple* (1950), pp. 21 ff.

[2] Cole, op. cit., pp. 18 f., who suggests that the syntactic form of the taunt (ὁ καταλύων . . . καὶ οἰκοδομῶν . . .) points to a claim that had been made more than once, or at least was well known.

she did not repent, and subsequently stated that the temple would be destroyed (Mark. 13. 2 pars.). One may suppose that the accusation expresses the conclusion Jesus must have reached towards the end of his ministry.[1] The temple, or the order represented by the temple, no longer served the purpose of God and would have to be replaced by another.

Assuming then that the accusation at the trial is based on an actual statement of Jesus, can we determine its original form? The couplet 'made with hands . . . not made with hands' and the time reference 'in ($\delta\iota\acute{a}$) three days' are generally regarded as Marcan additions for the purpose of bringing the saying into line with the resurrection predictions (Mark 8. 31, etc.).[2] This is doubtless true of the reference to the three days, though one would have expected the characteristic Marcan 'after ($\mu\epsilon\tau\acute{a}$) three days' and not 'in' ($\delta\iota\acute{a}$) (cf. the use of $\delta\iota\acute{a}$ in certain manuscripts at 13. 2), but there is less certainty in regard to the words 'made with hands . . . not made with hands'. The absence of the adjectives at Mark 15. 29 proves little, as it may only mean that the evangelist was simply abbreviating and understands the meaning as at 14. 58. Furthermore, the destruction of the existing temple and the erection of one of supernatural origin were, as we have seen, commonplace in Jewish eschatology, and the idea of a spiritual temple, i.e. a temple made without hands, as denoting the community, can no longer be considered novel since the publication of the Qumran writings.[3] On the other hand, if these adjectives are original it is difficult to understand why words so suggestive of the resurrection should have been omitted by Matthew. It does not seem adequate to say that with the fall of the temple in A.D. 70 Matthew considered the words redundant. Certainty as to the original form of the saying is obviously out of the question, but I think we may regard John 2. 19 as coming nearest to what Jesus said: 'Destroy this temple,

[1] Goguel, op. cit., p. 507.

[2] R. Bultmann, *The History of the Synoptic Tradition* (1963), p. 120, Goguel, op. cit., p. 509; Taylor, op. cit., p. 566; Lohmeyer, *Das Evangelium des Markus*, p. 336; Cranfield, op. cit., p. 442; Lindars, op. cit., pp. 68 f. Cf. C. F. D. Moule, 'Sanctuary and Sacrifice in the Church of the New Testament', *JTS*, N.S. 1 (1950), 29–41, who argues plausibly that 'made with hands . . . not made with hands' represents the church's reply to Jews and others who reproached her for not having a temple.

[3] See above chapters II–IV. Cf. M. Simon, 'Retour du Christ et reconstruction du Temple dans la pensée chrétienne primitive', in *Aux Sources de la Tradition chrétienne, Mélanges M. Goguel* (1950), pp. 251 ff.

and in three days I will raise it up' (λύσατε τὸν ναὸν τοῦτον, καὶ ἐν τρισὶν ἡμέραις ἐγερῶ αὐτόν).[1] It was the Jews themselves who would destroy their temple. By rejecting Jesus and the gospel they were committing themselves to the alternative programme of nationalism and war with Rome, one of the consequences of which would be the destruction of the temple (Mark 13. 2 ff. pars.).

In reproducing the saying at the trial the witnesses probably understood Jesus to mean that he would destroy and replace the temple by the use of magical powers (cf. John 2. 20). The idea, of course, was ridiculous, and Jesus is not reported as having taken the trouble to rebut it. But there is very likely another reason why neither Jesus nor the evangelists qualify the accusation. It was allowed to stand for the same reason that the high priest's question concerning Jesus' messiahship was allowed to stand, although it undoubtedly implied a quite different kind of messiahship from what Jesus meant when he answered the question in the affirmative. The accusation was, ironically, true. In a sense of which the witnesses were ignorant it asserted what in the event had taken place. The death of Jesus had resulted in the supersession of the old order and his resurrection had brought into being a new order. How much weight one should give this secondary and deeper meaning is not clear, but Mark's cryptic way of writing (cf. 15. 38) and the interpretative words 'made with hands . . . not made with hands' and 'in three days' rather suggest that he invites his readers to read between the lines.[2] That this was in fact what they did is strongly suggested by Matthew's omission of the reference to the false witness and John's ascription of the logion to Jesus himself.

In conclusion we may say that the accusation made against Jesus at his trial as reported by Matthew and Mark may be regarded as a garbled version of what Jesus actually said towards the close of his ministry. He saw that the temple, or, more correctly, the institution symbolized by the temple—for Jesus had no quarrel with the temple as such—had outlived its usefulness and was doomed to perish. In fact it would be destroyed because it was opposed to the purpose of God. At the same time, Jesus did

[1] Cf. Lindars, op. cit., p. 68. On the logion in the fourth gospel see below, pp. 78 ff.

[2] Note the connection between the erection of the new temple and the resurrection suggested by the use of the verb 'rise' (ἀναστήσεσθαι) (cf. Mark 8. 31 etc.) instead of 'build' (οἰκοδομεῖν) in the variant reading at Mark 13. 2.

not turn his back so completely on the old order as to envisage a formless worship of God. What he did was to unite loyalty to the traditional hope of Israel to the uniqueness of his own person. The new age would have its temple, and he as Messiah would erect it.[1]

According to Mark two things happened at the moment Jesus died, or rather one thing and its sequel: the veil of the temple was torn in two and the Roman centurion in charge of the execution was converted (15. 37–9; cf. Matt. 27. 51 ff.). How precisely the evangelist expects his readers to understand his narrative at this point is not very clear. Interpretation depends upon whether we are dealing here with history or symbol. Commentators have been in the habit of treating it as historical fact. Thus Lightfoot, whose exegesis has influenced much subsequent study, writes: 'For a single instant . . . we are transplanted from Golgotha to the Temple area, and then back again to Golgotha.'[2] Similarly, Dibelius suggestively states, 'While the Jews only scoff at the dying Jesus, the ancient holy place of the Jews bears witness that something decisive has happened.'[3] This line of thought is developed by Lightfoot. Rightly noting the close connection between the rending of the veil and the confession of the centurion in Mark, he states: 'In these two passages . . . we see and hear the testimony given to that death by the Jewish temple and the Gentile world respectively.'[4] Attempts are therefore made at identifying the veil. Some scholars think it refers to the veil that hung in front of the holy place of the temple of Jerusalem, i.e. the sanctuary (Jos. *Wars* 5. 211–14; cf. Exod. 27. 16; Num. 3. 25), and interpret the rending as a sign of the destruction of the temple (cf. Mark 13. 2).[5] Others (the majority) believe it is the inner veil, the one that covered the entrance to the holy of holies (Jos. *Wars* 5. 219; M. Yoma 5. 1; Exod. 26. 31–5), and think the

[1] Goguel, op. cit., p. 510.

[2] *The Gospel Message of St. Mark*, p. 55.

[3] M. Dibelius, *From Tradition to Gospel* (1935), p. 195. Parallels are found by commentators in Josephus' mention of the strange portents that happened in the temple of Jerusalem prior to its destruction (Jos. *Wars* 6. 288–300). Cf. 2 Bar. 8. 1 f.

[4] *History and Interpretation in the Gospels* (1935), p. 86.

[5] The Gospel According to the Hebrews (Jerome, *Ep.* 120. 8. 2; Matt. 27. 51) interprets the tearing of the veil as the destruction of the temple: 'In the gospel that is written in Hebrew letters we read, not that the veil of the temple was rent, but that a lintel of the temple of wondrous size fell' (M. R. James, *The Apocryphal New Testament* (1924), p. 5).

rending signifies the opening through the death of Jesus of the way to God.[1] The difficulty with both these interpretations, and especially the latter, is that it is hard to see how the rending would have the character of a public sign which would affect the centurion.[2]

It is important for interpreting the Marcan narrative to note that the tearing of the curtain and the confession of the centurion are a single event, and attention never for a moment shifts from the cross: Jesus breathed his last . . . the curtain of the temple was torn in two . . . the centurion saw . . . and said, 'Truly this man was a (the) son of God!' Compare Matthew and Luke, where the torn veil is one of a number of things that happen at the death of Jesus, and the centurion's confession is not linked directly to it. There is no doubt that these evangelists understood the destruction of the veil literally as referring to the temple of Jerusalem.[3] With Mark it is different. He fixes attention on the cross throughout, and describes a single event throughout. That being the case it seems we are obliged to interpret the rending in the second gospel as symbolic and interpretative. It would appear that we should regard the rent veil as the evangelist's way of telling his readers that the death of Jesus which he has already depicted as sacrificial means forgiveness and salvation for mankind. The destruction of the veil stands for the removal of what hides the face of God from mankind.[4] The barrier in question was of course nowhere more in evidence than in Judaism, but to think that it is the veil of the temple that is meant would be to set a limit to the grandeur of the evangelist's thought. What he has in mind undoubtedly includes the barrier in the temple of Jerusalem but it means much more as well.

In summary, we can say that the evangelists interpreted the ministry of Jesus as the fulfilment of the eschatological hope of

[1] For authorities see G. Lindeskog, 'The Veil of the Temple', *CN* xi (1947), 132–7; J. E. Yates, *The Spirit and the Kingdom* (1963), pp. 232–7.

[2] Yates, op. cit., pp. 234 f.

[3] There is this difference between Matthew and Luke: while Matthew, like Mark, regarded the centurion's confession as a confession of faith, Luke regarded it as a confession of Jesus' innocence. Schrenk suggests that Judas's casting of the thirty pieces of silver into the temple (ναός) at Matt. 27. 5 represents the permanent defilement of the temple (*TDNT* iii. 245 f.).

[4] Cf. Heb. 10. 20—'the new and living way which he opened for us through the curtain, that is, through his flesh'. So C. H. Dodd, *The Apostolic Preaching and its Developments* (1936), p. 51; Yates, op. cit., pp. 232 ff.

Israel. The coming of the kingdom of God, the Messiah, the re-gathering and reunion of the people of God, the advent of the Messiah at Jerusalem, the purification of the temple, and the inclusion of the Gentiles—all the time-honoured motifs are present in the gospels and interpreted in the light of Jesus Christ and his redeeming work. The focus of attention is no longer the temple of Jerusalem, but Jesus and those gathered around him. It is upon them that the divine presence rests (Mark 9. 7 pars.; cf. 1. 10 f. pars.). The temple made without hands has displaced the temple made with hands. There is much that one would like to know about the new temple which faithfulness to the limits imposed upon the evangelists by the nature of their task prevented them from telling their readers. They are concerned simply to state the fact of its existence and leave it to others to expound its meaning.

VI

FROM OLD TEMPLE TO NEW

THE fourth gospel and the book of Acts provide a convenient link between the introduction of the idea of the church as the new temple in the synoptic gospels and the fully developed treatment of the subject in the epistles. They show how the temple of Jerusalem surrendered its redemptive significance to Christ and his church and thereby dropped out of the plan of God.

The Fourth Gospel

In its treatment of Jesus' relations with the temple of Jerusalem the fourth gospel continues and develops the radical view of the Marcan interpretation. John, however, makes no attempt to convey the idea of contingency, which, according to Mark and the synoptics, surrounded Jesus' relations with the temple to the moment when Judaism irrevocably rejected Jesus. Here the temple and its festivals have value only as images of Christian truth. In one sense, therefore, interpretation of John is much more straight-forward, but in another sense it is much less so. Frequently an image will be found to be based upon various different associations so that interpretation is difficult. No one particular meaning can be confidently adopted to the exclusion of others. In such cases the most one can hope to do is to isolate the different discernible components of the image in question and point to their possible meaning.

John strikes out on his bold line of interpretation right at the beginning of his gospel. 'The word', he tells us, 'became flesh and dwelt (ἐσκήνωσεν) among us . . . we have beheld his glory (δόξα)' (1. 14). The sacral character of the language has long been recognized. The word σκηνοῦν can mean simply 'to dwell', but connected as it is with δόξα it should be accorded its full theological sense as denoting the presence of God with his people. The imagery of the feast of Tabernacles features so prominently in the gospel (4. 13 f.; 7. 37 f.; 19. 34) that one may take it as

virtually certain that it forms the basis of this text. The evangelist
wishes his readers to understand that the glory of God which was
present in the tabernacle (Exod. 40. 34 ff.) and (afterwards) in
the temple of Jerusalem (1 Kgs. 8. 10 f.; Isa. 6. 1 f.) and which, it
was believed, would be revealed to men in the new age (e.g. Isa.
40. 5), dwells in Jesus Christ, whose glorified body, as John will
tell us presently, is the new temple (2. 21). Now, however, there
is a new and greater degree of identity between God and men.
It is not only his glory, his name or *sh͏eḵhīnāh*, but God himself,
God the Word, who dwells with his people. Now at last the long-
standing tension between the transcendence and the immanence
of God is resolved. However, we are not yet at the thought of
God dwelling *in* his people, his new temple. That will come later.
For the moment John cannot think of the indwelling taking place
until Jesus has been glorified and the Spirit given.[1]

The advent of Jesus Christ has decisive consequences for
Judaism, as John proceeds to show.

At 1. 29 Christ is depicted as 'the Lamb of God who takes
away the sin of the world' (cf. v. 36). The image is highly complex. Interpretation is rendered difficult by the words 'who takes
away the sin of the world'. It is not present in the parallel text
1. 36, and may be a doctrinal comment. Universalism is certainly
characteristic of the fourth gospel, but the thought of atonement
for the world's sin does not fit well with any of the Jewish
sacrifices that may have influenced the text, except perhaps Isa.
53. 12, if it can be said that this text is in mind. Similarly the
expression 'lamb *of God*' is uncertain because it gives the text
a very wide meaning. Of the many explanations that have been
offered[2] the one which commends itself to most is that which sees
a reference to the Paschal lamb. The Passover is important for
John (2. 13; 6. 4; 11. 55; 12. 1; 13. 1 ff.; cf. 18. 28, 39; 19. 14)
and it would seem that the evangelist has altered the chronology
of the Passion so that the death of Christ should coincide with the
Passover (18. 28; 19. 14) and appear as a Paschal sacrifice (19.
36; cf. v. 29). On the other hand, the association of the Lamb of
God with the Messiah at 1. 35–42 and the over-all view of Christ
in this gospel makes the identification of the lamb with the slain
but triumphant lamb of the book of Revelation attractive. In

---

[1] A. M. Ramsey, *The Glory of God and the Transfiguration of Christ* (1949), p. 60.
[2] Cf. e.g. L. Morris, *The Apostolic Preaching of the Cross* (1965), pp. 129 ff.

such circumstances the most that one can say with any confidence
is that sacrificial ideas are in mind and the reference seems to be
of a general nature. At all events, the death of Christ is presented
as a new and better sacrifice.

The desire to depict Christ as the new temple may be in mind
at 1. 51, 'You will see heaven opened, and the angels of God
ascending and descending upon the Son of man.'[1] The allusion is
to Jacob's dream at Bethel (Gen. 28. 16). We know that the
rabbis identified the stone on which Jacob slept as the foundation-
stone of the temple of Jerusalem, and there is a tradition to the
effect that Jacob's ladder marked the site of the new temple (Gen.
R. 68. 12; 69. 7). What John would appear to be saying therefore is that the bond joining heaven and earth is no longer the
temple of Jerusalem, where the glory or presence of God was
hidden in the holy of holies, but Christ, in whom the divine glory
is made visible. God's intercourse with men, as the evangelist
will tell his readers plainly at 4. 21 ff., no longer takes place at
spot the marked by the historic rock in the holy of holies at
Jerusalem,[2] but through the person Jesus Christ, who is the sole
means of access to the Father (14. 6).

The abrogation of Judaism by the new order inaugurated by
Jesus Christ is powerfully expressed in the Johannine account of
the cleansing of the temple (2. 13–22). The crucial importance of
the cleansing is indicated by the fact that the evangelist puts it
at the beginning of his gospel and appends to it the logion on the
destruction and replacement of the temple which in the synoptics
belongs to the trial of Jesus. The connection between the cleansing
of the temple and its destruction which is hinted at in the
synoptics is thereby illumined.

The thoroughgoing nature of the cleansing is emphasized by
John. Whip in hand, Jesus authoritatively drives out not only
the offending traders and money-changers but also the animals
and birds destined for sacrifice (2. 15 f.). He tells the Jews, 'You
shall not make my Father's house a house of trade' (2. 16). The
words are reminiscent of Zech. 14. 21 ('there shall no longer be
a trader in the house of the Lord of hosts on that day') and, if
taken by themselves, might convey the impression that nothing
more than a reform of the cult is in mind; but clearly John's

---

[1] J. Jeremias, 'Die Berufung des Nathanael', *Ang.* 3 (1928), 2–5.
[2] Cf. Appendix A.

understanding of the cleansing is much more far-reaching. The disciples see Jesus' action as the fulfilment of Ps. 69. 9, 'Zeal for thy house will consume me'. The future tense is used instead of the perfect, since the outcome of Jesus' action, his death, still lies in the future. Jesus, like the righteous sufferer of the Psalm will pay dearly for his loyalty to God's house.[1] The Jews, for their part, question Jesus' right to interfere in the affairs of the temple and ask for a sign (2. 18; cf. Mark 11. 28). Their response indicates their incredulity, for the cleansing is itself a sign (cf. 2. 23). But although Jesus refuses their request he replies, by way of inviting them to see in the cleansing itself the sign they demand, 'Destroy this temple, and in three days I will raise it up' (2. 19). The saying should be distinguished from the interpretation given to it by the evangelist (v. 21). Plainly it refers to the temple of Jerusalem, not simply because the Jews understood it thus but because it is closely related to the cleansing, and reflects what we found in the synoptics to contain a genuine word of Jesus on the destruction and replacement of the temple. By throwing the sacrificial animals and birds out of the temple Jesus proclaims that the worship of Israel is at an end. As in the Marcan interpretation, the cleansing signifies the destruction of the temple to make room for a new type of worship: 'Take these things away . . . the hour is coming, and now is, when the true worshippers will worship the Father in spirit and truth, for such the Father seeks to worship him' (2. 16; 4. 23). But, as frequently in this gospel, a deeper meaning is given to Jesus' words. John states that 'He spoke of the temple of his body (ὁ ναὸς τοῦ σώματος αὐτοῦ)' (2. 21), adding that it was only after the resurrection that the disciples understood the deeper meaning.

Interpretation of the passage is notoriously problematical. The sense seems to be something like this: 'Even though you (Jews) by your unbelief destroy this temple,[2] that is, the tabernacle of the Word (cf. 1. 14),[3] (and thereby destroy the temple of Jerusalem),

[1] C. H. Dodd, *The Interpretation of the Fourth Gospel* (1953), p. 301. For the use of Ps. 69 in connection with the passion see Lindars, op. cit., pp. 99 ff.

[2] Even if 'destroy' (λύσατε) is an ironic imperative (cf. e.g. Amos 4. 4, 'Come to Bethel, and transgress'), our Lord's reply 'conveys the truth that the Jews in their unbelief will themselves become the instruments in bringing about the sign the Lord now offers them' (R. H. Lightfoot, *St. John's Gospel* (1956), p. 113).

[3] λύειν is used of the dissolution of life as well as the destruction of buildings (E. C. Hoskyns, *The Fourth Gospel*, ed. F. N. Davey (1947), i. 205).

in three days I will raise it up again,[1] but (we may fill out the
thought of the text) your temple will never be restored, for the
new temple of my body will become the rallying point of
the true worshippers of God.' That the evangelist equated the new
temple with Christ's glorified body is supported by the remark
that it was after Jesus was raised from the dead that the disciples
made the connection between the new temple and the body of
Christ. It is also supported, as we shall see, by the thought of 7.
37–8 and 19. 34.

It seems likely that we have preserved in John 2. 19 the *verbum
Domini* of which the false witnesses produced a garbled version at
Jesus' trial (Mark 14. 58 par.). It is the Jews themselves and not
Jesus who will destroy the temple. The identification of the
new temple as the body of Christ is a novelty, but, as we have
seen, the synoptics hint at it in the idea of the new temple as
a temple made without hands which comes into being three days
after the destruction of the temple made with hands. The conception of the church as the body of Christ is not indeed Johannine, but the union of believers with their Lord and their mutual
indwelling is fundamental to the gospel.[2] The teaching of 2. 19–21
is thus of a piece with what John has already told us about the
new mode of worship. But this significant development is present:
the new order of worship owes its existence to the death and
resurrection of Jesus Christ.[3]

The same thought of the supersession of the old mode of worship by the new is presented from a different point of view in
Jesus' encounter with the representative of the Samaritans at 4.
20–6. The woman raises the ancient controversy concerning the
primacy of Jerusalem or Gerizim as the place of the true worship
of God. Jesus retorts that the question is no longer relevant.
'The hour is coming when neither on this mountain nor in
Jerusalem will you worship the Father. . . . The hour is coming,
and now is, when the true worshippers will worship the Father in
spirit and truth, for such the Father seeks to worship him' (4. 21,
23 f.). These words, following as they do the account of the ex-
pulsion of the animals and vendors from the temple, suggest a

---

[1] ἐγείρειν, which is used of the resurrection of the dead, also denotes the erection
of buildings (Hoskyns and Davey, op. cit. i. 205).

[2] 'We abide in him, because we are his members; but he abides in us, because
we are his temple' (Augustine). Quoted by Hoskyns and Davey, op. cit. i. 337.

[3] O. Cullmann, *Early Christian Worship* (1953), pp. 73 f.

contrast between a cult that is spiritual and inward and one that is material and external to man. However, this is not what is meant. Christianity supersedes Judaism and Samaritanism not because it is spiritual whereas they are material but because it is centred in a person and not in a place. 'The mark of all true worship is that, centred round the Christ, it is permeated by his Spirit, and that, offered in his name, it is also in accordance with the truth; that is, with the true knowledge of God given to man in him.'[1] No more centripetal, the worship of God is available to all men everywhere. Hence Jesus' conversation with the woman leads to his mission to Samaria, whose inhabitants confess him to be the Saviour of the world (4. 42).[2]

Now since Jesus Christ takes the place of the temple of Jerusalem it is natural that ideas associated with the temple are transferred to him.

Thus at 7. 37–8 we have Christ (or the believer in Christ) depicted as the source of living water. The evangelist states that on the last day of the feast of Tabernacles Jesus proclaimed in the temple of Jerusalem, 'If any one thirst, let him come to me and drink. He who believes in me, as the scripture has said, "Out of his heart shall flow rivers of living water" ' (7. 37 f.). John adds, by way of interpretation, 'Now this he said about the Spirit, which those who believed in him were to receive; for as yet the Spirit had not been given, because Jesus was not yet glorified' (v. 39). Uncertainty surrounds the punctuation of the passage and the origin of the 'scripture' mentioned at v. 38. But whether with the eastern fathers (and the EV) we punctuate the text with a full stop after 'drink' (in which case it is from the believer that the living water is said to flow) or with the western fathers after 'me', 'let him drink who believes in me' (in which case Christ is the source of the waters), the meaning is the same: Christ is the dispenser of the water or river of life.[3] At 4. 10 Christ is described as the source of living water (cf. 6. 35), and believers by virtue of their union with him are fountains of this water (4. 14). In the case of the 'scripture', it is likely that the reference, like so many

---

[1] A. Corell, *Consummatum Est* (1958), p. 51.

[2] Ibid., pp. 51 f.

[3] Although both interpretations yield meaning which is true to Johannine thought, the latter is strongly suggested by (*a*) the texts 19. 34 and 20. 22, (*b*) the fondness of John for exodus typology, and (*c*) the imagery of Rev. 22. 1 (cf. 22. 17).

other texts on living (i.e. running) water in Jewish literature, goes back ultimately to Old Testament texts on the pool of Siloam (2 Kgs. 20. 20), though the immediate reference is probably to one of the eschatological texts based upon the historic pool. The pool is given a symbolic interpretation at Isa. 8. 6 and Ps. 46. 4 f., and Ezekiel and Zechariah developed the idea by representing the temple as the source of life and blessing for mankind in the new age (Ezek. 47. 1 ff.; Zech. 14. 8). Zechariah 14 was one of the readings at Tabernacles, and the 'scripture' mentioned by John may well be connected with it.

The imagery of our text is clearly modelled on the feast of Tabernacles, the most popular of all the temple festivals. The feast reached a magnificent climax on the evening of the final day when a golden flagon of water from the pool of Siloam was carried round the altar seven times and prayers for rain for the incoming year were offered. Illuminated by the great candelabra and in view of all the worshippers, the priests poured the water into the shaft at the side of the altar. Hence the altar, or more precisely the rock on which it rested, was said to mark the spot where the world's thirst was quenched.[1] Jesus' claim to supply living water could not fail to challenge Jewish readers. It meant that the centre and source of the world's life was no longer the temple of Jerusalem, but himself, the new temple (cf. below on 19. 34).

We recall, moreover, that the water-pouring at Tabernacles was interpreted eschatologically as the symbol of the outpouring of the Spirit of God in the messianic time.[2] So John, passing out of the realm of cosmology into eschatology, interprets the water Jesus offers as the gift of the Spirit (7. 39). It is the Spirit, according to John, who mediates the divine life to men (6. 63; cf. 3. 5), and it is Christ who imparts the Spirit (20. 22). The statement that the blessing of the Spirit still lies in the future because Jesus is not yet glorified (v. 39) is a further reminder that the coming of the new era is contingent upon the death and resurrection of Christ.

[1] Cf. Appendix A.
[2] Cf. Appendix A. The claim of Jesus at John 8. 12, 'I am the light of the world', which in the earliest manuscripts follows the Tabernacles incident, is probably made in relation to the temple. The light that flooded Jerusalem at Tabernacles (M. Suk. 5. 3) has given way to the true light (John 8. 12 ff.; cf. 1. 9, etc.), who gives sight (illumination) to mankind (9. 1–12). Cf. below, p. 175 on Rev. 21. 23.

Since Christ is the new temple we also have the idea of the ingathering and uniting of the people of God and the conversion of the nations associated with him. Jesus is portrayed as the messianic shepherd whose task it is to gather together the flock of God (those of Israel who hear his voice and those of other folds, i.e. non-Jews) 'so (that) there shall be (literally, they shall become) one flock, one shepherd' (10. 16). The same conception is expressed at 11. 52: Caiaphas, unwittingly moved by the prophetic gift belonging to his office, declares that Jesus 'should die for the nation, and not for the nation only, but to gather into one the children of God who are scattered abroad'. The latter text is taken by some exegetes to refer to the Gentiles, but the language is rather indicative of Jews of the dispersion.[1]

The wider ingathering alluded to under the mention of the 'other sheep' at 10. 16 is given fuller treatment in the record of the visit of the Greeks to Jerusalem to see Jesus (12. 20 ff.).[2] In John the coming of the non-Jews to Jerusalem takes the place of the cleansing of the temple in the synoptics and we should probably interpret the incident as the Johannine equivalent of the Marcan interpretation of the cleansing so that the temple may become 'a house of prayer for all the nations'. John has just described the entry of Jesus into Jerusalem in terms of the visit of the Messiah to Zion, and by inserting the visit of the Gentiles at this point he gives expression to his complementary theme of Jesus as the Saviour of the world. The coming of the 'Greeks' to Jerusalem in fulfilment of the scriptures concerning the eschatological pilgrimage to Zion is for Jesus the signal that he is about to enter into his messianic glory (12. 23). 'Behold, your king is coming (12. 15); . . . his dominion shall be from sea to sea, and from the River to the ends of the earth' (Zech. 9. 9 f.). Previously his mission had been to his own sheep, his own nation; but now (in a change of metaphor) the seed is to fall into the ground and die and bear much fruit (12. 24). The glorification of Christ through death is, once again, the means whereby he will draw the nations to himself (12. 27–33) and thus become the centre of unity predicted of the new temple.

[1] So J. A. T. Robinson, 'The Destination and Purpose of St. John's Gospel', *NTS* 7 (1960), 127 f. (= *Twelve New Testament Studies* (1962), pp. 120 f.).

[2] The 'Greeks' here are taken by J. A. T. Robinson to mean Greek-speaking Jews living outside Palestine (op. cit., pp. 120 f.), but the context is against this interpretation.

The other place where we have evidence of John's desire to reinterpret the ancient cultic images is his account of the circumstances attending Jesus' death. The evangelist states that as Jesus was already dead it was not necessary for the Roman soldiers to hasten his death by breaking his bones, but that in order to ensure that he was indisputably dead one of the soldiers thrust a spear into his side, causing an effusion of blood and water (19. 31–4). In both of these incidents prophecy is fulfilled (19. 36 f.). The scripture which John may have in mind in observing that none of Jesus' bones was broken may be Ps. 34. 20, which refers to God's care for the righteous; but it is much more likely to be the Passover requirement that no bone of the sacrificial lamb should be broken (Exod. 12. 46; Num. 9. 12). The evangelist evinces great interest in the Passover and would appear to have altered the chronology of the passion so as to represent Jesus as having died at the very hour of the Paschal offering. Presumably he wishes his readers to regard the death of Jesus as the true Passover, fulfilling and therefore terminating Jewish worship (1 Cor. 5. 7b). Similar ideas appear to be conveyed by the statement that at the spear-thrust blood and water flowed from Jesus' side. Ostensibly a witness to the humanity and actual death of Jesus (19. 35), it also has symbolic significance. What is this but the river of life which Ezekiel said would flow from the new temple—the living water which if a man drink he will never thirst again (4. 14; 7. 38), and the blood which is drink indeed (6. 55)?[1] No sooner has Jesus been glorified (cf. 7. 39) than the new life of the Spirit is made available for mankind (20. 22; cf. below on Rev. 22. 1, 17). The reference to the life-giving stream from the Saviour thus rounds off the thought of 4. 13–14 and 7. 37–8 by giving symbolic expression to the fact stated at 2. 19–21: the new salvation issues from Jesus' sacrificial achievement.

This concludes our examination of the fourth gospel. The gospel follows Mark closely in its interpretation of the work of Christ in relation to the temple of Jerusalem. The decisive and radical

---

[1] Dodd, *The Interpretation of the Fourth Gospel*, p. 428. Lightfoot makes the interesting suggestion that here from the cross our Lord hands over the dispensation of the Spirit (παρέδωκεν τὸ πνεῦμα), thereby fulfilling the prediction of 7. 38, ' "Out of his heart shall flow rivers of living water". Now this he said about the Spirit, which those who believed in him were to receive.' (*St. John's Gospel*, p. 319).

character of this work is now more than ever in evidence. Furthermore, we are not only shown clearly that the new temple owes its existence to the death and resurrection of Christ; we are also told precisely what the new temple is. The accomplishment of all this, far from being hindered by the death of Jesus, is in point of fact made possible by this very means. Jesus' death, followed by the resurrection, creates the new temple and the new worship, the gathering together of the children of God who are scattered abroad, the salvation of the Gentiles, and the life-giving stream for the renewal of the world. The old order is displaced by the new, not so much because the old is essentially bad—for salvation is of the Jews—but because Christ fulfils what it stands for so magnificently that it is necessary for it to have a completely new form.

The Acts of the Apostles

The value of the book of Acts as evidence in support of our thesis is less direct than indirect. It is true that some scholars have found the doctrine of the new temple in Acts, but this does not seem justifiable. The author of Acts is concerned simply to show how the temple of Jerusalem played its predicted role as the venue of the eschatological fulfilment and then gave way to the new salvation which is not confined to a particular topographical location.

It is at Jerusalem, as the prophets predicted, that the divine presence or Spirit is vouchsafed to God's people. But in place of the temple of Jerusalem to which men go is the Spirit-filled church which is sent out far and wide. 'You shall be my witnesses in Jerusalem and in all Judea and Samaria and to the end of the earth' (1. 8). Familiarity with these words blunts their great significance. The old world-centre is displaced by the church which mediates the blessings of the eschatological age to all men wherever they are.[1]

Such a revolutionary reinterpretation of the traditional outlook probably took time to be fully appreciated.[2] At any rate, Acts

---

[1] In one sense, of course, the difference between the centrifugal and centripetal movements is relative. The church goes out in order to gather in; it is dispersed in order to assemble. Cf. J. Blauw, *The Missionary Nature of the Church* (1962), pp. 91, 166.

[2] A. Hastings, *Prophet and Witness in Jerusalem* (1958), p. 179.

represents the young church as worshipping at the temple of Jerusalem for a time (2. 46; 3. 1 ff.; 5. 12, 42; cf. Luke 24. 53). Even when allowance is made for such Lucan apologetic tendencies as the desire to present Christianity as the heir of Judaism[1] and its innocence in respect of its relations to the authorities, this attachment to the Jewish cult is odd. Doubtless it had something to do with the nature of the church's commission: to the Jew first, and afterwards to the Gentile (Acts 1. 8; cf. Matt. 10. 5 f.; Rom. 1. 16); and the temple in Luke's writings is the place of proclamation (Luke 19. 47 f.; 20. 1, etc.; Acts 5. 20).[2] What we cannot do is to solve the problem by saying that the early Christians used the temple only for prayer and not for sacrifice.[3] Unsatisfactory also is the suggestion that the church was awaiting the gift of the Spirit, because Pentecost did not break the association with the temple. It may be that hope of an early *parousia* had something to do with it. Messiah and temple had been inseparable ideas, and Jesus himself had spoken of his exaltation in connection with the temple of Jerusalem (Mark 13. 2, 26; Matt. 23. 38 f.). There is some evidence that Paul thought of the final denouement as taking place at Jerusalem (Rom. 11. 26),[4] and the early Christians may possibly have stayed at Jerusalem in daily expectation of the return of their Lord. Whatever the particular reason or reasons for the attachment of the early church to Jerusalem it is important to observe that Acts shows that there existed alongside the worship at the temple specifically Christian gatherings, in particular the breaking of bread (2. 46), and the latter was destined to emerge as the essential expression and characteristic of the Christian community. One may say, therefore, that the apparent devotion of the first Christians to the temple of Jerusalem was a transitional phenomenon.[5]

[1] Acts, like the third gospel, depicts the new order as beginning at the place of the old (cf. Luke 2. 27 ff., 41 ff.; Conzelmann, op. cit., pp. 164 f.; 212 f.).

[2] Conzelmann, op. cit., pp. 164 f., 189.

[3] As is argued by F. C. Burkitt, *Christian Beginnings* (1924), pp. 62 ff.; Lohmeyer, *Lord of the Temple*, pp. 112 f.

[4] Cf. J. Munck, 'Israel and the Gentiles in the New Testament', *BSNTS* i–iii (1950), 26–38; *Paul and the Salvation of Mankind* (1959), chap. 9–11; below pp. 123 f.

[5] Cf. H. R. Boer, *Pentecost and Missions* (1961), p. 113. The view of E. Lohmeyer (*Galiläa und Jerusalem* (1936)) and L. E. Elliott-Binns (*Galilean Christianity* (1956)) that Galilee, as well as Jerusalem, was a centre of early Christianity has not won wide acceptance among scholars.

According to the author of Acts the first stage of the centrifugal movement of salvation was set in motion by the scattering of the church resulting from the persecution which followed the death of Stephen (8. 1). What it was that Stephen said that caused the church to be severed from Jerusalem is not explicit in Acts. It may, however, be inferred from the accusations brought against him by the Hellenist Jews: 'We have heard him speak blasphemous words against Moses and God' (6. 11). The charge is subsequently specified:

This man never ceases to speak words against this holy place and the law; for we have heard him say that this Jesus of Nazareth will destroy this place, and will change the customs which Moses delivered to us (vv. 13–14).

The charge is attributed to false witnesses (6. 13), but as in the case of Jesus in the gospels the falsity was probably due more to misrepresentation than perjury. There seems little doubt that Stephen taught something to the effect that Jesus said that the temple would be destroyed; the wording of 6. 13 (οὐ παύεται λαλῶν) suggests that it was a frequent theme of his preaching (cf. 21. 28). Luke evidently saw a connection between the accusation brought against Stephen and that brought against Jesus at his trial since he allows the former to serve for the latter, which he omitted from his gospel.

Parallels for the ideas expressed in the teaching of Stephen can be found in the various anti-cult movements within Judaism,[1] especially that at Qumran;[2] but if we are adequately to account for the high regard in which Stephen was so obviously held and the way in which the early church accepted and fulfilled the novel and far-reaching consequences of his ministry it seems necessary to say that his teaching was based, and was recognized as based, upon the teaching of the Lord himself. Luke is not unaware of the tradition that the temple would be destroyed (Luke 21. 5 f. pars.; cf. 19. 44). His omission of the logion on the destruction and replacement of the temple at the trial (Mark 14.

[1] M. Simon, 'Saint Stephen and the Jerusalem Temple', *JEH* 2 (1951), 127–42; *St. Stephen and the Hellenists in the Primitive Church* (1958).

[2] Cf. O. Cullmann, 'The Significance of the Qumrân Texts for Research into the Beginnings of Christianity', *JBL* 74 (1955), 213–26; 'A New Approach to the interpretation of the Fourth Gospel', *ET* 71 (1959), 39–43; A. F. J. Klijn, 'Stephen's Speech—Acts vii. 2–53', *NTS* 4 (1957–8), 25–31.

58; Matt. 26. 61) is due not to an oversight, but to the evangelist's developing scheme. The charge brought against Stephen serves for the one brought against Jesus. Luke evidently wishes us to understand that the judgement on Jerusalem (and its temple) is suspended till the gospel, duly fulfilled in the gift of the Spirit, has been offered and rejected, i.e. till the first stage of the dominical commission ('you shall be my witnesses *in Jerusalem*') has been executed (cf. Acts 13. 46; 18. 6; 28. 28). The tradition that Jesus would destroy the temple of Jerusalem, which, as we have seen, was preserved by the early community despite the possibilities of misunderstanding it contained, Stephen understood and expounded. The effect as Luke reports it, was instantaneous and decisive: the world mission of the church was under way.

Some exegetes think that if Stephen's teaching was based upon the logion of Jesus concerning the destruction of the temple, as seems likely, he must also have followed Jesus in predicting a new temple.[1] The suggestion is interesting; it not only gives Acts 7 a positive nuance but provides a link between the teaching of our Lord on the temple and that of Paul on the church as God's temple. It cannot be supported, however; though not because the original form of the logion in Mark 14. 58 pars. did not contain the promise of a new temple[2] or because there was no room in Stephen's eschatology for anything to take the place of the temple of Jerusalem,[3] but simply because it goes beyond the evidence of Acts 7. Not even Stephen's assertion that 'the Most High does not dwell in houses made with hands ($\chi\epsilon\iota\rho\sigma\pi\sigma\iota\dot{\eta}\tau\sigma\iota\varsigma$)' may be taken to suggest that he meant to say that God dwells in a temple made without hands ($\dot{\alpha}\chi\epsilon\iota\rho\sigma\pi\sigma\dot{\iota}\eta\tau\sigma\varsigma$). The contrast lies elsewhere. 'The counterpart of the "ekklesia" in the wilderness (7. 38) is not the new *ekklesia*, but the Jewish hope in the time of Jesus. It is not the church which is contrasted with the temple, as a house not made with hands, but rather the heavenly temple, the pattern that Moses saw on the mount.'[4]

The expansion of the church to Samaria which followed the death of Stephen (8. 4–8) was of considerable significance. It is

[1] Cole, op. cit., p. 44; F. F. Bruce, *Commentary on the Book of Acts* (1954), p. 158.
[2] As is argued by J. C. O'Neill, *The Theology of Acts* (1961), p. 74.
[3] As is argued by Simon, *Saint Stephen and the Hellenists in the Primitive Church*, pp. 76, 97.
[4] N. A. Dahl, *Das Volk Gottes* (1941), p. 196 (quoted by Simon, *Saint Stephen and the Hellenists in the Primitive Church*, p. 124).

true that the Samaritans were circumcised and observed the law of Moses, but there was little in common between them and the Jews (John 4. 9). They were regarded by the Jews as an inferior race of half-castes given over to schismatic worship and pagan tendencies. The chief bone of contention was the rival temple of Gerizim (John 4. 20 ff.). The admission of Samaritans to the church on an equal basis with ex-Jews must therefore have forced the congregation at Jerusalem to consider again the question of its relation to the temple. Were the Samaritan Christians to continue worshipping at Gerizim, or to abandon it in favour of the temple at Jerusalem, or were all concerned persuaded that the hour had come when the true worship of God would be offered without respect to either Jerusalem or Gerizim?[1] Whatever questions may have been in the minds of the Christians at Jerusalem, the fact that they welcomed the Samaritan believers into the church, and sought and received for them the essential hallmark of membership, the gift of the Spirit, without reference to the question of their worshipping at the temple of Jerusalem, goes to show that whatever importance the temple previously had for the Christian movement it was no longer seen to possess any essential importance. The principle thereby established was of paramount significance for the future expansion of Christianity. If some people could become fully accredited members of the church without worshipping at the temple of Jerusalem, it stood to reason that others should be similarly admitted to its membership. The way was thus opened for the inclusion of the Gentiles.[2]

But the final step was not easily taken. The story of the conversion of Cornelius and his friends, which anticipates the Gentile mission,[3] reflects the church's diffidence over the matter. Peter's question ('Can I and may I go to the Gentiles?'[4]) was decisively answered, however. The venture was in accordance with the will of God from start to finish (11. 9, 12, 15, 17). To oppose it would be to oppose God (cf. 10. 47). The Gentile mission thus began with the approval and blessing of the church at Jerusalem (11. 18). So the first Gentile church was established, at Antioch (11.

---

[1] W. L. Knox, *St. Paul and the Church of Jerusalem* (1925), p. 68.

[2] Ibid., pp. 69 f.

[3] The significance of the conversion of the eunuch of Ethiopia is due more to the fact that he was a eunuch than to his being a foreigner (cf. Deut. 23. 1) *contra* Simon, *Saint Stephen and the Hellenists in the Primitive Church*, pp. 31 f.

[4] Munck, *Paul and the Salvation of Mankind*, p. 231.

19–26), and Paul and his companions planted churches far and wide in Gentile lands (13. 1 ff.).

The conversion of large numbers of Gentiles through the labours of Paul proved too much for some of the Jewish Christians at Jerusalem. These contended that the Gentiles could not be saved unless they were circumcised according to the law of Moses (15. 2 ff.; cf. Gal. 2. 11 ff.), i.e. unless they first became Jews. Clearly the faith and unity of the church were in danger. A special gathering met at Jerusalem to discuss the matter, when it was decided that the Gentiles should not be required to comply with the requirements of the law. The issue, which obviously was of the greatest importance for the continued expansion of Christianity, was summed up by James, the leader of the Jerusalem congregation and chairman of the meeting, as follows:

> Brethren, listen to me. Symeon has related how God first visited the Gentiles, to take out of them a people for his name. And with this the words of the prophets agree, as it is written, 'After this I will return, and I will rebuild (ἀνοικοδομήσω) the dwelling (ἡ σκηνή) of David, which has fallen; I will rebuild its ruins, and I will set it up, that (ὅπως ἄν) the rest of men may seek the Lord, and all the Gentiles who are called by my name, says the Lord, who has made these things known from of old' (15. 13–18).

It is the use of Amos 9. 11 that is of chief interest to us.[1] The wording follows that of the LXX where the ingathering of the Gentiles is clearly to the fore ('that the remnant of men, and all the Gentiles who are called by my name, may earnestly seek me'). The argument reflects a familiar Old Testament theme: Israel is restored in order to fulfil her destiny to the nations; God has rebuilt the fallen dwelling of David and this is followed by the ingathering of the Gentiles. For Luke the first part of the prophecy (the rebuilding of 'the dwelling of David') had been fulfilled, and the second part (the ingathering of the Gentiles) was in process of fulfilment.

We come then to the question of what precisely our text means by the 'dwelling of David'. Does it denote the restoration of the Davidic kingdom or dynasty in a non-material form? Or does it refer more specifically to the resurrection of the body of the crucified son of David? The possibilities are by no means exclusive, since the restoration of the Davidic kingdom was

---

[1] Cf. the eschatological use of Amos 9. 11 in CD 7. 16; 4 Q Flor. 1. 11–13.

contingent upon a new David being raised up. The thought of the kingdom is just as congenial to Luke as the thought of the king (Luke 22. 18, 28 f.; Acts 1. 3; 14. 22; 19. 8; 28. 23, 31). It is true that the resurrection is set forth at 2. 25–31 and 13. 32–7 as the fulfilment of the promises made to, and the predictions made by David, but Luke does not view the resurrection as an individualistic phenomenon (9. 4b). It seems wisest therefore to interpret the rebuilding of the dwelling of David in a general sense as a figurative expression of the new economy of salvation brought into being through the death and resurrection of Christ. In other words, I do not think that one can take 'dwelling' here to mean new temple.[1]

The vindication of the universal character of the gospel by the council at Jerusalem is followed by the record of the further expansion of the church. The new faith is now widely planted in Macedonia and Greece (16. 6–19. 20). Concomitant with the increasing acceptance of the gospel by the Gentiles is its progressive rejection by the Jews. Towards the end of this period, Luke introduces the final phase of the centrifugal movement 'to the end of the earth' in Paul's journey to Rome (19. 21). From this point onwards Rome is the destination towards which the narrative unerringly moves until, after describing how the gospel overcomes every obstacle, Luke concludes by showing the apostle proclaiming the gospel in the heart of the Gentile world (28. 28 ff.). If Luke witnesses to Paul's determination to visit Jerusalem before he goes to Rome, as he does (19. 21 etc.), it is not because he believed that the city possessed theological significance for the apostle but because that is how he gets to Rome, namely, through his arrest and appeal to Caesar. Jerusalem had forfeited its right to a place in the plan of God (22. 18); the new movement is no longer dependent upon it. The book closes with attention fixed upon the mission to the Gentile world (28. 28).

Although Luke is concerned to give only the theological reason for the movement of Christianity from Jerusalem to the nations (Acts 1. 8), there is little doubt that other factors assisted the process. The rapid change in the composition of the church's membership must have been a cause. As the church became pre-

---

[1] *Contra* Cole, op. cit., pp. 48 ff. Amos 9. 11 is also spiritualized at CD 7. 16; cf. 3. 19; 4 Q Flor. 1. 11–12, but it is not used there either in relation to the idea of the spiritual temple.

dominantly Gentile in character the emotional attachment to Jerusalem would weaken and eventually cease to exist. One has only to look at the writings of the early fathers to see how dispassionately Jerusalem came to be viewed. Another historical circumstance which probably facilitated the psychological break with the temple, at least as far as Jewish Christians were concerned, was its destruction in A.D. 70. If there is a danger of the importance of this event being over-emphasized in some quarters,[1] there also is the danger of its being neglected altogether in others. This destruction must have been the occasion of theological reflection on the part of many Christians even though there does not appear to be any trace of this in the New Testament.[2] Christian writers of the third and fourth centuries interpreted the fall of Jerusalem as the effective out-working of Judaism's rejection of Christ, and one may reasonably assume that the event put an end to any lingering sentiments and hopes Jewish Christians may have entertained as to the role of Jerusalem in the new dispensation.

Acts then is the story of the church set free from its moorings at Jerusalem and carried by the winds of God's Spirit to the ends of the earth. It is the story of how the temple surrendered its redemptive significance to Jesus and his church. 'Mount Zion, then, is now different from what it was formerly, for wherever the doctrine of the gospel is preached, there is God really worshipped, there sacrifices are offered, there, in a word, the spiritual temple exists.'[3] Acts does not tell us anything about the new temple, but that the doctrine was already known and taught in the churches Luke writes about is evident from the epistles, to which we now proceed.

[1] As is done by S. G. F. Brandon, *The Fall of Jerusalem and the Christian Church* (1951).
[2] Luke 21. 20 may or may not refer to it. See C. H. Dodd, 'The Fall of Jerusalem and the "Abomination of Desolation" ', *JRS* 37 (1947), 47 ff.
[3] Calvin, Commentary on Micah, 4. 7.

VII

THE NEW TEMPLE IN THE EPISTLES OF PAUL[1]

THE teaching of Paul on the church as God's new temple marks an important stage of our inquiry. For the first time in the New Testament the conception is worked out at length. That is not to say, however, that we shall find anything like a formal treatment of the subject in Paul. It is rather a case of our collecting all the relevant texts, examining these in their contexts and in relation to one another, and attempting to form a general picture.

A preliminary point of some importance that should be kept in mind is the fact that the temple is only one of a whole series of images the apostle uses to describe the church, none of which can be properly studied or understood in isolation from the others.[2] Thus we shall find that intimately connected with the thought of the church as the temple ($ναός$) is the church as the building ($οἰκοδομή$), which in turn is connected with the church as the body ($σῶμα$). Although co-terminous, each of these images has its own particular nuance. The temple image, as we shall see, depicts the church under its divine aspect as the society of the redeemed, which through sanctification by the Holy Spirit constitutes the inviolable dwelling-place of God, whereas the image of the building points rather to the dynamic and organic character and processes of the church. Since we are concerned to understand the meaning of the temple as an eschatological phenomenon we shall be occupied chiefly with the idea of the sanctuary ($ναός$), examining the conception of the building ($οἰκοδομή$) only in those texts where the temple image fuses with it. For the church as the building the reader is referred to the various studies on the subject.[3]

---

[1] We include Ephesians as Pauline. If it was not written by the apostle it was written by someone who had imbibed his thought.

[2] Cf. P. S. Minear, *Images of the Church in the New Testament* (1960).

[3] P. Vielhauer, *Oikodome: Das Bild vom Bau in der christlichen Literatur vom Neuen*

The texts to be considered are 1 Cor. 3. 16–17; 6. 19; 2 Cor. 6. 16–7. 1; Eph. 2. 20–22. 2 Cor. 5. 1–5 will be studied later in relation to the subject of the heavenly temple. We begin with 2 Cor. 6. 16–7. 1, since it is the fullest of Paul's texts on the spiritual temple, and by examining it first we shall be better prepared for considering his other texts. Also it may be noted that 2 Cor. 6. 16–7. 1 is part of what is generally regarded as Paul's 'previous letter' to Corinth (2 Cor. 6. 14–7. 1),[1] and may therefore represent the apostle's earliest recorded exposition of the subject.

2 Corinthians 6. 16–7. 1

The description of the church as a spiritual temple at 2 Cor. 6. 16 is introduced by a series of (five) antitheses which is intended to demonstrate that permanent relationships between Christians and non-Christians are neither permissible nor possible. Apparently Paul is correcting an abuse of Christian freedom. He wishes his readers to understand that while it is a fact that the external regulations of the law of Moses, which were intended to secure the holiness of the chosen people of God through isolating them from contact with non-Jews, had been done away by Christ, ethical separation, which those regulations sought to achieve, still obtained for Christians, who in their newly found freedom had to learn that there are certain things which they might not do.[2] One may say that the power of the infant church to redeem society, even to survive, depended, humanly speaking, upon its understanding of itself as a people set apart from the rest of society and dedicated to the service of God.

Do not be mismated with unbelievers. For what partnership (μετοχή) have righteousness and iniquity? Or what fellowship (κοινωνία) has light with darkness? What accord (συμφώνησις) has Christ with Belial? Or what has a believer in common (μερίς) with an unbeliever? What agreement (συγκατάθεσις) has the temple of God

Testament bis Clemens Alexandrinus, diss. (Heidelberg, 1939), pp. 76 ff.; P. Bonnard, Jésus-Christ édifiant son Église (1948), pp. 28 ff.; J. Pfammatter, Die Kirche als Bau. Eine exegetisch–theologische Studie zur Ekklesiologie der Paulusbriefe (1961). For a theological exposition of the subject see K. Barth, Church Dogmatics, iv. 2 (1958), 626–41.

[1] The letter mentioned at 1 Cor. 5. 9.
[2] L. S. Thornton, The Common Life in the Body of Christ (1941), pp. 12 f.

(ναῷ Θεοῦ) with idols? For we (ἡμεῖς) are the temple (ναός) of the living God (vv. 14–16).

The last of the antitheses prepares the way for the formal statement of v. 16b, 'we are the temple of the living God'. The emphasis is on the pronoun ('*we* are the temple . . .'), and is probably intended to impress upon the readers their unique status. The alternative reading 'you' (ὑμεῖς) has good manuscript support, and suits the form of address in vv. 14, 17, 18 (i.e. 'you Corinthians . . .'), but it is very likely due to influence from 1 Cor. 3. 16. Yet although Paul undoubtedly includes himself under the 'we' and thinks of the temple image in a universal sense, the reference is primarily to the congregation at Corinth.

The collocation of 'temple of God' and 'idols' is very effective. It only needs to be made to indicate the utter incompatibility of the two things. To associate the temple of God (in which not even an image of God was permitted) with idols and the abominable practices connected with idols was the most heinous form of sin conceivable to the Jew (Dan. 9. 27; 11. 31; 1 Macc. 1. 54; Mark 13. 14 par.; cf. Ezek. 8. 8–17).[1] The incongruity is heightened still further if the contrast intended is between the temple of the living God and lifeless idols (cf. 1 Thess. 1. 9),[2] though the reference is probably to the false gods or no-gods from whom the Corinthians were delivered at conversion (1 Cor. 8. 4 f.; cf. 10. 19–22).

The designation of the church as God's temple is now supported by a catena of Old Testament quotations, each of which is helpful for our understanding of the apostle's thought. First we have:

> I will live in them (ἐνοικήσω ἐν αὐτοῖς)
>   and move among them (ἐμπεριπατήσω),
> and I will be their God,
> and they shall be my people (v. 16b).

This is based on the *locus classicus* of Old Testament texts on the divine indwelling in Israel, Lev. 26. 12. The church, like the tabernacle of old, is God's dwelling, and should therefore be set apart for its sacred purpose. More significant still, the priestly formula was also used of the eschatological dwelling of God with his people at Ezek. 37. 27 ('my dwelling place shall be with

---

[1] Cf. A. Plummer, *The Second Epistle of Paul to the Corinthians* (1915), p. 208.
[2] So C. F. G. Heinrici, *Der zweite Brief an die Korinther* (1900), p. 243.

them [ἐν αὐτοῖς]'; cf. Jer. 31. 33), which Paul, by his substitution
of the words 'in them' for 'in you' (of Lev. 26. 12), clearly has
in mind. But the apostle evidently understands God's presence in
the church as much more than a type of the divine indwelling in
the old sanctuary or the fulfilment of the prophecy that God
would again dwell with his people after the exile, for he supple-
ments the LXX verb 'walk among' with the much stronger verb
'live in'.[1] In other words, God no longer dwells *with* his people
in a sanctuary which they make for him; he dwells *in* them, and
they are his temple.

Lev. 26. 12 and Ezek. 37. 27 are combined in a prediction of
the new temple at Jub. 1. 17, and it is possible that Paul is using
testimonies already taken over by the primitive church. Some
scholars think that these Old Testament texts were used by
Jewish Christians against the admission of Gentiles to the church.[2]
Similarly, it is suggested that the apostle is quoting from a
Qumran proof-text used to support the sect's withdrawal from
Jerusalem.[3] The sequel (v. 17) is certainly not against either
possibility, but one cannot be certain. Whatever the origin of the
quotation, and we shall return to the question later, Paul puts his
own construction upon it. It is the Christian community that
fulfils the ancient prophecy, and its holiness must be preserved
from defilement by unbelievers (αὐτῶν).[4]

Still supporting his statement with quotations from the Old
Testament, Paul proceeds to draw out the practical implications
of the doctrine of the church as God's new temple:

Therefore (διό) come out from them, and be separate from them,
says the Lord, and touch nothing unclean; then I will welcome you,
and I will be a father to you, and you shall be my sons and daughters,
says the Lord Almighty (vv. 17–18).

The first quotation, which is from Isa. 52. 11, continues the
separation motif. The separation that the prophet had in mind

[1] The verb ἐνοικεῖν is never used of God in the LXX (H. Windisch, *Der zweite
Korintherbrief* (1924) p. 216).
[2] L. Cerfaux, *The Church in the Theology of St. Paul* (1959), pp. 151 f.; M. Fraeyman, 'La Spiritualisation de l'Idée du Temple dans les Épîtres pauliniennes', *ETL*
23 (1947), 391 n.
[3] K. G. Kuhn, 'Les rouleaux de cuivre de Qumrân', *RB* 61 (1954), 193–205;
J. A. Fitzmyer, 'Qumrân and the Interpolated Paragraph in II Cor. vi. 14–vii. 1',
CBQ 23 (1961), 271–80.
[4] Fraeyman, op. cit., p. 391, n. 39.

refers to priests and Levites in exile (but cf. Num. 16. 26; Rev. 18. 4), so Paul omits the words 'you who bear the vessels of the Lord' in order to make the reference apply to the Christian community. He intends to say that as the priests of old were to leave behind them in Babylon everything that was unclean in order that they might worthily fulfil their sacred duties on their return to the temple of Jerusalem, so Christians are to live sanctified lives that befit their vocation. This reference to holiness, which we shall find recurring in all Paul's texts on the spiritual temple, has an interesting parallel in the Qumran texts on the community as the spiritual temple, but the connection between holiness and the temple is so ancient and widespread that it would be unwise to attribute direct dependence upon Qumran to Paul.[1]

Then follow the blessings which those who obey the call to holiness may expect to receive (vv. 17b–18). The first ('I will welcome you') is very appropriately based on Ezek. 20. 34, since this Old Testament text has to do with the new people of God. The other ('I will be a father to you . . .') is from the significant text 2 Sam. 7. 14, and contains what was considered to be the ideal relationship of God to his people, that of father to son (Exod. 4. 22; Jer. 3. 4, 19; 31. 9; Hos 1. 10; 11. 1). The application of 2 Sam. 7. 14 is generalized by reading 'sons and daughters' (Isa. 43. 6) instead of 'son'. 2 Sam. 7. 14 is not the only Old Testament text on the *summum bonum* of Israelite faith which the apostle might have chosen, and its use may have something to do with the fact that the blessing was given to Israel in connection with the promise of the temple,[2] but this cannot be pressed, since at this point of the text the image of the temple (v. 16) has given way to that of the family (v. 18).

The section closes with an affectionate appeal to the Corinthians to make their high status as the recipients of God's promises the basis of their conduct.

Since we have these promises ($\tau a \acute{u} \tau a s$ $o \mathring{\upsilon} \nu$ $\H{e} \chi o \nu \tau \epsilon s$ . . .), beloved, let us cleanse ourselves from every defilement of body and spirit, and make holiness perfect in the fear of God (7. 1).

[1] As Gärtner does (op. cit., pp. 55 f.).
[2] The building of the temple and the duration of the kingdom (issuing from the filial relationship between David's son and God) are complementary ideas: 'He shall build a house for my name, and I will establish the throne of his kingdom for ever' (2 Sam. 7. 13). Cf. Ps. 132. 11–14.

The word 'these' is emphatic. 'These, then, being the promises
which we have.'¹ The nature and antiquity of the promises, the
recollection of who it is that made them, and the recognition
that it is they themselves who have the honour of fulfilling them,
should inspire the Corinthians to take seriously the ethical
obligations of their new life in Christ.² Although the temple
image has receded into the background it remains the basis of
Paul's appeal throughout. All the Old Testament proofs quoted
are related in one way or another to the divine presence in Israel
or to the ingathering of Israel at the eschatological temple, and
the cultic character and functions of the church hinted at by the
use of Isa. 52. 11 (at 6. 17) are taken up again at the conclusion
where the sacral language (καθαρίζειν and ἁγιωσύνη) reappears
(7. 1).

The similarities between 2 Cor 6. 16–17. 1 and the teaching of
Qumran have been noted by a number of scholars. Common to
both is the sharp contrast between the two communities, the
κοινωνία of fellowship of light and the κοινωνία of darkness and
evil, the emphasis on the need for separation from evil and the
preservation of the community's holiness and, most important of
all, the idea of the faithful as a spiritual temple. In fact, the only
known parallel to Paul's use of the temple image is in the scrolls.
More generally, the apostle employs the same *pesher* hermeneuti-
cal method as the sect in his use of the Old Testament, altering
the wording of the original to suit the purpose in hand.³ However,
impressive as the similarities undoubtedly are, they do not entitle
us to say for certain that Paul is here quoting from Qumran
material.⁴ Catenae are a feature of his writings. Only if a catena
identical to 2 Cor. 6. 16–18 were to turn up at Qumran would
certainty be established. Not only has such a catena not been
found, but nowhere does the significant couplet Lev. 26. 12 and
Ezek. 37. 27 used by Paul appear in the Qumran texts on the
spiritual temple so far published. This, of course, is not to deny
the possibility that Paul may have been influenced by ideas from
Qumran, but to question the assertion that the text before us is to
all intents and purposes a Qumran document.

---

¹ Plummer, op. cit., p. 210.
² R. V. G. Tasker, *The Second Epistle of Paul to the Corinthians* (1958), p. 100.
³ Cf. Kuhn, op. cit.; Fitzmyer, op. cit.; Gärtner, pp. 50 ff.
⁴ So Fitzmyer.

If the text we have been considering belongs to Paul's first letter to Corinth then it represents the earliest-recorded teaching of the apostle, if not of the New Testament, on the church as God's new temple. Perhaps the most significant feature of this text is its extensive use of the Old Testament. Clearly the church is viewed as the fulfilment of the ancient hope that God would one day dwell with his people in a new and more intimate way. Little is said, however, about the new temple beyond the fact that it is made of persons. We are not told what it is that makes the community of the faithful a temple, how God dwells in it, nor its relation to Christ. But what Paul does not say should not be taken to mean that his thought on the subject is still largely undeveloped. His presentation is to a great extent determined by the fact that he is using Old Testament testimonies, which may have been in catena form before he took them over.

1 Corinthians 3. 16–17

The designation of the Christian community as the temple of God at 1 Cor. 3. 16–17 is prepared for by the use of the allegory of the building (οἰκοδομή) in verses 9–15, which, in turn, is introduced by the figure of the field under cultivation (γεώργιον) in vv. 5–9, for οἰκοδομή can mean edifice as well as construction.[1] All three figures of speech are intended to combat party strife in the church at Corinth (1. 10 ff.; 3. 5 ff.). In the case of the field Paul shows what is the true relation between himself and Apollos: they are fellow workmen of God, who alone makes their respective labours worth while (3. 6 f.). The figure of the building extends the discussion on the equality and unity of the apostles: each builder has his own particular job in the building of the church (v. 10). But there is a shift of emphasis. Paul is not concerned to state his equality with others so much as to indicate the nature of his own particular ministry (v. 10a), and what this means for others engaged in the upbuilding of the church. His job is to see to the foundation (θεμέλιον ἔθηκα); this is his particular

---

[1] The figures of planting and building have more in common than the building and the temple (ναός), and are frequently found together (Jer. 1. 10; 18. 7–10; 24. 6; 31. 28; 1 QS 8. 4f.; 11. 8; Eph. 3. 17; Col. 2. 7). οἰκοδομή and ναός are also used together at Eph. 2. 21.

responsibility (Rom. 15. 20).[1] Commentators differ over the question whether the foundation denotes teaching concerning Christ (i.e. the gospel) or Christ himself. The latter seems preferable; θεμέλιος is very likely a reverential circumlocution. The apostle laid the (true) foundation by basing the Corinthians upon Christ and upon him alone (2. 1 f.).[2] Paul then directs a threatening glance at those who say they are building the superstructure (ἄλλος δὲ ἐποικοδομεῖ, v. 10). They are warned to make certain that they are building upon the right foundation, for there is only one foundation (cf. Gal. 1. 6: ὃ οὐκ ἔστιν ἄλλο; cf. 2 Cor. 11. 4), the one in fact which Paul the master builder has laid; and having ascertained that they are building upon this they should then examine the materials they are using for the superstructure, because these will be examined and tested at the judgement day. If the materials are not correct the builder may find himself with nothing to show for his work (vv. 12–15).[3] Then by way of intensifying his warning, Paul introduces the image of the temple. The church is no human institution. It is divine, and anyone who harms it will incur the judgement of God who dwells in it (cf. 11. 29):

Do you not know (οὐκ οἴδατε) that you are God's temple (ναὸς Θεοῦ ἐστε) and God's Spirit dwells in you (τὸ Πνεῦμα τοῦ Θεοῦ ἐν ὑμῖν οἰκεῖ)? If any one destroys (φθείρει) God's temple, God will destroy (φθερεῖ) him. For God's temple is holy (ἅγιος), and that temple you are (οἵτινές ἐστε ὑμεῖς) (vv. 16–17).

Although the use of ναός is to some extent anticipated in the use of οἰκοδομή, the reader is scarcely prepared for the shift of emphasis.[4] Not only is there a change of subject (contrast 'he will be saved' of v. 15 and 'God will destroy him' of v. 17); there is also a change of presentation. The architectural figure is abandoned, and the organic and dynamic character of the church,

[1] Cf. the use of οἰκοδομεῖν at 1 Cor. 14, where the image is used to defend the church against threats to its unity from a selfish and arrogant exercise of ministries.

[2] E. Best, One Body in Christ (1955), pp. 162 f. Cf. A. Fridrichsen, 'Themelios, 1 Kor. 3, 11', TZ 2 (1946), 316 f.; Bonnard, op. cit., p. 33. On the use of θεμέλιος at Eph. 2. 20 see below.

[3] Ancient building-contracts included penalties against contractors whose materials and workmanship did not meet with the specifications (cf. J. Armitage Robinson, St. Paul's Epistle to the Ephesians (1904), pp. 260 f.).

[4] Cf. J. Weiss, Der erste Korintherbrief (1910), p. 85, who, however, thinks that vv. 16–17 are an interpolation.

implied in the use of the figures of the field (αὐξάνειν, vv. 6, 7) and the building (ἐποικοδομεῖν, vv. 10, 12, 14), is lost to view. In its place is the highly evocative image of the temple or sacred dwelling. The emphasis is on the numinous character of the church, upon the Spirit who inhabits it. Also to be noted is the mode of address, 'Do you not know . . .?' The words, which imply challenge if not reproach, suggest that the apostle is returning to what is familiar and accepted. When one asks what it is that Paul is calling to the attention of the Corinthians, one does not have far to look. The section which we have just examined (2 Cor. 6. 16–7. 1) may well be what is partially or wholly in mind. The latter, in contrast to 1 Cor. 3. 16 and 6. 19, does not have the rhetorical question 'Do you not know . . .?'—which rather suggests that the teaching was new to the readers. It is not unlikely, of course, that the idea of the church as the temple of God, or at least the doctrine of the indwelling Spirit, was treated of by the apostle during his stay at Corinth (Acts 18. 1 ff.).

The passage before us adds to our knowledge of Paul's understanding of the church as the new temple in a number of ways.

In the first place, the novel character of the doctrine of the divine presence in the new era is brought out. 'God's Spirit', Paul says, 'dwells *in you*' (τὸ πνεῦμα τοῦ Θεοῦ ἐν ὑμῖν οἰκεῖ parallels ἐνοικήσω ἐν αὐτοῖς of 2 Cor. 6. 16). God's dwelling on earth is no longer a thing apart from his people; it is the people themselves. The essential difference between the divine indwelling in the new dispensation and the old is brought out well by Congar when he writes, 'It is no longer a *presence* that is involved, but an *indwelling* of God in the faithful.'[1] Qumran, of course, believed that God dwelt *in* the faithful,[2] but there is a vast difference between Paul's understanding of the idea and that of Qumran. For the apostle the divine indwelling is orientated Christologically: it issues from the work of Christ and the consequent gift of the Spirit.

Secondly, this text indicates what it is that makes the faithful in Christ a temple. It is God's Spirit. Old Testament and inter-testamental eschatology, as we saw repeatedly, linked together the new temple and the presence of God. Without the presence of

---

[1] *The Mystery of the Temple*, p. 237.
[2] Cf. above pp. 46 ff.; Gärtner, op. cit., p. 58.

God there can be no temple. It is against such a background that Paul works out his doctrine of the church: 'You are God's temple and God's Spirit dwells in you', or, more correctly (as the καί is explicative), 'You are God's temple since God's Spirit dwells in you.' The statement that it is the Spirit of God, i.e. the Holy Spirit, that dwells in the temple (cf. also 6. 19) also points to Paul's new understanding of the divine tabernacling upon earth, for the gift of the Spirit to his way of thinking is contingent upon the work of Christ, and he does not think of the Spirit without thinking of Christ. The role of the Spirit is essentially unifying.[1] As it creates one body (1 Cor. 12. 13), so it creates one temple. It is this unity, the unity of the new people of God, that the Corinthians must zealously guard.

Thirdly, the corporate nuance of the temple image is noteworthy (ὁ ... ναὸς ... οἵτινές ἐστε ὑμεῖς). The collective plural 'you' (ὑμεῖς) denotes the unique temple: 'You Corinthians—all of you—together constitute God's dwelling-place.'[2] Over against the splinter-groups in the church at Corinth Paul sets the picture of the church as God's temple. His Jewish-Christian readers would not fail to see the point. God does not dwell in a multiplicity of temples. He is one, and there can be only one shrine which he can inhabit (cf. 1. 13, 'Is Christ divided?'). To cause disunity in the church is to desecrate the temple of God, and desecration of a holy place leads to its destruction.

Finally, the sanctity of the new temple is again to the fore. Because the Spirit indwelling the Christian community is the Spirit of holiness, the community is holy (ἅγιος) unto the Lord (cf. Eph. 2. 21, ναὸς ἅγιος). Patently the apostle owes much to his Jewish background. The priestly writers thought of the divine presence as communicating holiness to the sanctuary and the adjacent camp (Num. 16. 3), Zechariah predicted that in the new age when God once again dwelt in the midst of his people all Jerusalem would be holy (14. 20 f.), and the Jews of the Dead Sea called their temple 'a holy house' and 'a house of perfection' (1 QS 8. 5, 9). The language Paul uses suggests that he thinks of the church in almost spatial terms. The church is God's holy

[1] See at length S. Hanson, *The Unity of the Church in the New Testament* (1946), pp. 75 f., 94–8.
[2] The uniqueness of the temple may also be implied if the omission of the article before ναὸς Θεοῦ at v. 16 reflects the Hebraic construct state (J. Héring, *The First Epistle of Saint Paul to the Corinthians* (1952), p. 24).

preserve, and evil must not be allowed to enter it. Weiss rightly detects the idea of taboo.[1] Schism is equivalent to profanation of the holy place,[2] which in ancient society was a capital offence, executed by the deity himself (cf. 1 Sam. 5. 1 ff.; 2 Sam. 6. 6 ff.).[3] 'If any one destroys God's temple, God will destroy him.' A stronger warning concerning the unity of the church is scarcely possible. The church is a divine institution and anyone who would attempt to destroy it by shattering it with divisions will incur divine judgement.

The thought of this text is thus similar to that of 2 Cor. 6. 16–7. 1: the Christian community is God's temple. The only difference lies in the nature of the danger to which the church is exposed; here it is internal (divisiveness), whereas at 2 Cor. 6. 16–7. 1 it is external (heathen society). As in the case of 2 Cor. 6. 16–7. 1, the text contains affinities with the teaching of the Dead Sea sect. All four of the points mentioned above have parallels in the scrolls. The origin of Paul's ideas therefore calls for attention. We shall consider this question after we have studied all the New Testament texts on our subject.

1 Corinthians 6. 19–20

The conception of the body ($\sigma\hat{\omega}\mu a$) of the individual Christian believer as the temple of God in this text is best explained as a particularization of the conception of the church as the temple (3. 16; 2 Cor. 6. 16–7. 1). In support of this is the introductory formula, 'Do you not know ($o\dot{v}\kappa$ $o\ddot{i}\delta a\tau\epsilon$)?' Paul is appealing to what the readers already know, or ought to know. At the same time, it is clear that the thought of the community is not far away (note the use of the plurals, $o\ddot{i}\delta a\tau\epsilon \ldots \dot{v}\mu\hat{\omega}\nu \ldots \dot{v}\mu\hat{i}\nu$). The Christian's body is not his own, but Christ's, which is the church, the dwelling-place of the Holy Spirit. We found a similar oscillation of thought between the community and the individual in the writings of Qumran.[4] The irregularity which Paul wishes to combat resembles that in mind at 2 Cor. 6. 16–7. 1. Apparently some converts had interpreted the apostle's gospel of grace to mean that they were free to do as they pleased (6. 12). Their

---

[1] Op. cit., pp. 85 f.

[2] Cf. 1 Clem. 2. 6, 'All schism was an abomination ($\beta\delta\epsilon\lambda\nu\kappa\tau\acute{o}s$) to you.'

[3] J. Moffatt, *The First Epistle of Paul to the Corinthians* (1938), pp. 42 f.

[4] Above, p. 52.

licentious behaviour also seems to have owed something to the Greek belief that what one does with one's body is of no concern since it is the soul that is the essential part of man (cf. vv. 13, [?] 18a).

Paul meets this situation in the first instance by using against the libertines what appear to be maxims which they themselves had adopted to justify their conduct (vv. 12, 13)[1] and, secondly, by three affirmations concerning the Christian's body: (a) it matters greatly what happens to the body because the resurrection of Christ has invested it with an eternal destiny (vv. 13b, 14); (b) since the body is 'for the Lord' it is his (united to him by virtue of the resurrection, cf. Rom. 6. 5), and union with a prostitute is out of the question (vv. 15, 18); (c) (which concerns us) the body is God's temple:

Do you not know that your body (σῶμα)[2] is a temple of the Holy Spirit within you (ναὸς τοῦ ἐν ὑμῖν ἁγίου πνεύματός), which you have from God? You are not your own; you were bought with a price. So glorify God in your body.

The temple image in this context is particularly appropriate. At the temple of Aphrodite in Corinth the sexual relations between the worshippers and the priestesses was regarded as a form of worship (consecration).[3] Paul would have his readers understand that for the Christian such conduct is nothing short of sacrilege, the desecration of God's holy temple. Dishonouring the body, one dishonours God whose temple it is. The apostle emphasizes the nature of the indwelling; it is holy (ἅγιος) and divine (ἀπὸ θεοῦ). In other words, there is the same idea of taboo as at 3. 16. The Christian's body is sanctified by the Spirit just as the temple of Jerusalem was sanctified by the divine presence (cf. Matt. 23. 17, 19), and it thereby acquires a numinous and sacrosanct character.[4]

---

[1] Cf. C. F. D. Moule, *An Idiom-Book of the New Testament* (1960), pp. 196 f., who thinks that the same device is also employed at v. 18. On this interpretation v. 18a ('Every other sin . . .') represents the libertine maxim, and v. 18b the apostle's reply. This suggestion has the merit of overcoming the difficulty which modern readers have with the statement (v. 18a) that fornication is a sin essentially different from other sins.

[2] A few manuscripts read 'bodies', but the emendation is late and serves at best to emphasize the individual nuance of the text.

[3] G. G. Findlay, 'First Corinthians', *EGT* ii (1900), 821; Moffatt, op. cit., p. 70.

[4] Cf. Barn. 4. 11; 6. 15.

Very naturally Paul adds that the Christian is God's possession, bought at a price. The figure is that of redemption, probably sacral manumission, and suits the temple image well.[1] Just as a slave won his freedom from his master by passing into the service of the god who purchased him (the ceremony took place in the temple of the god concerned), so the Christian, who has been purchased by the blood of Christ (cf. Eph. 1. 7), belongs exclusively to God (whose temple he is) and should render him obedient service (λατρεία). The allusion to the cult implicit in the image of sacral manumission is probably to be detected in the closing admonition, 'So glorify (δοξάσατε) God in your body'.[2]

Commentators have long been in the habit of explaining Paul's use of the temple image in the present text by reference to the teaching of Philo and the Stoics on man as the temple of God.[3] There is close similarity, and some Greek influence may be present,[4] but as Paul uses the image the difference is considerable. In designating Christian man as the temple of God the apostle's point of departure is not the individual (as in Stoic anthropology) but the community. To his way of thinking, God the Spirit does not dwell in the individual *qua* individual but as a member of the Christian community.[5] 'For by one Spirit we were all baptized into one body' (1 Cor. 12. 13). More specifically, it should be noted that it is the body (σῶμα) which Paul says is God's temple. Such a thought was foreign to the Greeks; and only in the case of Adam, the perfect man, was Philo willing to entertain the possibility. In this tradition it is the soul (ψυχή) or mind (νοῦς) which is the temple; the body is the prison of the soul.[6] Furthermore, the divine indwelling for the apostle is not the result of some natural endowment (the Stoics) or human achievement (the Stoics and Philo), but of grace. It is clear therefore that if one grants Greek influence to Paul, as one probably should, allowance must be made for considerable Hebraicizing and Christianizing.

[1] Cf. A. Deissmann, *Light from the Ancient East* (1927), p. 324.
[2] Δοξάζειν has cultic associations (Lev. 10. 3; Ps. 50. 23; Isa. 60. 7, 13; Cerfaux, op. cit., p. 148 n.).
[3] Cf. e.g. Weiss, op. cit., p. 166; Wenschkewitz, op. cit., p. 175; A. Robertson and A. Plummer, *The First Epistle of St. Paul to the Corinthians* (1911), p. 128.
[4] Cf. above, pp. 53 ff. Note the Stoic ring in the Vulgate reading, 'Glorify *and carry* God in your body.' See also on 2 Cor. 5. 8–9, below, p. 146.
[5] Cerfaux, op. cit., p. 148.
[6] Above, p. 55 f.

This concludes our exegesis of the texts from 1 and 2 Corinthians.

It will now be in place to state our conclusions. Before we do so, however, there is an outstanding question to be considered. The foregoing exegesis has assumed that the presence of the Spirit in the church is equivalent to the presence of God in the temple of Jerusalem. This needs to be justified, for nowhere in the Old Testament or Jewish literature is it said that the Spirit dwells in the temple.

Let us begin by noting that in the Old Testament the Spirit is never thought of as distinct from God. Although the Spirit is not spoken of as dwelling in the temple, it is thought of as dwelling in Israel (Ps. 51. 11; Isa. 63. 9), and a parallel is drawn between the Spirit and the 'angel of the presence' (Isa. 63. 9–11). Furthermore, in the post-exilic prophecies of the restoration of Israel the outpouring of the Spirit is the token of God's presence with his people (Isa. 32. 15; 44. 3; Ezek. 37. 14; 39. 29, etc.; Joel 2. 28 ff.). Thus in the book of Acts the advent of the messianic age coincides with the gift of the Spirit (1. 6–8). Pentecost is interpreted as the fulfilment of prophecy (2. 16 ff.). And the account of the subsequent life and activities of the church gives the reader the strong impression that the author saw a correspondence between the presence and activity of the Spirit in the church and the divine presence in Israel of old.[1]

When Paul says on the one hand that the Spirit dwells in the Christian community (1 Cor. 3. 16) and on the other hand that the community is the fulfilment of the promise that God would one day dwell with (in) his people (2 Cor. 6. 16–7. 1), he is really saying one and the same thing. The Spirit in the church is to his mind the equivalent to God's presence in the eschatological temple of Jewish hope.

Further support for equating the Spirit in the church with the divine glory in Israel is the close connection Paul posits between the Spirit and the glory (δόξα) of God. Jesus is the bearer of the divine glory as he is the bearer of the Spirit (2 Cor. 4. 6; cf. 3. 18), and Christians reflect this glory, which they have 'from the Lord who is the Spirit' (2 Cor. 3. 18).

---

[1] The Spirit is given to the church at Jerusalem, the place where the prophets said the presence of God would be revealed in the last days, and it leads the church after the fashion in which the divine presence (kâbhôdh-Yahweh) led Israel (Acts 1. 4; cf. Luke 24. 49; Acts 10. 19; 11. 12, 27 f.; 13. 2; 15. 28. Cf. 5. 1–11).

It may be safely concluded then that when Paul says that the Spirit dwells in the church he has in mind its eschatological status and is modelling his thought on the divine indwelling in the old dispensation. The church is God's new temple. His Spirit resides there just as his name or glory formerly resided in the temple of Jerusalem, though of course in a more profound way.

We may now make a summary of our findings thus far.

(i) The texts on the new temple in 1 and 2 Corinthians (1 Cor. 6. 19 excepted) refer primarily to the local church, the Christian community meeting at a particular place; whereas those still to be considered (Eph. 2. 20–2; 1 Pet. 2. 5 ff., etc.) refer, as we shall see, to the church universal. But this is a distinction that ought not to be pressed. The local implies the universal (just as the universal implies the local). This fact, which is present in all of Paul's thinking on the church, is particularly well illustrated by the temple figure. An orthodox Jew by upbringing, the apostle did not and could not think of many temples, but of one. The church at Corinth was, so to speak, the microcosm; the church universal the macrocosm. Just as the individual Christian is God's temple by virtue of his membership of the Christian community, so in turn the community is a temple by virtue of its belonging to the larger whole, the people of God as such.

(ii) The temple in these texts (and in Eph. 2. 20–2) is the place where God dwells and not (as in 1 Peter) the place where sacrifice is offered. The apostle does, it is true, connect the idea of sacrifice with the new temple (see (v) below) but this is a different matter. To his mind the new temple is fundamentally the place of the divine indwelling.

(iii) The temple is the temple of God or God's Spirit, and never the temple of Christ. The omission of all reference to Christ in these texts should not, however, be attributed to lack of development in Paul's thought,[1] but to the traditional theocentric orientation of the temple concept and to the nature of the argument in hand, in which the apostle is concerned to show the sanctity (2 Cor. 6. 16 ff.) and unity (1 Cor. 3. 16 f.) of the church. Already under the image of the foundation (of the building) (1 Cor. 3. 10 ff.) Christ's place in the church is stated. The way is thus

---

[1] So Wenschkewitz, op. cit., p. 179; and Vielhauer, op. cit., pp. 79 ff., 122 ff.

prepared for the idea of Christ as the cornerstone of the new temple at Eph. 2. 20 ff.

(iv) Intimately connected with the idea of the church as the temple is the thought of the church's oneness. Unity in Israel finds its complement in the unity of the church, and once again the temple is the symbol. Disunity is sacrilege, the dishonouring of him who graciously dwells in the church.

(v) To think of the new temple is to think also of the new cult. Christians are not simply God's temple; they have a sacrifice to offer him. The idea is no more than hinted at in the texts we considered above, but the fact that it is made in connection with the temple idea is interesting. Paul's teaching on the sacrificial nature of Christian life and practice is well known,[1] but its piece-meal character makes treatment difficult. It may be that the conjunction of the cult and temple at 1 Cor. 6. 19 f. gives us a clue to the coherency that Paul's thought apparently had for his readers.

(vi) The temple image is significant for its extensive Old Testament support. The wealth of scripture that lies at the back of the image, upon which Paul was evidently able to call and use with the greatest facility, must give this particular image a unique place in the apostle's repertoire of ecclesiological images. Here the church is seen in its greatness, for here it is seen as the realization of Israel's most cherished hope.

[1] Cf. 2 Cor. 2. 15; 9. 11 f.; Rom. 12. 1 f.; Phil. 2. 17; 4. 18; Col. 1. 22; also 1 Cor. 6. 20; Eph. 2. 18; 3. 12; Rom. 5. 2 (ἡ προσαγωγή).

VIII

NEW TEMPLE IN THE EPISTLES OF PAUL (*continued*)

Ephesians 2. 20–2

THIS text could in many ways be regarded as the conclusion towards which we have been working inasmuch as it depicts the church as the temple in which Jews and non-Jews are united as one people in the worship of the one God.

In this passage it is to be noted that (*a*) the church in its widest sense is in mind, the church universal; (*b*) the unity symbolized is that of the races; (*c*) unlike its use in 1 and 2 Corinthians, where it has to do with ethical exhortation, the image of the temple is used here for doctrinal instruction; (*d*) here for the first time the image of the temple (ναός) is fused with that of the building (οἰκοδομή), thereby enhancing its significance.

The description of the church as the temple at Eph. 2. 20–2 is directly connected with the thought of the preceding verses (cf. the ἄρα οὖν of v. 19), and can be properly understood only in the light of the discussion therein.[1] The section in question (vv. 11–19) is a description of the new status that the death of Christ has conferred upon the Gentiles (vv. 11–13), the reconciliation of both Gentiles and Jews to God and their consequent union as a single entity (vv. 14–18). In other words the subject under discussion, of which vv. 20–2 is the summarizing conclusion, is an historical phenomenon. Recognition of this fact is important for one's interpretation of the temple idea in this passage.

The author begins by recalling the former condition of his Gentile readers. They were 'Gentiles in the flesh' (τὰ ἔθνη ἐν σαρκί). The article (τά) should be given its full weight for it marks the Gentiles off as a group (lit. 'the Gentiles') in contradistinction to the Jews. The contrast intended is intensified by the additional words 'in the flesh'. This expression, as its use in regard to the Jews in the latter half of the verse (11b) indicates,

---

[1] S. Hanson, *The Unity of the Church in the New Testament*, pp. 141 f.

alludes to the ritual status of the Gentiles in relation to the Jews; they did not bear in their flesh the all-important mark and sign of the chosen race. In other words, the disunity of the races is essentially religious in character. The position of the Gentiles *vis-à-vis* the Jews is restated in the verse that follows; they were 'separated from Christ, alienated from the commonwealth (πολιτεία) of Israel, and strangers (ξένοι) to the covenants of promise, having no hope and without God in the world' (v. 12). Such was the condition of non-Jews in the old dispensation.[1]

Now, however (νυνὶ δέ, v. 13), with the advent of the eschatological age a completely new state of affairs obtains. In place of the two groups (δύο) there is one (ἕνα, v. 15). This single entity is variously described as 'one new man' (εἶς καινὸς ἄνθρωπος, v. 15), 'one body' (ἐν σῶμα, v. 16), and 'one Spirit' (ἐν πνεῦμα, v. 18). Its unity derives from the death of Christ, which destroyed the barrier that had formerly kept its members apart (v. 14).

What precisely the barrier (the 'middle wall of partition' of the AV) was is differently interpreted by scholars.[2] Many understand it to mean the balustrade of the temple of Jerusalem which segregated Jews and non-Jews. Some interpret it as the law, which instead of uniting Jews and Gentiles (cf. Isa. 2. 3; Mic. 4. 2; Zech. 8. 23) was turned into an instrument of division (cf. *Arist.* 139). Others think it refers to the veil that divided the holy of holies in the temple of Jerusalem (cf. Heb. 10. 19 f.; also 6. 19 f.). Still another interpretation is offered by Schlier, who argues that it alludes to the barrier which the Gnostics believed divided the earthly and heavenly worlds.[3] The choice seems to lie between the first and second interpretations, since the third is ruled out by the simple fact that the veil in question divided Jews, not Jews and Gentiles,[4] and the fourth forces a mythological interpretation upon the text that is in conflict with the plain

---

[1] Vielhauer suggests that separation from the commonwealth of Israel means separation from the church as the inheritor of the promises and privileges of Israel after the flesh (*Oikodome*, op. cit., p. 124). There is support for this in 2. 1 ff. and in the correspondence between 'without Christ' (χωρὶς Χριστοῦ) in v. 12 and 'in Christ Jesus' (ἐν Χριστῷ 'Ιησοῦ) in v. 13, but it posits a much too sudden and violent transition between v. 11 and v. 12. The break comes more naturally at v. 13 (νυνὶ δέ).

[2] See M. Barth, *The Broken Wall: A Study of the Epistle to the Ephesians* (1960), pp. 34 ff. Cf. the still-outstanding treatment by Armitage Robinson, op. cit., pp. 59 f.

[3] H. Schlier, *Christus und die Kirche im Epheserbrief* (1930), pp. 18 ff.

[4] T. K. Abbott, *The Epistles to the Ephesians and to the Colossians* (1897), p. 61.

historical sense of the context. In favour of understanding the wall to mean the law (the second view) is the wording of v. 15a ('by abolishing in his flesh the law of commandments and ordinances') which has all the appearance of being an epexegesis on the statement that Christ destroyed the wall of the partition.[1] On the other hand, the interpretation of the wall as the barrier in the temple of Jerusalem is supported by the imagery of v. 18 (ἡ προσαγωγή) and the figures of the house, the building, and the temple in vv. 19, 22. Moreover, it has the merit of adding colour to expressions used in the context. It was the barrier in the temple that visibly proclaimed to all and sundry the fact that non-Jews were 'without Christ', 'strangers', 'without God', and 'far off'. But on balance it seems wisest not to distinguish between these two interpretations and decide on one as against the other. The balustrade in the temple and the law of Moses were really symbols of one and the same thing that kept Jew and Gentile apart. The destruction of the temple barrier is equivalent to the abolition of the law (as it had come to be interpreted).[2] What the work of Christ in this respect means for the divisions of our modern world that are based on such things as class, race, and colour should be apparent.

The positive aspect of Christ's work on the cross is the union of Jews and Gentiles. This union is not simply the merging of the races but the creation of unity on a new and higher level. The 'one new man' who has come into being is neither Jew nor Gentile, for both Jew and Gentile have lost their old differentiating status and been given a new status; there is a new (καινός) being (cf. 2 Cor. 5. 17).[3] This means that although the distinction of race remains, it has lost its determinative religious significance (cf. Gal. 3. 28; Col. 3. 11; Rom. 10. 12). What matters now is not whether a person belongs to this race or that but whether or not he is a member of the new society, the people of

---

[1] Armitage Robinson, op. cit., pp. 63, 161.

[2] Ibid., p. 63.

[3] With the 'one new man' of 2. 15 compare the 'one body' (v. 16) and the 'one Spirit' (v. 18). As noted above, these are all parallel expressions of the one phenomenon. But it seems necessary to give the 'one new man' an individual nuance (cf. Armitage Robinson, op. cit., p. 65; Best, op. cit., pp. 152 ff.). To make his point the author personalizes the unity of the races; the new people are as a single person. Cf. Gal. 3. 28, 'You are all one (man) in Christ Jesus'. Underlying may be the idea of corporate personality. Cf. the *tertium genus* of Aristides (*Apol.* 2. 1) and the 'new people' of Barn. 5. 7; 7. 5; cf. 3. 6.

God who have come into being with the death (and resurrection) of Christ, i.e. whether he is a Christian or not. The same point is made at v. 16, where it is stated that Jews no less than Gentiles depend upon the reconciling work of Christ; and also at v. 18, which states that Christ is the means of access to the Father for both Gentile and Jew. The newly found unity of the races, it should be noticed, issues not simply from the fact that they are reconciled the one to the other but from their common reconciliation to God. Christ reconciled 'us both to God in one body (ἐν σῶμα) through the cross' (v. 16). Union in Christ is the basis of the union of the races.[1] Thus united, Jews and Gentiles share the same access (ἡ προσαγωγή) to the one Father in the one Spirit (v. 18, where ἐν ἑνὶ πνεύματι looks back to ἐν ἑνὶ σώματι at v. 16; cf. 4. 4a). A new mode of worship is therefore a further feature of the positive side of Christ's work on the cross.

The writer then summarizes what he has said (v. 19, ἄρα οὖν), and he does so in such a way as to introduce his conclusion (vv. 20-2). He uses the figure of a city comprised of two classes of people: citizens (πολῖται) and those (ξένοι and πάροικοι) who do not enjoy the rights and privileges of citizenship. Whereas formerly the Gentiles resembled the latter they now resemble the former; they are 'fellow citizens with the saints (συμπολῖται τῶν ἁγίων)'.[2] More intimately still, they are God's household (οἰκεῖοι). The reader is thus prepared for the formal description of the church as the building (οἰκοδομή) and temple (ναός) of God in vv. 20-2.

The language and ideas of vv. 11–19 similarly prepare the way for the temple image. The terms 'far' (μακράν) and 'near' (ἐγγύς) which are used to describe the status of the Gentiles (vv. 13, 17) are Old Testament designations for the Jews in regard to their relation with the temple of Jerusalem (Isa. 57. 19; Dan. 9. 7).[3] Again, the 'peace' between the races (vv. 14, 17) recalls

[1] S. Hanson, op. cit., p. 146.
[2] The 'saints' have been interpreted as Israel after the spirit (F. Mussner, *Christus, das All und die Kirche, Studien zur Theologie des Epheserbriefes* (1955), p. 105), or the inhabitants of heaven (G. Stählin, *TWNT* v. 29; cf. Cerfaux, op. cit., p. 345), but the contrast intended by the use of the image of the city and the term πολιτεία at v. 12 (with which συμπολῖται is undoubtedly connected) suggests that it is believing Jews, whose privileges converted Gentiles now share, that are in mind (M. Dibelius, *An die Kolosser, Epheser, an Philemon* (1927), p. 52.
[3] In rabbinic writings 'near' and 'far' are technical terms for the Jews and the Gentiles (Num. R. 8. 4; Dibelius, ibid., p. 53).

the eschatological peace which it was believed would prevail when Israel and the nations were united in the one cult at Zion (Isa. 2. 4; Mic. 4. 3; En. 90. 29–33; Sib. Or. iii. 755–76).[1] Belonging to the same complex of ideas very probably is the statement that Jews and Gentiles have common access to God (v. 18). One has only to ask where in Old Testament thinking one has access to God to discover what it is that determines Paul's thought; it is in the temple.[2] These allusions to the temple and the cult make it clear that the apostle to the Gentiles (3. 1–6) saw the inclusion of non-Jews in the church as the fulfilment of the great promises that in the eschatological age the nations would be graciously accepted by Yahweh in his house. The church is in truth 'a house of prayer for all peoples' (Isa. 56. 7; Mark 11. 17).

It is against this background that we are to understand the presentation of the church as the temple in the concluding verses of the section (20–2).[3] The Gentile converts are

built (ἐποικοδομηθέντες) upon (ἐπί) the foundation (θεμέλιος) of the apostles and prophets, Christ Jesus himself being the chief corner-stone (ὄντος ἀκρογωνιαίου), in whom (ἐν ᾧ) the whole structure (πᾶσα οἰκοδομή) is joined together (συναρμολογουμένη) and grows (αὔξει) into a holy temple (ναὸν ἅγιον) in the Lord, in whom (ἐν ᾧ) you also are built (συνοικοδομεῖσθε) into it for a dwelling place (κατοικητή-ριον) of God in the Spirit (2. 20–2).

The conjunction of the temple (ναός) and building (οἰκοδομή) images and the specification of different parts of the building marks an important development of our subject.

First we have the foundation. It is the apostles and prophets.[4] The use of θεμέλιος here is similar to its use in 1 Cor. 3, inasmuch as the apostle is thinking of those who are the foundation; but the correspondence does not extend any further, for here it is the persons who are built upon the foundation that are in mind, whereas in 1 Cor. 3 it is the builders and the kind of materials they use. To assert that the Gentile converts are built upon the

---

[1] Cf. also 1 Chr. 22. 8, where peace is a prerequisite for the building of the temple (cf. Deut. 12. 8 f.; Hag. 2. 9).

[2] Mussner, op. cit., p. 116.

[3] Failure to appreciate this is largely responsible for Schlier's excursion into Gnostic-Mandean cosmology to account for the thought of vv. 20–2 (*Christus und die Kirche im Epheserbrief* (1930), pp. 35 ff.). So also Vielhauer, pp. 129 ff., 155.

[4] τῶν ἀποστόλων καὶ προφητῶν is best understood as an epexegetical genitive. Cf. Abbott, op. cit., pp. 70 f.

apostles is equivalent to saying that their membership of the
church rests upon the bed rock of historic Christianity. The
'apostles' in question may refer to the twelve, the twelve and
Paul, or a wider number (cf. Rom. 16. 7). Identification would
be simpler if one knew whether the 'prophets' are Old Testament or New Testament personalities. If they are Old Testament
prophets, then 'apostles' refers more naturally to the apostles *par
excellence*, i.e. to the twelve. That it is the twelve who are in
mind is suggested by the fact that the foundation has been laid
and the superstructure ($\epsilon\pi o\iota\kappa o\delta o\mu\eta\theta\acute{\epsilon}\nu\tau\epsilon s$) is going up. Assuming
then that the 'apostles' refers to the twelve we may note the
affinity between the thought of this text and Matt. 16. 18, which
describes Peter as the rock upon which Christ will build his
church. The parallel depends, however, upon whether Peter is
likened to a part of the building (i.e. the foundation) and not to
the ground (i.e. rock) upon which the building will be erected,
which is uncertain.[1] A happier parallel is Rev. 20. 14, which
depicts the (twelve) apostles as the foundation of the new Jerusalem.[2] The 'prophets' mentioned in the text before us are understood by most commentators as New Testament prophets (cf.
Eph. 4. 11 and probably 3. 5): prophets were one of the earliest
orders of ministry in the church (Acts 11. 27; 13. 1, etc.). The
writer will therefore be simply restating what he has just said:
the inclusion of converted Gentiles in the church rests upon the
most primitive sanction. However, there is some justification in
the text for interpreting 'prophets' in the Old Testament sense.[3]
Compare the mention of the 'promise' at 2. 12 (cf. 2 Cor. 7. 1),
the allusion to Zech. 9. 10 ('he shall command peace to the
nations') in the description of Christ as the inaugurator of the
eschatological peace, and the clear reference to Isa. 57. 19 at
v. 17. On this interpretation the inclusion of the Gentiles rests
upon ancient prophecy (cf. 1. 4a) as well as historic Christianity
(the apostles). However one explains 'prophets', the meaning is
plain enough: ex-Gentile Christians have a great and sure

---

[1] Cf. Appendix B.

[2] Cf. below, pp. 172 f. The figure of the foundation is used in relation to the
spiritual temple in the writings of Qumran, though there it refers to the community
in general (cf. above pp. 46 ff.).

[3] Neither the word-order ('apostles and prophets') nor the absence of the article
before 'prophets' is necessarily against their being Old Testament figures (*contra*
Abbott, op. cit., p. 72).

foundation. None may call in question their membership of the church.

Nor is that all. The Gentiles are not built only on the apostolic tradition; more important still: they are built on Christ. Did the Messiah not cleanse the temple of Jerusalem, indicating that the hour for the salvation of the non-Jews was at hand? Or, in terms of the context, has the death of Christ not removed the obstacle to the free access of the Gentiles to God? So to the words 'built upon the foundation of the apostles and prophets' the author adds 'of which (ὄντος) Christ himself is the chief cornerstone (ἀκρογωνιαίου)'.[1] Traditionally ἀκρογωνιαῖος has been taken to be a stone at the foot of the building, but this is rejected by most modern scholars. They maintain that it is a stone at the top of the building. We have examined the question at some length in an appendix (to which the reader is referred at this point),[2] and do not think that there is any reason for abandoning the traditional interpretation. On the contrary, as we attempt to show, it is only when the stone is understood as belonging to the foundation that the meaning of the text is preserved and the sense of the context understood.

Ἀκρογωνιαῖος is connected with θεμέλιον at Isa. 28. 16 (LXX); and the new thought of the Gentiles also having Christ for their foundation would come easily to the writer's mind. 'He (Christ) himself, and neither apostle nor prophet, is at once the ultimate foundation and the head-stone of the corner.'[3] The Gentiles who believe are every whit as much the people of God as Jewish converts are since they are established not only on the apostles and prophets but also upon Christ. The position in the temple occupied by Christ approximates closely to the place in the building assigned to him in 1 Cor. 3. 11, except that here it is specified which particular stone of the foundation he is.[4]

But there is more than this in the author's designating Christ the cornerstone. Christ is the cornerstone 'in whom (ἐν ᾧ) the whole structure (πᾶσα οἰκοδομή)[5] is joined together (συναρμο-

---

[1] H. von Soden, *Die Briefe an die Kolosser, Epheser, Philemon, die Pastoralbriefe* (1893), p. 126; E. Haupt, *Der Epheserbrief* (1897), p. 95.

[2] Below, pp. 195 ff.

[3] S. D. F. Salmon, 'The Epistle to the Ephesians', *EGT* (1903), iii. 300.

[4] Cf. also below on 1 Pet. 2. 4 ff.

[5] The absence of the article in most manuscripts probably indicates a Semitism. The renderings 'the whole structure' (RSV) and 'the whole building' (NEB) are

λογουμένη)¹ and grows into a holy temple in the Lord'. In other words, the cornerstone also serves to unify the building. How precisely this unifying is effected is not very clear. For those commentators who interpret the cornerstone as a key-stone there is no difficulty, since the stone locks the arch over the entrance. But, as we have seen, this explanation depends upon an interpretation of the cornerstone which is not tenable. Some church fathers, doubtless thinking of the method used by builders for locking the walls of buildings at the corners (quoins and counters), suggest that Christ the cornerstone joins Jews and Gentiles as the two walls of a building.² This is an attractive idea, but it strains the metaphor and gives the context an unwarrantable interpretation. Jews and Gentiles are not distinguished like two walls of a building but are indifferently built into the one edifice (συνοικοδομεῖσθε).³ It seems probable that the writer's thought is governed as much by physiological as architectural ideas; the cornerstone unites the building because it is a 'living' stone (cf. below on 1 Pet. 2. 4 ff.). One recalls the physiological features attributed to the cornerstone of Isa. 28. 16, and how the Jews pictured the stone as the embryo from which the world grew and the bond which united the whole of creation.⁴ Such ideas may have influenced the author. Hence he can speak of the building 'growing' (αὔξει) from the cornerstone. The preposition 'in' (ἐν ᾧ) at v. 21 has more than an instrumental meaning; it has organic overtones and approximates in sense to the expression 'in Christ' (ἐν Χριστῷ: 2. 13). The building inheres, so to speak, in the cornerstone. One should compare 4. 15 f., where, in a similar mixing of metaphors, we have the converse of what is stated here, viz. the body is joined together (συναρμολογούμενον) and built up

much to be preferred to 'every several building' (RV), for the thought of the passage (the one society, the one foundation and cornerstone, and the single temple into which the building grows) is against the idea of several buildings. On the use of 'all' (πᾶσα) as a collective see Moule, *An Idiom-Book of the New Testament*, pp. 94 f. Cf. the fine description of the monolithic character of the new temple in Hermas, *Vis.* III. ii. 6; v. 1; *Sim.* IX. ix. 7.

¹ Armitage Robinson suggests that συναρμολογεῖσθαι is a technical term for the working of one end of a stone so as to fit the corresponding end of the stone next to it (op. cit., p. 262). Cf. the physiological use of the term at 4. 16.

² Athanasius (*PG* 27. 480); Augustine (*PL*, 38. 1159); Cyril of Alexandria (*PG* 72. 436); Theodoret (*PG* 82. 525); Bede (*PL* 92. 952 f.); Calvin (*CR* 79, 174–6). This idea is adopted by Fridrichsen, op. cit., p. 316.

³ Abbott, op. cit., p. 71.

⁴ Cf. Appendix A.

(εἰς οἰκοδομήν) from Christ the head (ἐξ οὗ). It is clear therefore that the cornerstone unites the building because it is organically as well as structurally bound to it. The statement that the building is 'joined together' (συναρμολογουμένη) will thus refer not simply to the union of one stone with another, but also to the union of the whole construction (πᾶσα [ἡ] οἰκοδομή) with (and in) the cornerstone.[1] As living stones Jews and Gentiles are not simply inserted into but are intimately joined together in a common life, the origin and source of which is Christ.[2] The point which the writer wishes to convey is the same as that made in the preceding verses (vv. 11–19), viz. unity in Christ.

The unity of Gentiles and Jews and their mutual dependence upon Christ is restated in the other relative clause (v. 22) which is connected to 'cornerstone': 'in whom (ἐν ᾧ) you also are built (συνοικοδομεῖσθε)'. This is a parallel and a particularization of v. 21a. Gentiles are joined with (σύν) others (i.e. Jews) in the same building. Compare the σύν in συμπολῖται at v. 19. The present tense ('are built') is probably related to 'grows' in the preceding clause. The building grows as further stones (the Gentile converts) are added to it.

The superstructure that rises upon the foundation is described under two images. (a) It is 'a holy temple in the Lord' (ναὸς ἅγιος ἐν Κυρίῳ v. 21b), and (b) it is 'a dwelling-place of God in the Spirit' (κατοικητήριον τοῦ Θεοῦ ἐν πνεύματι v. 22b). Clearly these are parallel descriptions of one and the same thing, for they follow as predicates of the parallel relative clauses just considered, which have the one subject (Christ the cornerstone). 'Temple' and 'dwelling-place' may therefore be taken as synonyms, the latter being expansive (τοῦ Θεοῦ).[3] In both cases it is the church universal that is in mind. The building, which up to this point is

---

[1] Cf. G. H. Whitaker, 'The Building and the Body (Eph. ii. 21 f.; iv. 16; Col. ii. 19),' *Theology*, 13 (1926), 335–6.

[2] Cf. Congar, pp. 165 f., who arrives at a similar conclusion by way of the formula 'in Christ'. He refers helpfully to Col. 2. 7, where the architectural and physiological images are blended (ἐρριζωμένοι καὶ ἐποικοδομούμενοι). Cf. also Eph. 3. 17 (ἐρριζωμένοι καὶ τεθεμελιωμένοι) and above (p. 47 and n. 6) on the favourite conjunction of the building and planting images in Jewish thought.

[3] To refer κατοικητήριον to the individual Christian as is done by some commentators (G. C. A. Harless, *Kommentar über den Brief Pauli an die Epheser* (1858), ad loc.; M. Meinertz, *Der Epheserbrief* (1917), p. 67; Max-Adolf Wagenführer, *Die Bedeutung Christi für Welt und Kirche, Studien zum Kolosser- und Epheserbrief* (1941), p. 116) is without justification.

not specified, is now said to be a temple, the dwelling-place of God. This fusion of the architectural (οἰκοδομή) and sacral (ναός) images, which appear separately at 1 Cor. 3, is fascinating, but not novel; it is also present in the Qumran scrolls.[1] The statement that the building grows (lit. is growing, i.e. is under construction) into a temple should not be taken to imply that the divine indwelling is a hope that will not be realized till some point in the future when the building is finished.[2] Once again the writer's thought is to be explained on the basis of his interpenetration of images. The figures of the building and the temple, which are distinct and stand for different ideas, are fused together to create a bivalent image. Viewed as the building the church is still under construction; viewed as the temple, however, it is an inhabited dwelling. This way of explaining the text seems preferable to that offered by Best, who writes, 'God already dwells in his temple although it is still growing and not yet complete; such is his gracious condescension.'[3] The character of the new dwelling is indicated by the use of the adjective 'holy'. As in 1 Cor. 3. 16 this holiness is not a virtue of those who constitute the temple. The temple is holy in the Lord (ἐν Κυρίῳ). Whether the character of the new temple (vis-à-vis the old material temple) is also signified by the use of the words 'in the Spirit' (ἐν πνεύματι), as is commonly supposed,[4] is not very certain: ἐν πνεύματι rather appears to be a parallel of ἐν Κυρίῳ, which it expands: ἐν Κυρίῳ = in God;[5] ἐν πνεύματι = in the (Holy) Spirit.

Eph. 2. 20-2 then is the picture of Christ and Christians together forming the church, in which God dwells. The total impression conveyed upon one is such that if the architectural motif is to be properly appreciated one must with the early fathers think of the building as a monolith.[6] The entire construction comprising cornerstone, foundation, and superstructure forms an indivisible whole.

The teaching of Ephesians on the new temple is thus more developed than that of 1 and 2 Corinthians.

---

[1] Cf. above, pp. 49, 52.

[2] So P. Ewald, Die Briefe des Paulus an die Epheser, Kolosser und Philemon (1905), p. 153, who incorrectly takes αὔξει as a future.   [3] Op. cit., p. 168.

[4] So Armitage Robinson, op. cit. p. 72; S. Hanson, op. cit., p. 134; Mussner, op. cit., p. 110, all of whom refer to the οἶκος πνευματικός of 1 Pet. 2. 5.

[5] Κύριος can hardly refer to Christ since the latter is already referred to under the ἐν ᾧ.   [6] Hermas, Sim. ix. 9.

In the first place, the imagery used is much more elaborate. The source of inspiration is no longer the closely knit and highly exclusive temple community of Ezekiel and the priestly writers, as in the Corinthian epistles, but the world-shrine of Isaiah and the intertestamental writers. In particular one calls to mind the great passage in Enoch which depicts the reconciliation of Jews and Gentiles and their union in the eschatological temple:

> The Lord of the sheep brought a new house greater and loftier than that first (house), and set it in the place of the first which had been folded up . . . and all the sheep were within it . . . all that had been destroyed and dispersed (i.e. the Jews), and all the beasts of the field and all the birds of the heaven (i.e. the Gentiles) assembled in that house. . . . And I saw till they laid down that sword (which had been given to the sheep to destroy the beasts and the birds) . . . and they brought it back into the house (90. 29–34).[1]

The presence in the church of those who formerly were not the privileged people of God is viewed as the fulfilment of the eschatological hope in its widest and most generous expression.

Of special interest is the Christological development present in the text. The temple is still the temple of God as in 1–2 Corinthians, but now for the first time we have a clear and definite relation posited between the temple and Christ. It is true that already at 1 Cor. 3. 11 Christ is represented as the foundation of the building, but the building is not specified. Here, as a result of the combination of the images of the building and the temple, Christ is not only shown to be part of the temple in which God dwells but its actual *fundamentum fundamentorum*.[2] As its living cornerstone, he creates, supports, and upbuilds the temple. In a sense Christ is the builder of the new temple. And, as ever, the work of the Messiah in erecting the temple is to provide God with a means of dwelling in the midst of his people. The traditional theocentric nuance which dominates the temple image is thus preserved.

The statement that the temple 'grows' is a new thought. It indicates that in Ephesians at least the conception of the church as the temple is conterminous with the church as the body, and

---

[1] Above, pp. 29 f. Cf. Sib. Or. iii. 755–76, which similarly describes the eschatological peace and unity of the races in the new temple.

[2] On the relation between the figures of the building and the temple at 1 Cor. 3 see above, pp. 98 ff.

prevents one from treating the image as in any sense static and concrete in comparison with images like the body and the flock. At this point, the meaning of the passage before us is similar to that of 1 Pet. 2. 4 ff. The church is made of living stones, and quantitatively and qualitatively it is growing, both as the various ministries engaged in its construction carry out their divinely appointed tasks (Eph. 4. 11 ff.) and as it upbuilds itself in love (4. 16). Thus the image of the temple approximates very closely to that of the body, and once again the idea of the building (οἰκοδομή) provides the link.[1]

A further development seen by some commentators in the present passage is the celestial character of the new temple.[2] Evidence for this is adduced from the statement that Christians are, by virtue of their union with their risen and ascended Lord, already in heaven (2. 4–6), and also from the words 'fellow citizens with the saints' (2. 19), which are taken to imply the existence of the heavenly city (and temple). The access to the Father (2. 18) is similarly interpreted to mean access to God in heaven. In this connection Schlier maintains that the thought of the text is best explained in terms of the heavenly building of Gnostic-Mandean mythology.[3] We have had occasion to reject Schlier's thesis on general grounds, and do not think, therefore, that it is applicable in this particular connection. That the epistle attributes a heavenly existence to the church is not to be doubted (1. 3; 2. 6). But the temple described at 2. 20–2 can hardly be regarded as heavenly in the same sense as the heavenly temple of the Jewish apocalypses, Hebrews, and Revelation. The temple conception of 2. 20–2 is directly connected with the discussion of the preceding verses (vv. 11–18) which, as we have noted, is concerned with the historical reconciliation of the races. It is the church as an historical actuality, the cult in which ex-Gentiles and ex-Jews here and now realize their oneness and enjoy common access to God the Father, which witnesses to this reconciliation.

The treatment of the new temple image in Ephesians, while it registers significant new features, is in a continuous line of

---

[1] Cf. the terminology of Eph. 2. 21–2; 4. 12, 15–16; Col. 2. 19.

[2] So Cerfaux, *The Church*, pp. 139, 345 ff., 352; Fraeyman, op. cit., pp. 394, 401.

[3] Schlier, *Christus und die Kirche im Epheserbrief*, pp. 35 ff., followed by E. Käsemann, *Leib und Leib Christi* (1933), pp. 59 ff.; Vielhauer, op. cit., pp. 129 ff. For criticism of Schlier see e.g. Mussner, op. cit., pp. 110 ff.

development with that of the earlier epistles and reflects the same Jewish milieu. Thus the figure of Christ as the cornerstone is (according to current architectural practice) really a development of the idea of Christ as the foundation at 1 Cor. 3. 11. Similarly the representation of the church as at one and the same time a building which is still under construction and a sanctuary inhabited by the deity is achieved simply by combining two figures which appear (separately) in 1 Cor. 3. The conception of the building is itself thoroughly biblical and Jewish, and the architectonic distinctions now introduced are inherent in the image (cf. 1 QS 5. 6). Ezekiel, the priestly writers, and the Jews of Qumran all made the architecture of the new temple symbolize the unity of the people of God of the end-time. Cosmological and physiological ideas are in evidence, but once again the background is Jewish. The popular composite biblical and post-biblical figure of the plant–building, and the rabbinic identification of the cornerstone in Zion as the embryo of creation go a long way to explaining the viable nature of the new temple. If the heavenly character of the new temple also is in mind, it can similarly be accounted for by reference to Jewish apocalyptic, which attributed to the eschatological temple a celestial character.

With the exception of Gal. 4. 26 and 2 Cor. 5. 1–5, which will be studied later in relation to the heavenly temple, we have now completed our study of the major texts on the spiritual temple in the Pauline corpus. A few miscellaneous texts of secondary importance from Paul are still outstanding, and will be considered towards the end of the next chapter. The remainder of this chapter will be devoted to a consideration of the factors which influenced Paul in his use of the temple image.

First and foremost undoubtedly was the influence of Christian tradition. The Jews of Qumran thought of the community as a spiritual temple long before Paul did, and it would *a priori* be surprising if he were the first Christian to do so. The case for believing that the idea of the church as God's new temple was in fact part of the tradition which the apostle received from the early church cannot be established until the other New Testament witnesses to our subject have been studied, but already the evidence is pointing in this direction. We refer to Paul's use of Old Testament *testimonia*. In the first place we have Lev. 26. 12 and Ezek. 37. 27 (2 Cor. 6. 16). These texts were already combined and used in Jewish teaching on the eschatological temple,[1] and the use of Ezek. 37. 27 at Rev. 21. 3 would suggest that Paul is drawing upon early Christian catechesis. More certain is the allusion to Isa. 28. 16 at Eph. 2. 20. The fusion of this text with Isa. 8. 14 at Rom. 9. 33 and the close resemblances between the latter and the catena of 'stone' texts at 1 Pet. 2. 6–8 make it virtually certain that the designation of Christ as the corner-stone of the new temple reflects a pre-canonical tradition. It would seem to follow therefore that the temple image, to which the 'stone' texts are attached, also comes from the same source.

Now, indebted as Paul was to his teachers in Christ, it is beyond doubt that his own background and education, as inter-preted in the light of his conversion, made its contribution here, as elsewhere. We should see two influences at work, or one influence with positive and negative aspects.

There was in the first instance the apostle's Jewish heritage.[2] Born in Judaism and reared and schooled in its strictest wing (Acts 22. 3; Phil. 3. 4 ff.), Paul gratefully carried his heritage into Christianity (Acts 23. 6) and never hesitated to testify to the faith of his fathers (26. 6 f.; 2 Cor. 11. 22). For one whose eyes were opened to Christ as the end of the law, conversion to Christianity was perhaps less revolutionary than is sometimes allowed. The promises of God had not failed (Rom. 9. 6); God had not rejected his people (11. 2). Now as always the ground of man's acceptance before God is faith (Rom. 3–4; Gal. 3. 17). Christians are sons of Abraham (Gal. 3. 7). As such they inherit the privileges of Israel. 'To them belong the sonship, the glory, the covenants, the giving of the law, the worship, and the promises' (Rom. 9. 4). In including the glory (δόξα) among the privileges of the people of God Paul is clearly referring to the divine presence. The same fact is to be adduced from the men-tion of worship (λατρεία), and also adoption and covenant, since the Old Testament thought of God redeeming (adopting) Israel and entering into a covenant with her in order that he might dwell among men (Exod. 29. 45 f.). More significantly, 'glory' and 'worship' both have strong eschatological associations: the prophets looked forward to the day when the divine glory would be more fully revealed and Israel would offer God acceptable worship. Hence the reference to the promises. The apostle would

[1] Cf. above, p. 95.   [2] Fraeyman, op. cit., pp. 381 f.

thus come to think quite naturally of God dwelling in the church as he once dwelt in his people of old. Viewed in this context the new indwelling was both type and fulfilment of the old. The thought would come all the more easily if the conception of the community of the faithful as a spiritual temple was already to hand.

The other influence, which we have called the negative influence in view of the circumstances of its inception, was the spiritualization of the temple conception. The Stoics and Philo on the one hand, and the Jews of Qumran on the other hand, spiritualized the idea of the temple. The extent to which Paul was influenced by one or other or both of these movements is not easily determined. Wenschkewitz in his treatment of the subject argued that the source of the apostle's spiritualizing is to be found in the Stoics,[1] but his work was published before the discovery of the Dead Sea scrolls. Fraeyman thinks that the influence was of a general nature.[2] Congar argues for a specifically Christian origin.[3] It seems necessary to allow for influence from both the Greek and Jewish traditions.

The conception of the individual as the temple at 1 Cor. 6. 19 and the view taken of the body at 2 Cor. 5. 2 ff. (on which see below) owe some debt to Greek thought, either directly or indirectly, while the conception of the church as the temple at 1 Cor. 3. 16, 2 Cor. 6. 16 ff., and Eph. 2. 20–2 is strongly reminiscent of Qumran. Having said this, one should note that in each case Paul's presuppositions are quite different from those of his mentors. The Stoics and Philo spiritualized the idea of the temple and cult because the thought of God dwelling in a temple made by men and accepting blood and other material offerings was intolerable to them, while the Jews of Qumran did so because they could not worship at the temple of Jerusalem. Paul's spiritualization rests upon a much more positive basis, the new and pneumatic order of worship that issues from the death and resurrection of Jesus Christ and the gift of the Spirit.

It is clear therefore that, influential as Christian and non-Christian traditions were upon the thinking of Paul, what contributed most to the apostle's teaching on the church as God's new temple was his own personal experience and understanding of Jesus Christ and his work. Everywhere we have evidence of

[1] Wenschkewitz, op. cit., pp. 175 f., 180.
[2] Fraeyman, op. cit., p. 411.   [3] Congar, op. cit., pp. 148 f.

a new and creative mind at work, selecting and reshaping traditional images and ideas.

The foregoing two chapters have attempted to show how the doctrine of the new temple adumbrated in the teaching of our Lord and the early church was expounded by Paul. In conclusion it may be asked whether the apostle regarded the new temple as having effectively and finally superseded the old temple. The texts we examined above present the church as the fulfilment of the ancient hope of the eschatological indwelling at Jerusalem. One would therefore expect that an answer in the affirmative could unhesitatingly be given; but one hesitates to do so.[1] While one may say with certainty that the apostle thought of God's dwelling in the church in parallel fashion to his dwelling in the temple of Jerusalem, one is reluctant to deduce that (therefore) the temple of Jerusalem ceased to have religious significance for him. The author of the Acts of the Apostles certainly believed that it no longer possessed such significance for the apostle,[2] but that is another matter. A straightforward reading of Paul's own writings can hardly be said to bear this out. At the point where one expects the apostle to carry his teaching to its logical conclusion one finds instead a certain ambivalence.

The text that gives us pause is Rom. 11. 26: 'All Israel will be saved; as it is written, "The Deliverer will come from Zion ($\dot{\epsilon}\kappa$ $\Sigma\iota\dot{\omega}\nu$), he will banish ungodliness from Jacob"' (cf. Isa. 59. 20). With this Rom. 9. 26 should probably be compared: 'In the very place where it was said to them, "You are not my people", they (lit. there [$\dot{\epsilon}\kappa\epsilon\hat{\iota}$] they) will be called "sons of the living God".' The last part of the latter text is from Hos. 1. 10 (= 2. 1 in the LXX), and if the adverb 'there' which may have been part of the LXX version used by the apostle[3] or have been added by him, signifies Jerusalem,[4] the sense is akin to Rom. 11. 26; but it may be that it refers more generally, as in Hosea, to the holy land.[5] At any rate, 11. 26 clearly refers to Jerusalem, and unless

[1] Cf. above p. 85; and J. T. Townsend, *The Jerusalem Temple in New Testament Thought*, diss. (Harvard, 1958), pp. 40 f., who, however, fails to do justice to Paul's doctrine of the Spirit dwelling in the church.
[2] Above, pp. 90 f.
[3] Rahlfs prints $\dot{\epsilon}\kappa\epsilon\hat{\iota}$ in his edition of the LXX.
[4] As is held by Munck, *Paul and the Salvation of Mankind*, pp. 306 f.
[5] Cf. W. Sanday and A. C. Headlam, *The Epistle to the Romans* (1902), p. 264.

one writes it off as a vestige of Jewish apocalypticism one is obliged to interpret it.

Munck, who believes that Paul attributed great significance to the temple of Jerusalem, is in no doubt that Paul is here referring to the imminent *parousia* of Christ at Jerusalem, and is thus attributing an eschatological role to the city.[1] Ellis is of the opinion that the apostle's words '*out of* Zion' (ἐκ Σιών) instead of '*for the sake of* Zion' (ἕνεκεν Σιών) as in the LXX, betokens a contrast between the true and the faithless Zion and suggests that the apostle is spiritualizing Zion as a symbol of the church as the '*locus* (and perhaps the instrument) from which the Redeemer goes forth'.[2] Sanday and Headlam incline to the view that it is the heavenly city that is signified.[3] Interpretation thus turns on the question whether the text is to be taken literally or figuratively. This is not very clear from the context. That it should, however, be interpreted literally is suggested by 2 Thess. 2. 3–4.[4] But if Paul is referring to Jerusalem (and its temple) it is difficult to see what role he attributed to it beyond that of its being the venue of the final salvation. The significance that Jerusalem had for the apostle (as for others) derived from the fact that it was the place where historically God met his people in judgement and mercy, and anything in the way of a redemptive role seems to be ruled out by the logic of the apostle's doctrine of salvation through faith in Christ. More than this one cannot safely say. Interpretation of Rom. 11. 26 depends upon interpretation of the context (chapters 9–11) and the relation of the latter to Paul's theology as a whole and to New Testament eschatology generally, which are still matters of debate.

[1] Munck writes, 'The quotation from Isaiah in Rom. xi. 26 is presumably meant literally, when it says, "There shall come out of Zion the Deliverer; he shall turn away ungodliness from Jacob", etc. That is: Christ shall come from the hill of the temple, and destroy the antichrist' ('Israel and the Gentiles in the New Testament', p. 30). Cf. Munck *Paul and the Salvation of Mankind*, pp. 131, 285, 306. Cf. also Lindars, op. cit., p. 245.

[2] E. E. Ellis, *Paul's Use of the Old Testament* (1957), p. 123, n. 5. Cf. p. 138.

[3] Op. cit., p. 337.

[4] See below, pp. 135 f.

IX

THE NEW TEMPLE IN 1 PETER AND MISCELLANEOUS TEXTS

THE extent to which the church of New Testament times saw itself as inheriting the promises, enjoying the privileges, and conducting the functions of the people of God of the Old Testament is nowhere more clearly in evidence than in the First Epistle of Peter. Writing to Christians of the spiritual dispersion in Asia Minor, the author places great emphasis on their status: 'You are a chosen race, a royal priesthood, a holy nation, God's own people. . . . Once you were no people but now you are God's people' (2. 9). The words form the conclusion of a string of Old Testament quotations which is intended to reinforce the paraenesis in the earlier part of the section (vv. 4–5). In bold but familiar imagery the preceding section depicts believers as babes who breast-feed on Christ their mother (1. 22–2. 3). If the writer is drawing upon Deutero-Isaiah, as he certainly is elsewhere, it is natural for him to switch to the temple image (οἶκος) since the prophet frequently used the image of the nursing mother to represent Zion (Isa. 49. 14 ff.; 54. 1 ff.). The new image introduces a second line of thought, which is intended to set forth some of the consequences of salvation. Christians are to grow up not as individuals in isolation but as a community; they are joined to Christ and to one another. The individualistic aspect of Christian faith recedes into the background and attention is directed to its institutional character. The passage is unique in what it has to teach us concerning the church's nature and function.

Come to him (πρὸς ὃν προσερχόμενοι), to that living stone (λίθον ζῶντα), rejected by men but in God's sight chosen and precious (ἐκλεκτὸν ἔντιμον); and like living stones (λίθοι ζῶντες) be yourselves built up (οἰκοδομεῖσθε)[1] into a spiritual house (οἶκος πνευματικός), to

---

[1] οἰκοδομεῖσθε should be taken as indicative: 'in coming to him . . . you are built.' The reading ἐποικοδομεῖσθε is epexegetical and due possibly to influence from Eph. 2. 20.

be a holy priesthood (εἰς ἱεράτευμα ἅγιον), to offer spiritual sacrifices acceptable (εὐπροσδέκτους) to God through Jesus Christ (διὰ 'Ἰησοῦ Χριστοῦ). (2. 4–5)

The thought of Jesus Christ as the stone is then taken up and expanded in a midrash:

(For it stands in scripture)
'Behold, I am laying in Zion a stone, a cornerstone chosen and precious (λίθον ἐκλεκτὸν ἀκρογωνιαῖον ἔντιμον)
and he who believes in him will not be put to shame.'

To you therefore who believe, he is precious, but for those who do not believe,

'The very stone which the builders rejected
has become the head of the corner (εἰς κεφαλὴν γωνίας)',
and
'A stone that will make men stumble (λίθος προσκόμματος),
a rock that will make them fall (πέτρα σκανδάλου)';

for they stumble because they disobey the word, as they were destined to do. But you are a chosen race (γένος ἐκλεκτόν), a royal priesthood (βασίλειον ἱεράτευμα), a holy nation (ἔθνος ἅγιον), God's own people (λαὸς εἰς περιποίησιν), that (ὅπως) you may declare the wonderful deeds of him who called you out of darkness into his marvellous light. Once you were no people but now you are God's people; once you had not received mercy but now you have received mercy. (vv. 6–10)

One cannot fail to be struck by the corporate nature of the terms used throughout the passage. Christians form a house built of many stones, a priesthood,[1] a race or nation,[2] a people. Spörri finely comments: 'They (the terms) present the church as a cohesive unit, a strong fellowship of persons of common origin, with a common experience and self-consciousness, a common possession and responsibility.'[3] The same idea of the gathering together of mankind into one society is also present at 2. 25, 'For you were straying like sheep, but have now returned to the Shepherd and Guardian of your souls.' This is also true of 5. 2 f., which describes the church as 'the flock of God'. The language is traditional and reflects the ancient hope of the eschatological ingathering and reunion of God's scattered people, but the

[1] Reading βασίλειός as a substantive (cf. E. G. Selwyn, *The First Epistle of St. Peter* (1946), pp. 165 ff.).
[2] The national idea of ἔθνος should not be pressed.
[3] T. Spörri, *Der Gemeindegedanke im ersten Petrusbrief* (1925), p. 38.

author interprets it in the light of Christ's work. It is not only the Jews who find unity, but also the Gentiles who had hitherto been divided and fragmented by their worship of 'gods many and lords many' (1 Cor. 8. 5 AV). Quite appropriately then the church is described as the house or temple of God.

First, Jesus Christ is depicted as the living stone (λίθον ζῶντα, v. 4). In ancient thinking a 'living' stone was one that had not been hewn or broken and which, therefore, retained its numinous power. But our author employs the epithet 'living' in a general sense (cf. 1. 3, 23; 2. 5), and the other epithets he uses suggest that the stone is cut and dressed. In further describing the stone as 'chosen and precious' the author reveals the source of his thought. The words are from the famous 'cornerstone' text Isa. 28. 16 (LXX). By connecting to this stone the stone that makes men stumble of Isa. 8. 14 the writer indicates (as is explicitly shown by the actual use of the term ἀκρογωνιαῖος at v. 6) that he is referring to a stone at the foot of the building. The same is true of the stone of Ps. 118 (117). 22: by associating this too with the stone of Isa. 8. 14 the writer shows that he took it to mean a stone at ground level. The substitution of the indeterminate word 'men' for 'builders' points to a stage in the transmission of this *testimonium* in Christian apologetics subsequent to that represented by its use at Mark 12. 10 and Acts 4. 11. Those who reject the stone now signify all who attempt to build society or their own lives without reference to Jesus Christ.[1] But Christ cannot be set aside. Hence the addition of the text on the stone of stumbling. Thus for those who believe in him Christ is the sure foundation and determining fact of their existence (Isa. 28. 16; Ps. 118. 22), while for those who reject him he is (as the angle of the corner) the cause of their downfall (Isa. 8. 14).

In calling Christ the stone, alias the corner- or head-stone, First Peter is thinking primarily of the relation of Christ to his church. The nature of the relationship is probably alluded to in the adjective 'living' (stone) (v. 4; cf. 'living stones', v. 5). Since the rock or stone in Zion was traditionally a living stone, our author, like Paul in Eph. 2. 20, would easily apply the idea to Christ, who by virtue of his resurrection is both living and life-giving (cf. 1. 3). At this point the thought of the text is thus similar to that of Eph. 2. 20–2: Christ is the source of the

[1] F. W. Beare, *The First Epistle of St. Peter* (1947), p. 99.

church's life and growth. For this reason believers are exhorted to keep coming (προσερχόμενοι) to him.

The conception of Christ as the living stone leads naturally to the conception of Christians as living stones.[1] 'In coming to him . . . you are built up as living stones into a spiritual house.' This is one of the points at which our author develops the new temple image. Although the Jews of Qumran thought of the spiritual temple in terms of a building they do not appear to have extended the image to include the idea of individuals as stones. The presence of the idea in 1 Pet. 2. 4 ff.; Eph. 2. 20–2 (by implication) and Ign. *Eph.* 9. 1 ('You are as stones of the temple of the Father') suggests that it appealed to Christians, by serving, one may suppose, to convey the close relationship and likeness between Christ and his followers. Bigg thinks that the present participle (προσερχόμενοι) suggests the idea of stones being added one after another, and he refers to Hermas' description of stones 'coming up' (ἀναβαίνειν) to be built into the house of God (*Sim.* ix. 3. 4 f.),[2] but this strains the metaphor too much. The meaning is rather that of stones adhering to the cornerstone Christ and thereby forming a building. As believers continuously come to Christ and are progressively built up in him they form God's house.

When the writer calls the building which Christ and Christians together form a 'house' (οἶκος) it is clear that he means a temple, as his mention of priesthood and cultus indicates. What he means by calling it a spiritual (πνευματικός) house is not so obvious. Selwyn, who discusses the term πνευματικός fully, thinks that it means 'God's true temple',[3] but this tends to introduce a polemical note that can hardly be said to be present in the epistle.[4] Nor can one say that the contrast is with temples made with hands, i.e. material, whether of Judaism or paganism.[5] Also unsatisfactory is the suggestion that the temple is spiritual because it is indwelt by God's Spirit,[6] since this author does not think of the new temple as the place of the divine indwelling but as the

---

[1] On the writer's doctrine of the *imitatio Christi* see Selwyn, op. cit., pp. 90 ff.

[2] C. Bigg, *The Epistles of St. Peter and St. Jude* (1910), p. 128.

[3] Op. cit., pp. 160, 286 ff.

[4] H. Windisch mistakenly regards the section (2. 4–10) as an anti-Jewish polemic (*Die Katholischen Briefe* (1930), p. 61).

[5] So Beare, op. cit., p. 96.

[6] So C. E. B. Cranfield, *The First Epistle of Peter* (1950), p. 47.

place of sacrifice. It seems wisest to interpret the epithet in the light of what is said in the context concerning the nature of the church's offering. The sacrifices are spiritual because they are the Christian's self-oblation (2. 5). The new temple may therefore be said to be spiritual because it is built of consecrated persons.[1] The sense of the passage approximates closely to Rom. 12. 1, and if one wishes to find the link connecting the two passages one may find it in the use of the word 'spiritual' (λογικός) at 1 Pet. 2. 2.

The conception of Christ and Christians as stones in the new temple is highly suggestive for understanding the relation between Christ and the church, and one could wish that it were more developed. But the writer passes on to what is of greater interest to him: the purpose of the temple. In place of a great edifice built of numberless stones we see priests offering sacrifice.[2] Priesthood and sacrifice of course were inseparable from ancient places of worship, and in the Dead Sea writings the concept of the spiritual temple is nicely balanced with the concept of spiritual sacrifice, so the new thought would come easily. Paul does indeed connect the new cult and the new temple, but since the temple for him is essentially the place of the divine indwelling he does not develop the idea. Clearly this author is primarily interested in the new temple as the place of worship (vv. 2, 9). He thus completes the circle of ideas represented by the temple image that the covenanters of Qumran hesitated to complete,[3] reinterpreting priesthood as well as temple and sacrifice.

We note that it is the church *in toto* that is priestly. This is seen both from the representation of the stones as priests (v. 5) and the quotation of Exod. 19. 6 (cf. 23. 22 LXX) (v. 9), which refers to the whole of Israel. The holiness of the priesthood (v. 5) is the holiness of the church (1. 15). What the sacrifices are that the new priesthood offers we are not told, but it is likely that our author thought of them as including such things as purity of soul (1. 22), the proclamation of the evangel (2. 9), good works (2. 12), suffering (2. 19 ff. etc.), prayer (3. 7; 4. 7), hospitality (4. 9), and humility (5. 5). In short, imitating Christ is to the author's

---

[1] See further Congar, op. cit., pp. 179 f.
[2] Cf. L. Cerfaux, 'Regale Sacerdotium', *RSPT* 28 (1939), 5–39 (= *Recueil Lucien Cerfaux*, 1954, pp. 283–315); Selwyn, op. cit., pp. 291 ff.; T. F. Torrance, *Royal Priesthood* (1955), pp. 1–22; C. Eastwood, *The Royal Priesthood of the Faithful* (1963), pp. 26 ff.
[3] Cf. above, p. 52.

way of thinking the sacrifice that is well-pleasing to God. In other words, the whole of life is the offering up of sacrifice. Thus the offering is called spiritual (cf. Rom. 12. 1). The statement that the church presents its offering to God 'through Jesus Christ' (v. 5) is a further indication of the distance separating our author from the sectarians of Qumran and from Judaism in general. Cultus, no less than temple, is dependent upon Jesus Christ. The words 'through Jesus Christ' (διὰ ᾽Ιησοῦ Χριστοῦ) are connected by some commentators with the verb 'to offer up' (ἀναφέρειν) and by others with the adjective 'acceptable' (εὐπρόσδεκτος). In the case of the former, the sacrifices are acceptable because they are spiritual, i.e. the worship of voluntary, rational, and moral beings (cf. Heb. 10. 1–10); in the latter because they are offered through Christ (cf. Heb. 13. 15). Both senses are supported by the context: the former by what we have seen is the probable meaning of the word 'spiritual', the latter by the form of the exhortation as a whole ('In coming to him . . . the sacrifices you offer are certain of acceptance'). One may therefore take the words 'through Jesus Christ' to refer both to the nature of the new cult and the ground of its acceptance before God. Christ is the heavenly priest who presents the sacrifices of the church upon earth, which, thereby, acquire worth in God's eyes. The acceptability of sacrifice was a matter of fundamental importance for the ancients, and the reference to it in this text may echo the popular belief that in the eschatological age worship would be pleasing to God (Mal. 3. 1–4; Ps. Sol. 17. 32 f.).

The new cult, thus offered, will 'declare (ἐξαγγέλλειν) the wonderful deeds (ἀρεταί) of him who called you out of darkness into his marvellous light' (v. 9). That is to say, the church is commissioned to do the task which Israel failed to do.[1] The allusion is to the Isaianic prophecy of the restoration (43. 20 f.), and when we ask where the prophets envisaged Israel prosecuting her missionary task we have an insight into the thought of the text before us. It was at the new temple (Isa. 2. 2–4 etc.). Even so, our author suggests, the new temple, raised now at the end of the times, is for the purpose of witnessing to the saving act of God in Christ. The temple image thus has some-

---

[1] The church's evangelical vocation is also implied in the writer's use of Exod. 19. 5 f., which continues, 'You shall be my own possession among all peoples; *for all the earth is mine*'. Cf. generally Blauw, op. cit., pp. 126 ff.

thing to teach us of the purpose as well as the nature of the church.

To summarize. The doctrine of the church as the new temple in 1 Peter is in close agreement with that of Paul. Interest in eschatological fulfilment, while not as strong as it is in Paul (2 Cor. 6. 16–7. 1), is nevertheless present (1 Pet. 2. 6–10). Although the conception of the building (οἰκοδομή) is implied in the author's description of Christians as stones, the thought is not nearly so important for him as it is for Paul. At other points, however, the treatment by this author fills out that of Paul. The complementary ideas of priesthood and sacrifice now receive attention. In fact, it is as the place of worship that 1 Peter is most interested in the new temple. To be noted in this connection is the pronounced spiritualization of the author's treatment. Earlier lines of spiritualization are drawn together and stamped with an unqualifiedly positive character. The temple is spiritual and its worship is spiritual. The place of Jesus Christ in the church is also elaborated. Temple and cult alike issue from his redemptive work. At the same time, the crucial importance of Christ for the destinies of those outside the church also is stated. Finally, the function of the new temple is now described as worship and witness.

The presence of the temple image in First Peter is evidence of its widespread currency. Obviously the conception was familiar in churches outside the range of Paul's influence. It is clear that both First Peter and Paul drew upon earlier material. First Peter uses Old Testament proofs (Isa. 8. 14 and 28. 16) that are also used by Paul (Rom. 9. 33). One must therefore assume that either one writer borrowed from the other or both used a common source. That Paul borrowed from First Peter is not of course impossible,[1] but not probable. First Peter could have used Romans,[2] but, as Dodd has indicated,[3] this hypothesis requires us to believe that First Peter disentangled his sources, supplementing them with bits of Isa. 28. 16 that Paul had omitted, which did not come from the LXX. The view that has won widest acceptance therefore is that First Peter and Paul used a pre-canonical *florilegium*

---

[1] So E. Kühl, *Die Briefe Petri und Judae* (1897), ad loc.

[2] So F. J. A. Hort, *The First Epistle of St. Peter I. 1–II. 17* (1898), ad loc.; Beare, op. cit., ad loc.

[3] C. H. Dodd, *According to the Scriptures* (1952), pp. 42 f.

of Old Testament proof-texts,[1] or possibly a strophe from an early Christian hymn.[2] The unique formula with which the quotations are introduced (ἐν γραφῇ and not ἐν τῇ γραφῇ, i.e. 'in the scripture') certainly commends one or other of these hypotheses. There remains the difficulty of explaining the differences between the *testimonia* as they appear in the two writers. The fact that First Peter gives the two Isaiah texts in an unconflated form would suggest that his is the earlier version. On the other hand, the triple form of the catena (Isa. 28. 16—Ps. 118. 22—Isa. 8. 14) is in favour of a more developed and later version. Also significant in the same connection is the conflation of Ps. 118. 22 and Isa. 28. 16 (2. 4). But if, as seems fairly certain, Ps. 118. 22 is the most important of the three proofs for our author, and the Isaiah texts represent a midrash on it, then his version of the catena probably is an early and widely used form. The use of Ps. 118. 22 links us with a widely representative tradition (Mark 12. 10 pars. and Acts 4. 11). Particularly significant for our purpose is the fact that First Peter brings the stone *testimonia* into relation with the doctrine of the new temple. Whether he was the first to do so one cannot say. At all events, the epistle shows that the conception of the church as the new temple rests upon very early tradition. Furthermore, the use of the stone testimonies in connection with the temple image means that we have to reckon with the possibility that wherever the stone texts occur in the New Testament the idea of the church as the temple may not be far away.

This completes our examination of the principal New Testament texts on our subject. To round it off, however, we add a number of related references.

In several texts the term house (οἶκος) is used in a spiritualized sense not unlike that of 1 Pet. 2. 4 ff., and in other places there are what some commentators take to be allusions to the church as the spiritual temple.

In the case of the former there are 1 Pet. 4. 17; 1 Tim. 3. 15; and Heb. 3. 1–6.

---

[1] H. Volkmar, *Die alttestamentlichen Citate bei Paulus* (1896), p. 41; Sanday and Headlam, *The Epistle to the Romans* (1902), pp. 281 f.; Bigg, op. cit., p. 20; J. Rendel Harris, *Testimonies* (1919), i. 30 ff.; H. J. Cadbury, *The Beginnings of Christianity* (1933), v. 373 f.; Dodd, op. cit., pp. 41 f.; Lindars, op. cit., pp. 177 ff.

[2] Selwyn, op. cit., pp. 268 ff.

1 Peter 4. 17

For the time has come for judgment to begin with the household of God (τοῦ οἴκου τοῦ Θεοῦ); and if it begins with us, what will be the end of those who do not obey the gospel of God?

The Revised Standard Version translation 'household' reflects the sense in which οἶκος in this text is generally interpreted by commentators,[1] but some compare its use here with that at 2. 5 and understand it as a reference to the church as the spiritual temple.[2] It is clear that the prophetic perspective, according to which divine judgement strikes first at the temple, is in view. If the language of the text is moulded by Ezek. 9. 6 ('begin [the judgement] at my sanctuary' [ἀπὸ τῶν ἁγίων μου ἄρξασθε]), as seems fairly certain, it is likely that its thought also is influenced by it. The prophet notes that the judgement 'began with the elders who were before (in) the house' (9. 6). Our author would therefore think of the judgement beginning on those who are the temple (2. 5). The new temple has precedence like the old even in condemnation. This is a possible interpretation, though one does not wish to press it.

1 Timothy 3. 15

I am writing these instructions to you so that, if I am delayed, you may know how one ought to behave in the household of God (ἐν οἴκῳ Θεοῦ), which is the church of the living God, the pillar (στῦλος) and bulwark (ἑδραίωμα)[3] of the truth.

That οἶκος in this passage means temple[4] is prima facie suggested by the mention of the pillar and foundation, but this is clearly a case of mixed metaphor; οἶκος here looks back to its use at 3. 4, 5, 12, where, in similar exhortation, it clearly means household (cf. 2 Tim. 1. 16; Titus 1. 11).

---

[1] So Spörri, op. cit., p. 36; Selwyn, op. cit., pp. 226, 290.
[2] So E. H. Plumtre, *The General Epistles of St. Peter and St. Jude* (1893), p. 150; O. Michel, *TWNT* v. 129; Beare, op. cit., p. 168.
[3] ἑδραίωμα is a synonym for θεμέλιος (cf. Col. 1. 23). Its use in the present text may be explained by reference to the use of θεμέλιος at 2 Tim. 2. 19. Cf. the expression 'foundation of truth' at 1 QS 5. 5; 9. 3 f.; Gärtner, op. cit., pp. 68 f.
[4] So Michel, op. cit., p. 129.

Hebrews 3. 1–6

Therefore, holy brethren, who share in a heavenly calling, consider Jesus, the apostle and high priest of our confession. He was faithful to him who appointed him, just as Moses also was faithful in God's house (ἐν [ὅλῳ] τῷ οἴκῳ αὐτοῦ). Yet Jesus has been counted worthy of as much more glory than Moses as the builder of a house has more honour than the house. (For every house is built [κατασκευάζεται] by some one, but the builder [ὁ κατασκευάσας] of all things is God.) Now (καί) Moses was faithful in all God's house (ἐν ὅλῳ τῷ οἴκῳ αὐτοῦ) as a servant, to testify to the things that were to be spoken later, but Christ was faithful over God's house (ἐπὶ τὸν οἶκον αὐτοῦ) as a son. And we are his house (οἶκός ἐσμεν ἡμεῖς) if we hold fast our confidence and pride in our hope.

Selwyn in his special treatment of the 'spiritual house' (of 1 Pet. 2) interprets οἶκος in Heb. 3. 1–6 as 'household' or 'family' and considers it significant that 'the distinctive architectural word οἰκοδομεῖν is avoided, and κατασκευάζειν, a much more general word covering equipment and administration as well as construction, is used instead',[1] though he leaves the question open. The argument from lexicography alone is not convincing. In the LXX uses of κατασκευάζειν listed by Hatch and Redpath the term as often as not has the sense of 'to erect', 'make', 'build', and in Josephus it is frequently used for the building of the temple of Jerusalem (*Vita*, 65; *Ap.* 1. 127, 193, 228; 2. 12). As a matter of fact it is the word employed by our author for Noah's building of the ark (11. 7; cf. 1 Pet. 3. 20). One cannot rule out the possibility, therefore, that it has this sense in the text we are now examining.

The superiority of Jesus over Moses (and therefore of Christianity over Judaism) is asserted in two ways. (*a*) Moses, faithful as he was, was himself a part of the household of Israel, whereas Jesus, as God's pre-existent creative agent (1. 2), is the builder of the house, and therefore distinct from it and greater than it (v. 3). (*b*) Moses, faithful though he was, served in God's house (ἐν τῷ οἴκῳ), whereas Jesus is Son (and heir) over it (ἐπὶ τὸν οἶκον, vv. 5 f.). If, as seems probable, the argument is influenced not only by Num. 12. 7 but also 2 Sam. 7,[2] the author may well have

---

[1] Op. cit., p. 290.

[2] J. Meier, *Die Texte vom Toten Meer*, ii (1960), 46; S. Aalen, ' "Reign" and

regarded the household of faith as the house (temple) Yahweh's son would build (2 Sam. 7. 13). Support for this may be found in the association of the 'house' with Jesus the high priest (Heb. 3. 1): the same combination is present at 10. 21 (ἱερέα μέγαν ἐπὶ τὸν οἶκον τοῦ Θεοῦ), where οἶκος definitely means temple, even if it is the temple in heaven.

Finally, there are a few texts where some commentators have found allusions to the church as the temple.

Galatians 2. 9

The description of James, Cephas, and John as pillars (στῦλοι) of the church in this text may have in mind the church as a spiritual edifice.[1] At 1 Tim. 3. 15 'pillar' means witness,[2] and one naturally interprets the term as applying to the leading apostles as witnesses of the unique events of the life of the Lord (Mark 5. 37; 9. 2; 14. 33 pars.; cf. Acts 1. 21 f.). However, the reference to Peter under the image of the rock or stone (πέτρος—κηφᾶς) and the use in the context of the term 'build' (οἰκοδομεῖν) may indicate that Paul is thinking of the church as God's building. In this case one should compare the use of 'pillar' at Rev. 3. 12, where the believer who overcomes in the name of Christ (i.e. the martyr) is promised a place as a pillar in the heavenly temple. On this showing there is a touch of irony in Paul's words. Peter who is reputed to be a pillar of the church, i.e. supporting it, is actually undermining it. But this interpretation of 'pillar' in this text remains uncertain.

2 Thessalonians 2. 3–4

The temple of God (ναὸς τοῦ Θεοῦ) in which the man of lawlessness is said to sit in the end-time has been taken by some commentators as a reference to the church, God's new dwelling. The man of lawlessness or sin was interpreted in early times as

"House" in the Kingdom of God in the Gospels', NTS 8 (1962), 236 f. Cf. the use of 2 Sam. 7. 14 at Heb. 1. 5.

[1] So C. K. Barrett, 'Paul and the "Pillar" Apostles', Studia Paulina, ed. J. N. Sevenester and V. C. van Unnik (1953), p. 12; J. Munck, Petros und Paulus in der Offenbarung Johannis (1950), p. 26; Michel, TWNT iv. 892.

[2] Similarly 1 Clem. 5. 2 refers to the martyrs Peter and Paul as pillars (στῦλοι).

ferring to heresy, and in later times as the papal office.[1] Each in its own way was regarded as a threat to the sanctity of God's holy dwelling-place. But this interpretation is seriously to be doubted. The whole section (2 Thess. 2. 1–12) is so demonstrably apocalyptic in tone and so clearly based on the prophecies of Daniel concerning the temple of Jerusalem that it can only be the latter, or possibly the temple in heaven (the blasphemy in the temple in Jerusalem signifying the ultimate blasphemy, cf. Rev. 13. 6), that is intended. It may be argued that a cosmic clash between good and evil would affect the church, but it cannot be said that disorder in the church is what is uppermost in Paul's mind.

1 Corinthians 10. 4

(Our fathers) all ate the same supernatural ($\pi\nu\epsilon\upsilon\mu\alpha\tau\iota\kappa\acute{o}\varsigma$) food and all drank the same supernatural ($\pi\nu\epsilon\upsilon\mu\alpha\tau\iota\kappa\acute{o}\varsigma$) drink. For they drank from the supernatural ($\pi\nu\epsilon\upsilon\mu\alpha\tau\iota\kappa\acute{\eta}$) Rock ($\pi\acute{\epsilon}\tau\rho\alpha$) which followed them, and the Rock was Christ.

This passage, in which Paul seeks to rebuke the complacency of the Corinthians by pointing to the experience of the Israelites in the wilderness, seems to allude to a Jewish legend which connected the well of water mentioned in Num. 21. 16–18 with the water from the smitten rock of Num. 20. 10–11.[2] It is no easy matter to thread one's way through the maze of legend which Jewish piety and imagination attached to the rock from which Israel drank, or to understand what the connection was with the temple of Jerusalem. However, whether the thought is, on the one hand, of the rock following Israel and supplying water (Tos. Suk. 3. 11 f.) or, on the other hand, of a stream or river flowing through the desert (Midr. Sifre to Num. 11. 21), it is reasonably clear that when the rabbis spoke of the rock in the desert they were often thinking of the rock in the temple of Jerusalem. Thus the rock is described as sending forth a river of water that runs to the sea (Tos. Suk. 3. 11 ff.), all manner of vegetation and fruit grow along its banks (Deut. R. 6. 11), and its waters have

---

[1] For authorities see E. von Dobschütz, *Die Thessalonicher-Briefe* (1909), p. 276.
[2] S–B iii. 406 ff. The connection apparently was known to the editor of Num. 21. 16, since he identifies the well with the rock from which Moses caused the water to flow miraculously, although it is stated that the leaders of Israel dug the well. See also Ps. 105. 41.

curative properties (Nu. R. 18. 22). Further evidence of the connection may be found in the fourth gospel, where in a section based on the desert epic (6. 31 ff.; 7. 40), Jesus is identified with the rock that featured in the feast of Tabernacles (i.e. the rock in the temple).[1] It may be safely assumed that Paul is making use of ideas that were associated with the temple in Jewish cosmology and eschatology. But it would be hazardous to infer that he is thinking of the church as the spiritual or new temple.

This concludes our study of the texts on the new temple from the epistles. The presence of the conception in such widely divergent traditions as Paul, First Peter, and Hebrews points to its early currency in Christian circles. It seems clear therefore that if the idea of the spiritual temple was of Jewish (Qumran) origin the borrowing took place at a fairly early stage. Now, since it is practically certain that the New Testament writers drew upon pre-canonical traditions in their use of the stone *testimonia*, it would seem to follow that the temple image, with which the stone images are connected, also comes from the pre-canonical period. In this case the New Testament writers were not directly influenced by Qumran. The extent to which the creators of the pre-canonical tradition were influenced from this quarter is to a great degree bound up with the question whether the ideas found in the scrolls were exclusive to the writers or shared, if not at the time then subsequently, by other Jews. That the ideas in question were in fact exclusive to Qumran is suggested by the fact that they do not appear anywhere else. But this does not imply that the link between the early church and the sect is a direct one. The similarity between the teaching of Stephen and that of Qumran rather suggests that the ideas and tenets of the latter filtered through various groups and movements before they entered Christianity.

I think one must say that the point at which the early church began its thinking on the new temple was the *verbum Domini* concerning the destruction of the temple of Jerusalem and its replacement by another. The importance of this logion for the infant church is clear from its presence in the synoptics, the

---

[1] Cf. above, pp. 80 ff. For the view that 1 Cor. 10. 4 is based upon some such saying as that recorded at John 7. 37 f. see Jeremias, 'Golgotha und der heilige Felsen', op. cit., p. 124; O. Cullmann, *TWNT* vi. 96.

fourth gospel, and Acts. As the first Christians ruminated upon the word of their Lord in the light of the outcome of his ministry, viz. the emergence of the new people of God, i.e. the church, the dwelling-place of God in the Spirit,[1] the conception of the eschatological community as a spiritual temple, offering God a spiritual sacrifice, doubtless appeared eminently suited to their catechetic and apologetic needs. Thus they began to speak of the new temple which Jesus had promised as a temple made without hands, i.e. a spiritual temple (Mark), and identified it with Christ's body which is the church (John, Paul, 1 Peter). It is at this point that the conception appears in the pages of the New Testament. Clearly the image underwent a considerable amount of reshaping before it reached this stage. In all this the person of Jesus Christ was pivotal.[2] Just as it was his word that encouraged the church to utilize existing ideas in order that people might more readily understand the outcome of his work, so it was the tremendous effect of his personality upon the church's self-understanding that obliged the church to fill these ideas with new meaning and content. Hence, while one may with profit trace the similarities that undoubtedly exist between the New Testament and Qumran one cannot postulate any essential relationship.

In summarizing the foregoing chapters on the New Testament treatment of our subject we may say that the relation in which the New Testament stands to the Old Testament is, in the first place, that of fulfilment to hope. The church is the expected temple of the traditional hope. Now at last God dwells in the midst of his people. Through the life, death, and resurrection of his Son Jesus Christ and the gift of the Holy Spirit, God has made good the ancient promise to his people, 'I will live in them and move among them, and I will be their God, and they shall be my people'. But there is something else we must say. The new temple is not like the old temple. The old temple was made for God by men; the new temple God makes for himself; it is made without hands. God now no longer dwells with his people; he dwells in them. It is God himself, God the Holy Spirit, not his

---

[1] Cf. Gärtner, op. cit., p. 139.
[2] Cf. D. Flusser, 'The Dead Sea Sect and Pre-Pauline Christianity', *SH* 4 (1958), 266; Gärtner, op. cit., pp. 138 f.

name or glory or *sheखkhînāh*, who, as his people are able to receive him, dwells in his church as in a temple. The divine indwelling of the Christian era, while it looks to the past, is thus different in both nature and degree from that of the old dispensation. The difference is due to the change which the incarnation has made in the relations between God and his creatures.

The object of our study is therefore largely accomplished. But before we draw together our findings in the concluding chapter an important question has to be considered. It concerns the doctrine of the heavenly temple, which in Jewish thought came to hold such a place of importance that in the end it was identified with and indistinguishable from the new temple. The fact that this development was largely due to the theological problems created, on the one hand, by the shortcomings of the earthly temple, and, on the other, by the doubt whether it was possible at all for men to build a temple worthy of God or impervious to the vicissitudes of history, would suggest that one need not look for the conception of the heavenly temple in the New Testament. Were not such problems resolved in the incarnation and gift of the Spirit? And in any case the new temple, established as it is by the resurrection of Jesus Christ, is a temple made without hands, that is to say, of supernatural or heavenly origin. Whatever the conclusions of the argument of logic would appear to be, the fact of the matter is that the conception of the heavenly temple is in the New Testament. It will therefore be the purpose of the next chapter to examine the New Testament doctrine of the heavenly temple and its relation to the Jewish doctrine on the one hand and the new temple of Christianity on the other.

X

THE HEAVENLY TEMPLE IN THE NEW TESTAMENT

To think of the heavenly temple in connection with the New Testament is to think of the epistle to the Hebrews and the book of Revelation. The doctrine is also present, however, in a number of other places in the New Testament, and we shall look briefly at these before considering the more formal treatment of the subject in Hebrews and Revelation.

The Fourth Gospel

We begin with John 1. 51, which was studied above in another connection.[1] In this text Jesus tells Nathanael that he will see 'heaven opened, and the angels of God ascending and descending upon the Son of man'. The allusion is to Jacob's stone at Bethel (Gen. 28. 10 ff.). It will be recalled that Jewish exegesis on Gen. 28. 10 ff. identified the spot on which Jacob lay as the site of the temple of Jerusalem and interpreted the ladder in the dream, on which the angels ascended and descended, as the bond joining the temple of Jerusalem and its heavenly counterpart. One may also note that the rabbis liked to think that the distance between the two temples was less at this point than at any other point (Gen. R. 69. 7). It may be that the evangelist is drawing upon this tradition and alluding to the heavenly temple, with which Jesus is in unbroken communion and to which he is the divinely appointed means of access (John 14. 6).

The other passage in the gospel where some commentators have seen a reference to the heavenly temple is 14. 2–3. The followers of Jesus are consoled concerning his departure out of this world:

In my Father's house (οἰκία) are many rooms (μοναὶ πολλαί); if it were not so, would I have told you that I go to prepare a place

---

[1] Cf. above, p. 77.

(τόπος) for you? And when I go and prepare a place (τόπος) for you, I will come again and will take you to myself, that where I am you may be also.

The expression 'my Father's house' (οἶκος) is used of the temple of Jerusalem at 2. 16, and prima facie its repetition here would suggest that it is the heavenly counterpart which is intended. But it is not easy to determine whether 'house' refers to God's dwelling in heaven, i.e. the temple, or to heaven itself. The idea of heaven or the heavens in a general sense as the habitation of God and the righteous was a commonplace in Judaism. The Enochian literature in particular contains frequent mention of the 'many mansions' of the saints in heaven (2 En. 61. 2; 1 En. 45. 3; cf. 1 En. 39. 4, 7 f.; 41. 2). That it is something similar which John has in mind is suggested by the fact that he states that God's house has 'many rooms'. For the ancients the temple is the dwelling of God alone. If, on the other hand, 'room' (μονή) has the indefinite sense of 'place' (τόπος, 14. 2) then 'house' may refer specifically to the temple in heaven, in which the friends of Jesus are promised places. But this interpretation savours more of the modern idea of a sanctuary as the place in which people assemble for worship than the ancient conception of the temple as the dwelling-place of the deity. On the whole is seems wisest not to find a reference to the heavenly temple in this passage.

Galatians 4. 26

The conception of the heavenly Jerusalem is of interest to us since one does not think of Jerusalem without thinking of the temple. The thought comes at the end of a piece of allegorical parallelism intended to set off the difference between the Christian life of faith and life under the law.[1] Earlier in the chapter Paul deals with the servitude caused by the law, from which Christ delivers men (4. 1–7). He now returns to the theme. In what must be his sharpest polemic against Judaism, the apostle begins by representing the Jews as the descendants of the slave girl Hagar and traditional enemies of Israel (Gen. 25. 12–18; 1 Chr. 5. 10, 19 ff.; Ps. 83. 6), whereas Christians are descendants of the free-born woman Sarah. Now in Isaiah and derivative literature Jerusalem, the symbol of Israel, was frequently

[1] Cf. J. C. de Young, *Jerusalem in the New Testament* (1960), pp. 103 ff.

represented as a mother, and the apostle easily extends the allegory by drawing a contrast between the city to which the Jews belong and the city to which Christians belong.

Tell me, you who desire to be under law, do you not hear the law? For it is written that Abraham had two sons, one by a slave and one by a free woman. But the son of the slave was born according to the flesh, the son of the free woman through promise. Now this is an allegory: these women are two covenants. One is from Mount Sinai, bearing children for slavery; she is Hagar. Now Hagar is Mount Sinai in Arabia;[1] she corresponds to the present Jerusalem ($\dot{\eta}$ $\nu\hat{\upsilon}\nu$ $\dot{I}\epsilon\rho o\upsilon\sigma a\lambda\dot\eta\mu$), for she is in slavery with her children. But the Jerusalem above ($\dot\eta$ $\check a\nu\omega$ $\dot{I}\epsilon\rho o\upsilon\sigma a\lambda\dot\eta\mu$)[2] is free, and she is ($\dot\epsilon\sigma\tau\acute\iota\nu$) our mother. For it is written,

> 'Rejoice, O barren one that does not bear;
> break forth and shout, thou that art not in travail;
> for the desolate hath more children
> than she who hath a husband' (4. 21–7).

Underlying Paul's argument is the ancient law that a slave woman can give birth only to slaves. The earthly Jerusalem which is under the law can produce only slaves of the law; the heavenly Jerusalem is not under the law and therefore begets free men.

Paul has taken over a familiar piece of Jewish imagery and given it a new and radical interpretation. He means to say that the heavenly city of Jewish hope does not simply replace the earthly city, as original replaces copy; it is in opposition to it. Contrary to Jewish belief the heavenly Jerusalem has nothing in common with the earthly Jerusalem. It belongs to Christians; it is *their* mother. The Jews (and Judaizers) have no right to it. The apostle carries his interpretation still further. In v. 27 he takes one of the great Old Testament promises regarding the earthly Jerusalem (Isa. 54. 1) and boldly transfers it to the city of those

---

[1] The text is uncertain at this point. The best-attested reading is that adopted by Nestle, 'and Hagar is Mount Sinai in Arabia'. So read, the text repeats v. 24, the new element being 'in Arabia'. The old covenant, made as it was in the land of the Hagarites, can result only in bondage. Cf. the similar contrast at Heb. 12. 18–24.

[2] The parallelism is not formally correct at this point. With the 'present Jerusalem' one would expect 'Jerusalem that is to be' (cf. Heb. 13. 14), or, more appropriately (since the heavenly Jerusalem already exists), 'Jerusalem above' with 'Jerusalem below'. It is important for Paul's argument that the heavenly Jerusalem also is the present, existing Jerusalem. Note the use of the present tense ($\dot\epsilon\sigma\tau\acute\iota\nu$): this Jerusalem is free; she is our mother (v. 26). Cf. de Young, op. cit., p. 131.

who live by faith in Christ; the children of the heavenly Jerusalem are not only free but infinitely more numerous than those
of the terrestrial city.

What does Paul mean by the Jerusalem 'above'? We shall be in
a better position to answer this question if we first understand
what he means by Jerusalem 'now'. Although the apostle probably has in mind Jerusalem's historic rejection of Christ and his
judgement upon it, he is employing the word in a broad sense.
This is suggested by the comprehensive terms used ('her children,' v. 25, 'children of the slave', v. 31). By the 'present
Jerusalem' Paul means the legalistic system that Judaism became,
Israel after the flesh. Thus the heavenly Jerusalem, used at it is in
connection with the comprehensive terms 'children of promise'
(v. 28) and 'children of the free woman' (v. 31), must refer to the
household of faith, i.e. the church. That Paul thought of some at
least of those who comprised the heavenly Jerusalem (the dead in
Christ) as existing in heaven is not to be disputed, but they are
not primarily in mind. The emphasis is on the nature of the
church, not the place where it is located. In designating the
church as the Jerusalem above, the apostle is referring to its
spiritual and supernatural character (cf. Phil. 3. 20). Nor does
Paul's use of the image here by implication tell us anything about
the destiny of the terrestrial city. It may be that he, like Jesus,
believed that Jerusalem's fate was sealed by the nation's rejection
of its Messiah, but there is nothing in the text to permit one to
say that the apostle was repudiating all eschatological hopes
concerning the city.[1]

Similar in thought to Gal. 4. 26 is Phil. 3. 20, 'our citizenship
is in heaven' (RV). Unlike the Judaizers (3. 2–19) who are
'earthy' (ἐπίγειος) Christians are of heaven (οὐράνιος), where
their citizenship (πολίτευμα) is. The word πολίτευμα is capable of
different renderings ('citizenship' RV, 'citizens of heaven' NEB),
but its meaning in this context is probably best expressed by
Moffatt, who translates the sentence thus: 'we are a colony of
heaven'. The Christian community is a colony whose life and
constitution reproduce the life and constitution of heaven.[2]
Nothing is to be inferred, however, as to the nature of the
heavenly Jerusalem or its temple.

---

[1] As is argued by de Young, op. cit., p. 119.
[2] M. Dibelius, *An die Thessalonicher I II an die Philipper* (1925), p. 71.

In the present connection one should also compare those texts which liken Christians to exiles. First Peter addresses its readers as 'exiles of the dispersion' (1. 1; cf. 1. 17; 2. 11), and James calls Christians 'the twelve tribes of the dispersion (1. 1)'.[1] We witness a remarkable semasiology here. The nomenclature of the old church is converted and put to Christian use. Christians, like Jews of the dispersion, are separated from their homeland, but the *civitas Dei* to which they belong is not in Palestine, and their hope of survival is not dependent upon restoration to that centre. Their city is in heaven, and their exile is life on earth. This language and imagery, as we shall see, is carried a stage further in the epistle to the Hebrews, which describes Christians as pilgrims.

2 Corinthians 5. 1–5

This section forms a kind of conclusion to the contrast drawn in the preceding verses between the Christian's present life of hardship and suffering and the future glorious life he is destined to enjoy (4. 7–8). The respective modes of existence are depicted under the images of a perishable earthly dwelling (a tent), on the one hand, and an enduring heavenly dwelling (a building) on the other:

For we know that if the earthly tent we live in is destroyed (ἡ ἐπίγειος ἡμῶν οἰκία τοῦ σκήνους καταλυθῇ), we have (ἔχομεν)[2] a building from God (οἰκοδομὴ ἐκ Θεοῦ), a house not made with hands (οἰκία ἀχειροποίητος) eternal in the heavens. Here indeed we groan, and long to put on (ἐπενδύσασθαι) our heavenly dwelling (τὸ οἰκητήριον ἡμῶν τὸ ἐξ οὐρανοῦ), so that by putting it on we may not be found naked. For while we are still in this tent (οἱ ὄντες), we sigh with anxiety; not that we would be unclothed, but that we would be further clothed, so that what is mortal may be swallowed up by life. He who has prepared us for this very thing is God, who has given us the Spirit as a guarantee.

---

[1] N. A. Dahl thinks that the same concept is implied at Acts 8. 1, 4: the scattering of the church (διασπείρεσθαι) means a new diaspora (*Das Volk Gottes* (1941), p. 196). Cf. Acts 11. 19. It is to be doubted, however, whether in these texts διασπείρεσθαι has this technical sense.

[2] ἔχομεν is taken by J. A. T. Robinson (*The Body* (1952), p. 77) as an unconditional present tense, but it seems wisest with Best (op. cit., p. 161, n. 1) to regard it as an eschatological present, otherwise the longing for this habitation in v. 2 is unintelligible.

A new exegesis of this old *crux interpretum* offered in recent times finds a reference here to the heavenly temple.

The correspondence between the terminology of this passage and that of the famous logion of Jesus on the destruction of the temple of Jerusalem and its replacement by a different one (Mark 14. 58), which has been noted on a number of different occasions,[1] is taken by Feuillet to mean that Paul's thought is based upon this *verbum Domini*.[2] He suggests that the apostle, like the fourth evangelist, saw a connection between the destruction of the earthly body of Christ, followed by the raising of his new body (or temple), and the destruction of his own body, followed by a new body (or temple). The present temple is earthly (ἐπίγειος), that is to say, 'made with hands', and therefore destined for destruction (καταλυθῇ).[3] The new temple is the heavenly building (οἰκοδομή) or dwelling.[4] It is not made with hands, i.e. eternal and heavenly (αἰώνιον ἐν τοῖς οὐρανοῖς)[5]—the house not made with hands of 2 Cor. 5. 1 being equivalent to the spiritual body of 1 Cor. 15. 44.[6] The heavenly building is the resurrected body of Christ. The Christian thus reproduces the destiny of his Lord.

This line of exegesis is closely followed by Ellis,[7] who develops the corporate nuance of the body image as set forth by Robinson.[8] He maintains that the heavenly dwelling is not the spiritual body of the individual believer but the corporate body of Christ. Ellis argues that since the terms building (οἰκοδομή) and house (οἰκία and its cognates) are used elsewhere in the writings of Paul to denote the church it is reasonable to assume that they have this corporate sense in the present passage.[9] He writes:

[1] Selwyn, op. cit., p. 290; R.F. Hettlinger, '2 Cor. 5. 1-10', *SJT* 10 (1957), 174-94.

[2] A. Feuillet, *Destinée des Chrétiens et Fondements de l'Eschatologie paulinienne*, Institut Catholique de Paris, no date given (= *RSR* xliv [1956], 161-93, 360-402).

[3] The earthly habitation suffers destruction not simply because it is of perishable material (2 Cor. 4. 7) but because it is 'in Adam' (1 Cor. 15. 22; Rom. 5. 12. 18).

[4] Οἰκοδομή has the meaning of process of construction, but since it is paralleled by the term 'house' (οἰκία) the sense here is clearly that of a finished and habitable dwelling.

[5] 'From heaven' is the expression used by Paul in connection with eschatological events (1 Cor. 15. 47; cf. 1 Thess. 1. 10; 2 Thess. 1. 7).

[6] Feuillet, op. cit., p. 34.

[7] E. E. Ellis, 'II Corinthians v. 1-10 in Pauline Eschatology', *NTS* 6 (1960), 211-24 (= *Paul and His Recent Interpreters* (1961), pp. 35-48).

[8] J. A. T. Robinson, *The Body*, passim.

[9] Op. cit., p. 217.

It is most probable then that in II Cor. v. 1 ff. Paul has in mind the concept of the New Temple which views the Messianic Community in terms of the 'house of God'. In an interchange of the two images, New Temple and Body of Christ, the house from heaven (οἰκητήριον, II Cor. v. 2) or building of God (κατοικητήριον, Eph. ii. 22) here refers to those ἐν Χριστῷ as they are incorporated into the Body of Christ in whom the new aeon has been fully actualized and who alone is individually present in the heavenlies.[1]

This interpretation is attractive. In the first place, it provides a clear and intelligible answer to the question of what the heavenly temple is: it is the community of the faithful. Secondly, it posits an interesting continuity between the new temple and the heavenly temple (cf. v. 5); as on earth the Christian community constitutes 'a dwelling place (κατοικητήριον) of God in the Spirit' (Eph. 2. 22), so in heaven it forms the building, i.e. the dwelling (οἰκητήριον) of God (2 Cor. 5. 2). Thirdly, it explains the introductory 'we know' (οἴδαμεν) by connecting it with the use of the term at 1 Cor. 3. 16 and 6. 19 and finds here evidence of a well-known tradition.[2] But it is an interpretation which rests upon an uncertain foundation. It depends upon a corporate interpretation of the resurrection body of the believer, which is by no means established.[3]

One can say that the heavenly building is the resurrection body and grant a certain corporeity of nuance, but to equate it with the church simply on the ground that the terms 'building' and 'house' denote the church in other texts is not warranted.[4] In the first place, the use of the clothing image (which is fused with the building image) and the likelihood of Greek influence in the view taken of the body in vv. 8–9 strongly suggest that the sense of the text is individualistic rather than corporate. Secondly, if the heavenly building is the new temple it is difficult to understand why the apostle should long to possess it, since, according to his teaching elsewhere in the Corinthian letters (1 Cor. 3), the church on earth is the new temple. At 2 Cor. 5. 1 ff. Paul is manifestly looking forward to something which he and his fellow

[1] Op. cit., p. 218. Similar in many respects to this interpretation, though resting upon different premisses, is that of Vielhauer, who suggests that the building in question is the heavenly building of gnostic mythology (*Oikodome*, pp. 107 ff.). Cf. Michel, *TWNT* v. 150.

[2] Cf. Michel, ibid., pp. 149 f.

[3] Cf. D. E. H. Whiteley, *The Theology of St. Paul* (1964), pp. 192 ff. Cf. pp. 254 ff.

[4] Cf. Best, op. cit., p. 161, n. 1.

Christians do not yet possess and will not possess so long as they are in their present bodies.[1] Thirdly, the correspondence between the terms used in the passage and those found at Mark 14. 58, while interesting, cannot carry a great deal of weight.[2] It seems wisest therefore not to see a reference to the heavenly temple at 2 Cor. 5. 1 ff.

The Epistle to the Hebrews

The doctrine of the heavenly sanctuary in the epistle to the Hebrews is well known. The conception is one of a number of ways used by the author to demonstrate the superiority of Christianity over Judaism. The author, doubtless in keeping with his favourite motif of the life of faith as a pilgrimage or because it suits his doctrine of model and pattern, employs the figure of the tabernacle; but it is quite clear that he is basing his ideas on the Jewish cultus in its most fully developed form in the temple of Jerusalem:

The first covenant had regulations for worship and an earthly sanctuary (ἅγιον κοσμικόν). For a tent (σκηνή) was prepared, the outer one (ἡ πρώτη), in which were the lampstand and the table and the bread of the Presence; it is called the Holy Place (ἅγια). Behind the second curtain stood a tent (σκηνή) called the Holy of Holies (ἅγια ἁγίων), having the golden altar of incense and the ark of the covenant covered on all sides with gold, which contained a golden urn holding the manna, and Aaron's rod that budded, and the tables of the covenant; above it were the cherubim of glory overshadowing the mercy seat (9. 1–5).

The writer does not intend his readers to go into the question of the furnishings of the tabernacle, or the difficulties he creates by his description of these.[3] As he himself says: 'Of these things we cannot now speak in detail' (v. 5).[4] His main point is still to come:

These preparations having thus been made, the priests go continually into the outer tent (lit. first tent, πρώτη σκηνή), performing their ritual duties; but into the second only the high priest goes, and

[1] Cf., e.g., R. P. C. Hanson, *II Corinthians* (1954), p. 59.
[2] Note the juxtaposition of καταλύειν and σκηνή at Isa. 38. 12.
[3] On the problem created by the author's placing the altar of incense inside the holy of holies instead of in the holy place (Exod. 30. 6) see the commentaries.
[4] A. Cody, *Heavenly Sanctuary and Liturgy in the Epistle to Hebrews* (1960), pp. 146 f.

he but once a year, and not without taking blood which he offers for himself and for the errors of the people. By this the Holy Spirit indicates that the way into the sanctuary is not yet opened as long as the outer tent (πρώτη σκηνή) is still standing (which is symbolic for the present age). According to this arrangement, gifts and sacrifices are offered which cannot perfect the conscience of the worshipper, but deal only with food and drink and various ablutions, regulations for the body imposed until the time of reformation (vv. 6–10).

The writer is manifestly bent upon exposing the unsatisfactory character of the old temple. The division of the sanctuary into two parts so that the first or outer part formed a kind of barrier to the second or inner, the prohibition of all worshippers from entering the inner part except the high priest once a year and then only after the greatest possible precautions had been taken, the ineffectiveness of the sacrifices offered—all this indicated the inadequacy of the traditional cult. In fact, as long as the previous temple 'stood' (i.e. retained its status) access to God was not possible.[1] Thus the old temple itself pointed to the need for a new and better temple (v. 9).

The new temple has in fact been erected:

Christ appeared as a high priest of the good things that have come,[2] then through the greater and more perfect tent (διὰ τῆς μείζονος καὶ τελειοτέρας σκηνῆς) [not made with hands (οὐ χειροποιήτου), that is, not of this creation] he entered (εἰσῆλθεν) once for all into the Holy Place (εἰς τὰ ἅγια), taking not the blood of goats and calves but his own blood, thus securing an eternal redemption (9. 11–12).

In mentioning the new sanctuary or temple the author is returning to a theme he introduced earlier. At 6. 19–20 he says that

---

[1] Understanding τῶν ἁγίων of 9. 8 to mean the presence of God (cf. 10. 19; A. S. Peake, *Hebrews* (1902), p. 179; J. Moffatt, *The Epistle to the Hebrews* (1924), p. 118), and translating the verse thus: 'By this the Holy Spirit indicates that the way into God's presence is not yet opened as long as the first (i.e. the old) tent is still standing' (i.e. is the only mode of worship). Cf. B. F. Westcott, *The Epistle to the Hebrews* (1889), p. 252. Cody comments, 'The first tent becomes the old, earthly tent in its entirety, including both the Holies and the Holy of Holies, and the second tent, the "better and more perfect tent" of vs. 11, becomes the celestial sanctuary' (op. cit., pp. 147 f.).

[2] Reading γενομένων instead of μελλόντων. Although the former has good manuscript support, it is rejected by most commentators. It agrees, however, not only with the contrast present in the context but with the tenor of the epistle as a whole. Christians have already tasted the powers of the age to come (6. 5) and share in the celestial worship (12. 22), although the full realization of these things undoubtedly lies in the future (1. 14; 2. 5; 13. 14).

Jesus has entered the holy of holies as our high priest, and at 8. 2
he describes Jesus as a 'minister in the sanctuary and the true
tent (τῶν ἁγίων λειτουργὸς καὶ τῆς σκηνῆς τῆς ἀληθινῆς) which is
set up not by man but by the Lord'. The conception of a heavenly
temple which is the archetype of the earthly as we have seen was
familiar to Judaism, but in referring to the heavenly sanctuary as
'true' (ἀληθινή) (8. 2 ; 9. 24), and its earthly counterpart as a copy
(ὑπόδειγμα) and shadow (σκιά) (8. 5; 9. 23), the author reveals
his indebtedness to Greek thought, or, what is probably more
likely, to the interpenetration of Jewish thought by Greek thought
which was a feature of his times.[1] The conception is used to good
effect. By representing the heavenly sanctuary as the true sanctuary and its earthly counterpart as its shadow the writer very
effectively demonstrates the transcendence and superiority of
Christianity over Judaism. The old temple is superseded by the
new, and the true and genuine temple contrasted with what is
imperfect and inadequate for salvation. The same point is made
in the statement that the heavenly sanctuary has been erected by
God and not man (8. 2 ; 9. 11).[2]

What is the new and heavenly temple of which our author
writes? It is, in the perspective of the epistle, the presence of
God (cf. τῶν ἁγίων of 9. 8 and 10. 19 f.) ; and when one proceeds
to ask where, to this writer's way of thinking, the presence of
God is, the answer is that it is in heaven, so that in a sense
the heavenly temple is heaven;[3] but it is not only in heaven that the
presence of God is to be located. What the author says about the
death of Christ indicates that he thought of the new or 'heavenly'
temple as encompassing both heaven and earth.[4] He writes:

We have confidence to enter the sanctuary (εἰς τὴν εἴσοδον τῶν ἁγίων)
by the blood of Jesus, by the new and living way which he opened for
us through the curtain (διὰ τοῦ καταπετάσματος), that is, through his
flesh (τοῦτ' ἔστιν τῆς σαρκὸς αὐτοῦ) (10. 19–20).

[1] See Appendix D.   [2] Cf. Mark 14. 58; Acts 7. 48; 17. 24.
[3] Cf. 9. 24, also 8. 1 f., where the heavenly session of Christ and his ministry in
the heavenly sanctuary are parallel ideas. But one cannot easily systematize what
Hebrews says about heaven and unqualifiedly speak of the heavenly temple as
heaven, as Cody (op. cit., pp. 156 ff.) does. The epistle uses the word heaven in so
many different ways that one hesitates to say that one consistent scheme is in mind
(U. Luck, 'Himmlisches und irdisches Geschehen im Hebräerbrief', NT 6 [1963],
207 f.). At 4. 14 Jesus is said to pass through the heavens, at 7. 26 he is exalted
above the heavens, at 8. 1 he is in heaven, and at 9. 24 he enters into heaven.
[4] Luck, ibid., pp. 209 ff.

The imagery is based upon the entry of the high priest into the holy of holies on the Day of Atonement but it has woven into it a piece of allegory on the flesh of Jesus, which is not at all easy to interpret. Some scholars connect 'flesh' with 'veil' ('the veil of his flesh'), while others, following Westcott,[1] connect it with 'way' ('a new and living way through the veil, that is, the way of his flesh').[2] Since the reference to the flesh looks back to the mention of Christ's blood at v. 19 and has to do with our Lord's death, it seems necessary to understand 'flesh' to mean the body of Jesus (cf. v. 5; 5. 7). As the body on the cross was pierced and torn apart, the veil hiding God was torn open. It is Jesus' (rent) flesh (v. 20) and shed blood (v. 19) that make access to God possible. To look upon Christ's dying is to look upon God's un-veiling. No better commentary on the text before us is to be found than the Marcan version of the rending of the veil and the confession of the centurion at Jesus' death.

The meaning of 9. 11–12 thus becomes clearer. The 'greater and more perfect tent' through which or by means of which[3] Christ 'entered once for all into the Holy Place' refers to God's presence as related to the work of Christ. Hence it is described as 'not made with hands, that is, not of this creation'.[4] It refers on the one hand to what Christ did on the cross[5] and on the other hand to what (on the basis of his historic work) he now does in heaven. In other words, the new temple of the epistle embraces heaven and earth.

According to our author Christ is a high priest for ever (7. 17). His priestly work has not ceased with his exaltation. 'We have (ἔχομεν) a high priest, one who is seated at the right hand of the throne of the Majesty in heaven, a minister in the sanctuary and the true tent which is set up not by man but by the Lord' (8. 1–2).

---

[1] Westcott, op. cit., pp. 319 ff.

[2] Cf., e.g., G. Lindeskog, 'The Veil of the Temple', *CN* 11 (1947), 132–7.

[3] On the different interpretations of διά . . . διά at 9. 11 see, e.g., H. W. Montefiore, *The Epistle to the Hebrews* (1964), pp. 152 f.

[4] Much of the difficulty experienced in interpreting 9. 11 f. results from contrasting the holy place and the holy of holies. It is unlikely that the distinction was important for our author, if in mind at all. It is not present at 8. 2. Cf. Montefiore, ibid., p. 153. Let us bear in mind that the heavenly temple is curtainless.

[5] Cf. the thought of Rom. 3. 25: the mercy seat is set forth (προτίθεσθαι) for all (A. Nygren, *Commentary on Romans* (1952), pp. 157 f. Cf. K. Barth on Rom. 3. 25: 'The life of Jesus is the place in history fitted for God for propitiation and fraught with eternity' (*The Epistle to the Romans* (1933), p. 105).

Again, 'Christ has entered, not into a sanctuary made with hands, a copy of the true one, but into heaven itself, now (νῦν emphatic) to appear in the presence of God on our behalf' (9. 24). Now the function of a high priest, as our author observes, is to offer something; hence it is necessary for Christ to have an offering to make (8. 3). What is Christ's heavenly sacrifice? It is the perfect and unrepeatable oblation of himself (7. 27; 9. 25 f., 28; 10. 12). Thus the writer says that Christians have an altar (13. 10). There is no suggestion that the permanency of Christ's priesthood consists in his repeating the sacrifice which he offered on the cross; the epistle is quite definite on this point (10. 11–14). The offering which Christ now makes on behalf of men issues from and depends upon his sacrifice upon the cross. One particular aspect of Christ's heavenly offering that is of interest to us is his offering of his people's worship to God the Father (13. 15 f.). The close connection between the worship offered in heaven and that offered upon earth is important in the mind of this writer, and will reappear presently.

The idea of Christ entering the presence of God as the forerunner and head of the faithful connects with another theme of the epistle which we have to consider. It is the pilgrimage of the people of God to the heavenly Mount Zion. This is found in the sections 3. 7–4. 16 and 10. 19–12. 29. It is also supported by a number of other images throughout the epistle: achieving salvation (1. 14), lordship in the world to come (2. 5–10), pressing on to perfection (6. 1), inheriting the promises (6. 12; cf. 10. 36; 11. 13), receiving the eternal inheritance (9. 15), gaining the soul (10. 39), receiving the kingdom that cannot be shaken (12. 28). With very good justification Käsemann has given his study of the epistle the title *Das wandernde Gottesvolk*. It is clear, however, from the thought and imagery of the epistle that what is at the back of the author's mind is not the general peripatetic character of Israel in its formative period but the eschatological pilgrimage to Zion. (One only has to glance at his interpretation of the entry into Canaan at 3. 7–4. 16 to see this.) This journey of journeys becomes a symbol of the life of faith. Reviewing the history of the people of God in Old Testament times, the author writes:

These all died in faith, not having received what was promised, but having seen it and greeted it from afar, and having acknowledged that they were strangers and exiles on the earth. For people who speak thus make it clear that they are seeking a homeland. If they had been thinking of that land from which they had gone out, they would have had opportunity to return. But as it is, they desire a better country, that is, a heavenly one. Therefore God is not ashamed to be called their God, for he has prepared for them a city (11. 13–16).

Now, says our author, Christians also are on a pilgrimage. At their head is Jesus, the forerunner or *voortrekker* (12. 2; cf. 6. 20), who leads them to the homeland and city which God has prepared for them. This city is not Zion in Palestine, any more than the city desired by Abraham and his descendants was; it is the city 'which is to come' ([τὴν] πόλιν ... τὴν μέλλουσαν [13. 14]), 'the city which has foundations, whose builder and maker is God' (11. 10; cf. v. 16). That is to say, the goal of their pilgrimage is the heavenly Jerusalem (12. 22). In keeping with the motif Christians are exhorted to press on in the course that lies ahead of them (12. 2; cf. 4. 1 ff.).

Still drawing upon traditional ideas, the author, in a magnificent piece of imaginative writing, runs ahead of himself and depicts the pilgrims as already gathered at the heavenly Mount Zion and joined in worship:

You have come to (προσεληλύθατε) Mount Zion and to the city of the living God, the heavenly Jerusalem, and to innumerable angels in festal gathering (πανήγυρις), and to the assembly (ἐκκλησία) of the first-born who are enrolled in heaven, and to a judge who is God of all, and to the spirits of just men made perfect, and to Jesus, the mediator of a new covenant, and to the sprinkled blood that speaks more graciously than the blood of Abel (12. 22–4).

The dramatic picture owes its inspiration to the great festivals at Jerusalem, which, as we have seen, brought together literally or symbolically the whole of Israel.[1] All the joy and the sense of

---

[1] πανήγυρις is the term used in the LXX for such gatherings (Amos 5. 21; Hos. 9. 5; Ezek. 46. 11; cf. C. Spicq, *L'Épître aux Hébreux* (1953), ii. 406 f.). It is rightly translated 'festal gathering' by the RSV following Thayer–Grimm and Moffatt (op. cit., p. 214). The same corporate idea is conveyed by ἐκκλησία. There is some uncertainty over the number and identity of the groups mentioned in the passage before us, but whether one connects πανήγυρις with 'angels' or 'first-born', or treats it on its own, the union of earthly and heavenly worship is clearly implied. For the church's participation in worship with the angels cf. E. Peterson, *The Angels and the Liturgy* (1964), pp. x–xi. The text bears striking resemblances to the Qumran scrolls, which depict the faithful on earth sharing worship with the angels. See above, pp. 36 ff.; cf. Gärtner, op. cit., pp. 91 ff.

triumph and fulfilment associated with the end of the pilgrimage, the arrival at the holy city, and the joining together in worship before the face of God become symbolic and antitypal of Christian worship.

What is the heavenly Zion, this place of joy and festivity, that is contrasted with the earthly mountain of gloom and fear? It is, as the contrast indicates, the new economy of salvation, the new covenant of which Jesus is mediator. One is curious to know what connection there is, if any, between the author's heavenly Zion or city and his true tent. It has only to be asked what is the central idea of the passage under consideration to see that there is an intimate connection. The chief feature of the new order of salvation, in contrast to the old, is nearness to God. So while the images of the heavenly Zion or city and the true or archetypal tent represent thought-forms that are basically different, they symbolize one and the same idea: access to God and nearness to him through Jesus Christ, and all the blessings which this means.

But how can the writer say 'You have come to Mount Zion . . .' when he has just said that the people of God are pilgrims to the heavenly city? Montefiore argues that the translation of προσεληλύθατε by 'have come' (i.e. arrived) does not suit the general futuristic outlook of the epistle, and he renders it 'have drawn near'.[1] The answer to our question lies in a paradox that this epistle shares with the New Testament generally, the paradox of future hope and present realization, of the 'not yet—even now'. More particularly, the translation 'You have come to Mount Zion . . .' (or 'You stand before Mount Zion . . .' NEB) is required by the context: (a) vv. 22–4 are a parallel to the preceding verses, the point of which is that Israel *had* come to the mount; (b) the imagery of the verses describes the church at worship; (c) προσεληλύθατε is itself a cultic *terminus technicus* in the epistle for the access of Christians to God (4. 16; 7. 25; 10. 22; 11. 6; cf. 10. 1; 12. 18).[2]

The pilgrimage motif employed by the author goes some way towards explaining his thought. The great annual pilgrimage festivals, as will be recalled, derived much of their significance

---

[1] Op. cit., pp. 229 f. Cf. Barrett, 'The Eschatology of the Epistle to the Hebrews', *The Background of the New Testament and its Eschatology*, pp. 363–92.

[2] Cf. M–M, *VGT*, p. 547; Spicq, op. cit., i. 281.

from the fact that they were national occasions. The whole of Israel was united in worship, the diaspora Jews sharing in the temple worship through their appointed representatives and through the synagogue services which were timed so as to coincide with the temple offerings.[1] Some such idea may be in the mind of the writer. Through Christ, who is the forerunner, consummator, and high priest of the faithful, Christians are even now sharing in the life and worship of the world to come (6. 5).

Characteristic, then, of the Christian life is the idea of polarity. On the one hand, Christians are pilgrims; the end of their journey lies in the future; and in this respect they resemble their counterparts of the old order, who sought a city which was to come. On the other hand, they are already enjoying God's presence and sharing in the worship of the heavenly world, even though the full realization is not yet experienced. The new people of God are thus in a much happier position than Israel of old. To know that the goal of one's hope and endeavour has already been achieved, to enjoy the first fruits of it here and now, make all the difference.

The reinterpretation undertaken by the writer to the Hebrews has turned full circle. Pilgrimage, assembly at Zion, temple, vision of God, priesthood, and cult—all are converted and put to Christian use. The thoroughgoing nature of the conversion is apparent. For while it is a fact that many of the ideas of the epistle which we have been studying have parallels in the literature of the Old Testament, of the Jews of Qumran, and of Plato, the differences are so considerable as to make what dependence there is purely formal. These differences all have to do in one way or another with Jesus Christ and his work. It is Christ who leads the caravan to the heavenly city, Christ who enters the true tent on behalf of men, and Christ who joins the worship of the faithful on earth with that of the faithful in heaven. The main interest of the epistle for us is its extension of the image of the new temple to embrace both heavenly and earthly realities. There is no suggestion that the new temple or heavenly Jerusalem is the community of the faithful. The image is used rather to convey the nature of life under the new covenant: access to God and nearness to him.

[1] Cf. above, p. 5.

The Book of Revelation

Two subjects call for our attention in the book of Revelation; the heavenly temple (chapters 4–20) and the new Jerusalem (chapters 21–2). The author, it is well to note, for all his flights of inspiration and his occupation with other-worldly matters, writes with a very practical aim. His purpose is to strengthen the church so that it may faithfully serve its Lord during the time of trial; the result is that his work comes close to being a Christian interpretation of history. After pointing to the church's need for renewal (chapters 1–3), John proceeds to brace its members for their ordeal of suffering, firstly, by reminding them that God is sovereign and in control of all that happens upon earth, and, secondly, by describing the rewards which the faithful may expect to receive. In both instances the figure of the temple was eminently suited to his purpose, for it traditionally symbolized God's action in history, just as it represented the *summum bonum* of every Jew, i.e. communion with God. From the great library of Jewish eschatology and oriental cosmology, John selects images and motifs which he makes the framework of a comprehensive liturgical drama in which heavenly and earthly realities are played out in relation to one another. In attempting to interpret the book we should not be surprised therefore if we find ourselves going over familiar ground. That is not to say that we shall not discover anything new. Far from it. Our author is of much too original a mind to reproduce his sources woodenly. Moreover, he writes as a Christian. His Christian viewpoint imprints itself on practically everything he handles.

In attempting to understand the imagery of the Apocalypse the interpreter has to be clear as to the methodology of the author. Is he interpreting the author's conscious or unconscious literary motivation? The point may be illustrated by reference to philosophical exegesis. One school of thought believes that the interpreter has provided a satisfactory statement of an author's thought if he relates it convincingly to specific current intellectual issues, which can be presumed to be uppermost in the scholar's consciousness.[1] New Testament students are generally of the opinion that the book of Revelation is to be treated as a pre-

[1] Thus in the case of Berkeley most interpreters relate his philosophy to the questions raised by Lockian empiricism, occasionalism, and late seventeenth-century scepticism as represented by Boyle.

meditated work of art.[1] On the other hand, there is the psycho-
analytic interpretation, which holds that the author works
from an unconscious motivation.[2] Is this what John does? Is
this what Dr. Farrer says that he does?[3] Surely not. If this were
the case John's students would be in a largely hopeless position,
for everything in the way of effective criteria would be ruled
out. But clearly the content of John's visions is generally re-
cognizable to any serious student of the Bible. We must say
that the seer of Patmos works with deliberation; he 'thinks with
his pen'.[4] He has the scriptures both as the source of his
inspiration and the model of his images. His visionary expe-
riences fall into certain shapes and patterns, which can be
identified and studied. Students of the book of Revelation
may hopefully explore the religio-historical milieu in which
the author had grown up. Thereafter they may consider what
new meaning the images are given and the realities they are
intended to convey. This is what is important, and the exegete
can hope to achieve it only if he has uncovered and examined
the author's sources.

We begin by taking note of the cosmological setting of John's
visions. Without doing so, much of what Revelation contains is
obscure.

The visions are prefaced by the account of the prophet's
translation to the heavenly world (4. 1 f.); one is reminded of
Enoch's visit to the heavens (En. 14. 8 ff.). In heaven John sees
the throne of God (4. 2 ff. etc.). Near by is the sea, or what
appears as such (4. 6), and the altar,[5] under which are the souls
of the righteous dead (6. 9). Presently John sees the sacred mount
(14. 1; cf. 21. 10), then the sea of glass again, now mingled with

---

[1] Cf. most recently J. Comblin, 'La liturgie de la Nouvelle Jérusalem (Apoc.
XXI. 1–XXII. 5)', ETL 29 (1953), 5–40.

[2] So J. O. Wisdom, The Unconscious Origin of Berkeley's Philosophy (1953).

[3] A. M. Farrer, The Glass of Vision (1948), pp. 35–56; A Rebirth of Images (1949);
The Revelation of St. John the Divine (1964). Thus Farrer writes, 'St. John simply
yields himself to the images, that is to say, to the Holy Ghost' (A Rebirth of Images,
p. 18). 'Divine truth is supernaturally communicated to men in an act of inspired
thinking which falls into the shape of certain images' (The Glass of Vision, p. 57).

[4] Farrer, The Revelation of St. John the Divine, p. 24.

[5] The immediate source of John's inspiration at this point may have been the
laver which stood close to the altar (1 Kgs. 7. 23 ff.), but it is clear from 15. 2 that
what he has in mind is the cosmic ocean. In any case the laver was intended to
symbolize the great deep (Pedersen, Israel, iii–iv. 243; Jos. Ant. 8. 79–87).

THE BOOK OF REVELATION

fire, and, safely beyond its reach, the redeemed host singing the
song of Moses and the Lamb (15. 2 ff.).[1] When we fit together
these various elements and ask what it is that determined John's
thought, the answer is clear. It is the representation of heaven in
terms of the world view of his day. The ancients, let us recall,
likened the world to a great mountain rising out of the sea. On
top of this mountain was the sacred rock, alias the altar, which,
among other things, marked the spot where the saints rest in
peace beyond the encroachments of the mighty deep.[2] What
our author has done is to project this world picture into the
the heavens.[3] The sea which John beholds is the heavenly sea (the
'waters above the firmament' of Gen. 1. 7)[4] and the mount,
the heavenly mount. Thus John juxtaposes the altar and the
throne and tells us that the dead are beneath the altar. That is
why he can say of the latter: 'Therefore are they before the
throne of God, and serve him day and night within his temple'
(7. 15). Similarly, in the final vision he will tell us that from the
throne of God and of the Lamb flows the river of life (22. 1).
We shall arrive at the same conclusion regarding John's cosmology if we remind ourselves that since the divine dwelling is in
heaven the holy mountain must be in heaven, for one cannot
have the one without the other. Such a background for the
author's visions of the heavenly temple and city would be familiar
to his readers. Enoch used it before him,[5] and the rabbis loved
the idea of correspondence when thinking of the heavenly world.[6]
Its use by John alerts us to expect a more formal and comprehensive description of the heavenly temple than we have so far
encountered in the New Testament.

[1] Cf. Isa. 51. 9–11, where the defeat of the primeval monster is connected with
the crossing of the Red Sea.

[2] See Appendix A.

[3] It is not always easy to determine whether John receives his visions in heaven
or on earth. At 21. 10 he seems to view the new Jerusalem from earth, but in fact
the mountain in question is the site of the city, not the place from which it is
viewed. One cannot agree with Charles (*The Revelation of St. John* (1920), ii. 1 ff.)
that the scene described at 14. 1 f. is on earth.

[4] According to T. Levi 2. 7 these waters hang between the first and second
heavens. Some commentators rightly noting the temple imagery which forms the
background of chapter 4 interpret the 'sea' of 4. 6 as the laver of 1 Kgs. 7. 23–6, but
the association of the sea with the exodus at Rev. 15. 2 ff. is rather in favour of the
interpretation adopted above. However, since the laver was the symbol of the
primeval ocean the interpretations are not mutually exclusive.

[5] Above, pp. 28 f.   [6] Above, pp. 34 ff.

Before we examine what John says about the heavenly temple we should take note of the fact that he, like other New Testament writers, thinks of the church on earth as God's temple. It is central to the theology of Revelation that the Paschal victory of Christ and his subsequent reign in heaven are not only the ground of salvation for the faithful, but also invest them with a unique character and destiny: 'Because he is Lord of lords and King of kings those with him are also called and chosen and faithful' (17. 14). In particular, Christians are kings and priests, and a temple. It is the latter that we are concerned with here. The conception comes in a very condensed bit of symbolism in the third vision:

> Then I was given a measuring rod like a staff, and I was told: 'Rise and measure the temple (ναός) of God and the altar and those who worship there, but do not measure the court outside the temple; leave that out, for it is given over to the nations, and they will trample over the holy city for forty-two months. And I will grant my two witnesses power to prophesy for one thousand two hundred and sixty days, clothed in sackcloth' (11. 1–3).

The writer has in mind (as the mention of the forty-two months indicates) the savage attack of Antiochus Epiphanes on the people of God, which reached its horrifying climax in the desecration of the temple of Jerusalem (Dan. 7. 25; 12. 7). This is taken as a type by John (cf. Mark 13. 14 par.) and applied to the persecution which God's people are once again about to undergo. The imperilled church is appositely depicted under the guise of the temple of Jerusalem, or more correctly the holy of holies (ναός), for the forecourt, i.e. the profane part, is excluded from the measuring. Zechariah predicted that God would protect his holy city like a wall of fire (2. 5); so the Christian prophet is told to draw a divine protecting line around God's new dwelling.[1] Although the measuring in Revelation symbolizes preservation rather than the intention to build, the thought of Ezekiel's measuring the new temple may not have been far from the author's mind: the prophet's vision of the eschatological city

---

[1] The altar is included with the sanctuary in the measuring presumably because it was not part of the outer complex of buildings, but why it should be singled out for specific mention is not obvious. Possibly it has something to do with the fact that the altar is an important item in John's temple in heaven. On the other hand, 'altar' and 'temple' may be one idea, the καί in this case being explicative.

certainly was important for him. At any rate, he wishes his readers to know that, although the new temple will be exposed to dangers like the old temple, it will not suffer the same humiliating fate.[1] Only the outer and profane part of the temple, that is, the people on its fringe, will perish in the approaching crisis. Whether those on the church's fringe are faithless Christians or Jews is not easy to determine. If they are Jews the passage probably carries a *double entendre* and alludes to the destruction of Jerusalem and its temple (cf. Luke 21. 24).[2] There is some support in the context for this (11. 8), but the thought of the Apocalypse generally (esp. 2. 1–3. 22) rather favours our interpreting the 'fringe ones' as Christians who are not fully committed. Just as the pagans trampled upon the temple of Jerusalem profaning it, so the world will invade and secularize those who say they are Christ's and are not.

The meaning of the passage is further elucidated if we take with it the verses that follow (11. 3–13), as the repetition of the forty-two months suggests that we should. Drawing upon a late-Jewish tradition concerning the experience of Elijah and Moses[3] and symbolism from the book of Zechariah, John illustrates what he has just said about the inviolability of the church. The 'two witnesses' are explained to be the 'two olive trees and the two lampstands which stand before the Lord of the earth' (11. 4). In other words, they recall Zerubbabel and Joshua (Zech. 4), and thus symbolize royalty and priesthood. That is to say, the two witnesses stand for the church, which is royal and sacerdotal in character (1. 6; 5. 10; 20. 6; cf. Exod. 19. 5 f.).[4] So, following what he has already said regarding the inviolability of the faithful under the image of the temple, John proceeds to state that nothing will hinder the two witnesses in the execution of their divinely appointed mission; and when their testimony is consummated in martyrdom they will not have perished as their jubilant enemies mistakenly suppose, but will continue their indestructible life in heaven. The section on the two witnesses thus makes it clear beyond reasonable doubt that it is the church that is depicted

---

[1] The thought is the same as that of the sealing of the 144,000 at 7. 1–8. The church is inviolable because it is numbered, i.e. measured.

[2] Somewhat similar is the thought of Heb. 9: the outer part of the tabernacle represents Judaism, the inner Christianity.

[3] Cf. S–B iii. 811 f.

[4] Cf. G. B. Caird, *The Revelation of St. John the Divine* (1966), p. 134.

under the image of the temple in the immediately preceding
verses.[1]

Other allusions to the church on earth as God's temple may
possibly be found at 20. 9 ('the camp of the saints') and 1. 12–13,
where Christ seems to be represented as wearing the garments of
a priest and standing in the churches as an officiating priest.
Congar takes 14. 15 to refer to the church on earth as a temple,[2]
but the idea of an angel residing in the earthly church does not
particularly commend itself. The context strongly suggests that
it is the heavenly temple that is intended.

We proceed to the conception of the heavenly temple.

John does not describe the heavenly temple in anything like
the detail that we might expect from one so familiar with Jewish
liturgy. In fact, one is not always sure whether it is a temple
which John has in mind, or a palace, or even a synagogue, or
whether he thinks of heaven itself as a temple. First we have
a picture of God enthroned as king (4. 2 ff. etc.). Twenty-four
elders are seated on thrones after the fashion of elders of the
synagogue (4. 4 ff.), and a scroll is produced like the scroll kept in
the ark of the synagogue. Then we hear of the angels of the
presence (7. 11; 8. 2 ff.; cf. Tob. 12. 15), the tent of witness (15.
5; cf. 13. 6), and the ark of the covenant (11. 19). One can
harmonize the ideas of the throne, the temple, the tent, and the
ark, for the holy of holies was traditionally regarded as God's
throne, and in any case ancient temples were as much palaces as
sanctuaries.[3] Also to call the temple a tent (σκηνή), i.e. a dwelling,
as John frequently does (13. 6; 15. 5; cf. 21. 3), is not a problem
either.[4] But to fit in the twenty-four elders and their thrones is
no easy matter. It is true that the synagogue was a replica of the

---

[1] The connection between the two sections may be closer than at first sight
appears, if hovering at the back of John's mind is the tradition concerning the
fate of the temple of Jerusalem in 587 B.C. that was popular in Jewish circles. It was
believed that the temple was not really destroyed, as its enemies thought. God had
miraculously intervened and arranged for its essentials (the tabernacle, ark, and
altar of incense) to be secreted away to the mountain where the pattern of the
sanctuary had been revealed, and to be preserved there (2 Macc. 2. 4 ff.; 2 Bar.
6. 5–10; 80. 2; 4 Bar. 3. 18).

[2] op. cit., p. 212.

[3] Cf. the interesting example of how John combines the ideas of the temple and
throne at 7. 15 and 16. 17.

[4] The curious expression ὁ ναὸς τῆς σκηνῆς τοῦ μαρτυρίου (15. 5) is best rendered
with Bousset, 'der Tempel, nämlich die Stiftshütte' (Die Offenbarung Johannis
(1906)⁶, p. 394).

temple, and perhaps one should allow for a certain interpenetration of images. But if in fact a temple is in mind, then one wishes to know what sort of a temple it is in which all the worshippers are inside and have free access to God (7. 9, 15). One can, of course, say that the writer is a visionary and it would be unwise to expect too much from him in the way of logical consistency, but such a conclusion should be adopted only as a last resort. I think that provided one is not unduly concerned about particular details it may safely be said that it is a temple which John is describing. Evidence for this is to be found not only in the prominent place occupied by the altar (6. 9; 8. 3 ff.; 9. 13; 14. 18; 16. 7) and the angels of the presence (7. 11; 8. 2 ff.) but preeminently in the liturgical scenes (esp. 7. 15). However, precise identification is not essential for our purpose. In this section of the book (chapters 4–20) John is not interested in the heavenly temple as such; as we shall see, the symbolism of these chapters should not be too closely connected with that of chapters 21–2. The temple idea is used here simply as a piece of stage scenery or background for the author's *dramatis personae*.[1] No attempt is made to convert the image and give it new meaning as is done in the vision of the new Jerusalem. Thus in the great vision of chapter 7 the redeemed are depicted as worshipping in the temple, with no suggestion that they are themselves the temple, even though John has already prepared the way for this reinterpretation of the heavenly temple image (3. 12) and the vision of the twelve-fold people of God on Mount Zion at 14. 1 ff. provided him with an excellent opportunity for introducing it. Only in the final vision does the heavenly temple and city move into the foreground and have crucial importance for the interpretation of the book.

In the heavenly temple John witnesses a magnificent liturgy. It is presented in seven scenes, in accordance with the sevenfold symbolism of the book: 4. 2–11 (the elders and the four living creatures worshipping God); 5. 8–14 (the four living creatures,

---

[1] For example, in 7. 9–17 where we have the novel picture of the martyrs standing before the throne of God, i.e. in the holy of holies, attention is directed not at the temple but at the status of the faithful, who enjoy the privilege previously reserved for the high priest (see further below). The only place in this section (chapters 4–20) where possibly the faithful in heaven are depicted as a temple is 13. 6, but in the present state of uncertainty over the text one cannot be sure. Cf. Farrer, *The Revelation of St. John the Divine*, p. 153.

the elders, and angels worshipping the Lamb); 7. 9–17 (the great multitude gathered out of every nation, clothed in white with palms in their hands and worshipping God); 11. 15–19 (the elders worshipping God); 14. 1–5 (the Lamb and the 144,000 gathered on Mount Zion); 15. 2–4 (the redeemed host standing at the edge of the dangerous sea and singing the song of Moses and the Lamb); 19. 1–8 (the great multitude, the elders, and beasts heralding the marriage of the Lamb). Interspersed between these scenes are various visions, actions, and movements in heaven, between heaven and earth, and upon earth, in which the whole moves forward to a grand climax in the last judgement. Our concern is the heavenly worship as depicted in the seven scenes.

To understand this we must first attempt to identify the imagery used. First, there are the nations worshipping God 'within his temple', the Messiah on Mount Zion and God's flock now at last united and safely gathered at Zion. There is also the appearing before God, the worshipping company, music, and singing. What is this but the ancient motif of the festal gathering at Zion put to Christian use? Our author has done precisely what the writer to the Hebrews did. He has selected what was the supreme moment in the life of every Jew and interpreted it spiritually in the light of Christ's paschal victory and subsequent reign. The writer to the Hebrews saw a long caravan with Jesus at its head; John sees the pilgrims assembled at Zion and in their midst the Lord. Each writer interprets the motif according to his own particular thesis. The writer to the Hebrews draws attention to the pilgrimage to the sacred mount and the need for perseverance in reaching it; John describes the gathering together of the worshippers in the great festival at Zion. Common to both writers is the reinterpretation of the motif in terms of spiritual and heavenly realities. The prophetic hope is divested of its material and national character and given a new orientation and transferred from the earthly to the heavenly plane. It is the reward of those who keep the faith, just as it is the goal of those who journey by faith.

We have now to ask what particular Jewish festival, if any, John has used as the model for his heavenly liturgy. This is no easy task. For John frequently combines ideas which in their sources are quite distinct, and on occasion invests images with features which they did not previously have. Moreover, even when one has identified John's imagery it is not always clear to what extent the details should be pressed.

It is to the merit of Comblin that he has shown that the imagery of the concluding section of the Apocalypse (21. 1–22. 5) is based upon the Feast of Tabernacles, the Jewish feast *par excellence*.[1] There is good reason for believing that Tabernacles also is the dominant image of the seven liturgical scenes.[2] To start with, the faithful at 7. 9 ff. are described as bearing palm branches; this is a feature of Tabernacles.[3] Their rubric, 'Salvation belongs to our God', recalls the cry *hosanna* of Ps. 118. 25, which was used at the feast (M. Suk. 4. 5). The description of the heavenly host in the posture of worship, the palms, the trumpets, and the Hallel is not in itself conclusive, but appearing together as these do and in conjunction with other details of the visions (see below) they make it reasonably certain that the reference is to Tabernacles. Quite explicit in fact is the allusion to the tabernacling presence: 'Therefore are they before the throne of God, and serve him day and night within his temple; and he who sits on the throne will shelter them with his presence (σκηνώσει ἐπ' αὐτούς)' (7. 15; cf. 21. 3; John 1. 14). This leads naturally to the thought of God's care and provision for Israel in the wilderness. Finally, there is the promise of 'springs of living water' (7. 17), alluding to the central rite of Tabernacles, the water-pouring, which from the time of Zechariah had an eschatological orientation (Zech. 14. 8 ff.; cf. Rev. 22. 1). Similarly in the sixth vision, Tabernacles once again appears to be the source of John's inspiration. Thus the representation of the saints as victors standing beside the forbidding sea singing praises to God recalls the psalms sung at Tabernacles on the 'steps of Tehom'.[4] Again, the marked universal thrust of the liturgy accords well with Tabernacles (Zech. 14. 16 f.). Many of these elements we shall find reappearing in the vision of the new Jerusalem, where Tabernacles is clearly in mind.

That John should have selected the Feast of Tabernacles for his imagery is not surprising. As the symbol, on the one hand, of the

---

[1] Op. cit., pp. 28 ff.

[2] This was suggested by V. Burch, *Anthropology and the Apocalypse* (1939), but not worked out in detail.

[3] Palms were the principal item of the *lulab* (M. Suk. 3).

[4] The superscription of the Targum on the 'Songs of ascent' (Pss. 120–34) reads 'A Song Sung on the Steps of Tehom'.

presence of God with his people, and, on the other hand, of the vindication of God's people and their triumph over their enemies and the conversion of the nations to God (Zech. 14. 16–19), the feast was peculiarly suited to his purpose. Thus the martyrs shelter under God's presence (7. 15; cf. 21. 3) the four living creatures and the elders ascribe praise to the Lamb who was slain and 'didst ransom men for God from every tribe and tongue and people and nation' (5. 9); and the palm-bearing worshippers are 'from every nation, from all tribes and peoples and tongues' (7. 9). Similarly, the 144,000 on Mount Zion are the first fruits of mankind (14. 4); and the victors over the beast cry, 'All nations shall come and worship thee' (15. 4). That John's use of the motif also had an apologetic aim is not impossible. Certainly his references to the festival would have more than an antiquarian appeal. The temple of Jerusalem no longer stood, but the vibrant memories and hopes associated with the feast were kept alive by the synagogue, and it may be to such memories and hopes, expressed year after year in the synagogue liturgy, that John is making an appeal.

The heavenly priesthood is an interesting feature of the Apocalypse. We have met the conception already in the third cultic scene:

> They have washed their robes and made them white in the blood of the Lamb.
> Therefore are they before the throne of God, and serve him (λα-τρεύουσιν αὐτῷ) day and night within his temple (ναός) (7. 14–15).

That is to say, the faithful in heaven are in the posture of priests; compare the statement in v. 9 that they are 'standing'. Although John is thinking primarily of the martyrs (7. 14a) it is clear that he thinks of the new priesthood as including all Christians (1. 5–6; cf. 5. 9).[1] This priestly service begun on earth is continued in heaven, and, as we shall see presently, in a profounder way. Its basis is the priestly work of Christ on the cross; it is this that makes the faithful priests (1. 5 f.; 7. 14). Ideally all Israelites were priests, and John, like 1 Peter, makes use of Exod. 19. 6. But where the LXX reads 'a kingdom of priests' (βασίλειον ἱεράτευμα = מַמְלֶכֶת כֹּהֲנִים), John has 'a kingdom and priests' (βασιλείαν καὶ ἱερεῖς, 5. 10), alternatively, 'a kingdom, priests'

---

[1] Cf. 1 Pet. 2. 9, on which see above, pp. 129 f.

(βασιλείαν ἱερεῖς, 1. 6), thus distinguishing the ideas of priesthood and kingship. Charles has shown that this was a Jewish way of treating the text,[1] so it may not be significant. But since the royal status of the faithful is one of the author's leading conceptions (3. 21; 5. 10; 20. 6; 22. 5) one suspects that it is important for him and ought to be interpreted as an attempt to balance the notion of priesthood with that of kingship. There would be no difficulty here for John's readers, since in their day kings acted as priests. The idea of the redeemed as priest-kings is congenial to John (20. 6; 22. 5). But more fruitful for our understanding of his thought is the imagery he uses. The reinterpretation is remarkable. In the first place, those represented as priests in the heavenly temple are 'from every nation' (7. 9; cf. 5. 9).[2] Admission to the new priesthood depends no longer upon racial descent, but upon the blood of the Lamb (7. 14 f.). Furthermore, those who comprise it are not simply priests, but high priests: they stand before the throne of God (7. 9, 15), i.e. inside the holy of holies (cf. 22. 3–4). In similar vein possibly is the description of the faithful as dressed in white robes: white was the colour worn by the high priest when serving in the holy of holies (M. Yoma 3. 6; 7. 4), and John's priest-angels are similarly dressed (15. 5). The new priesthood cannot be fully understood without reference to its offering, but before we consider this, two points are to be noted. (a) Priestly functions belong to the four living creatures, the twenty-four elders (5. 8; 7. 11), and the angels (8. 3 ff.; 15. 5; cf. Tobit 12. 15).[3] (b) Nowhere does the Apocalypse call Christ a priest. If the author entertained the thought,[4] it apparently was not important. What is uppermost is the idea of Christ receiving the offering of those whom he has made priests. Contrast the epistle to the Hebrews, where Christ makes the offering.

We come now to the sacrifice offered in heaven. As might be expected, John's spiritualizing is most clearly in evidence here, for it was in regard to worship that the writers of the Old

---

[1] *Apocrypha and Pseudepigrapha*, ii. 38; *Revelation*, i. 16.

[2] Although some commentators believe that Isa. 66. 21 refers to the Gentiles, it is very improbable that the Jews ever contemplated the possibility of non-Jews exercising sacerdotal functions.

[3] For the part assigned to heavenly beings in the worship of heaven in Jewish literature see above, pp. 36 ff. and T. Levi 3. 7; B. Hag. 12b; B. Zeb. 62a; B. Men. 110a. On their functions in Revelation see Peterson, *The Angels and the Liturgy*.

[4] It may be implied in 1. 13.

Testament and their successors showed the greatest tendency to spiritualize,[1] and Jewish apocalyptic habitually described the heavenly sacrifice as spiritual.[2] John follows this tendency by describing the worship of the saints in terms of praise, thanksgiving, and prayer. Hence the altar in heaven becomes the altar of incense (8. 3 ff.; cf. 5. 8).[3] Our author's Christian viewpoint is nowhere more apparent than in the repeated assertion that the worship is offered to God *and to the Lamb* (4. 10 f.; 5. 8 f.; 7. 10; 15. 3; 19. 7; cf. 3. 21; 22. 3). The faithful are priests of God and of Christ (20. 6). The difference of the new worship from the old may also be seen in the statement that it never ceases ('they . . . serve him day and night', 7. 15; cf. 22. 3 f.).[4]

The Apocalypse has the same vivid sense of the union of heavenly and earthly worship which we noted in Hebrews. The writer depicts the angelic ministrants at the golden altar as joining the incense, that is, the celestial sacrifice, with the prayers of the faithful on earth (ταῖς προσευχαῖς τῶν ἁγίων, 8. 3–4; cf. 5. 8). This can scarcely be taken to mean that the martyrs have a mediatorial function in so far as their worship gives acceptance to the worship offered from earth, but rather that the faithful in heaven and the faithful on earth are joined in one and the same liturgical action. The unity of their worship may also be signified by the four worshipping creatures and the twenty-four elders, if the former represent creation and the latter the church on earth.[5] The close connection between what takes place in heaven and on earth is dramatically illustrated by the effects which the worship of heaven has for those who are upon earth. We are shown how the prayers offered in heaven return to earth in the form of judgements upon the enemies of God and his people (8. 5 ff.). The voice from the altar, in response to the prayers of the faithful,

---

[1] Cf. above, pp. 43 ff.   [2] Cf. above, pp. 31 f.

[3] Most commentators find two altars in heaven, one the altar of burnt offering (6. 9; 8. 3a, 5; 14. 18 [?]; 16. 7), and the other the altar of incense (8. 3b; 9. 13). This is unnatural. Jewish apocalypticists and rabbis thought of only one altar in heaven, the one corresponding to the altar of burnt offering, otherwise the *'ébhen sheᵉthiyyāh*. John, who follows Jewish cosmology, can have only one altar in mind when he speaks of 'the altar', the altar of burnt offering (= the sacred rock), which he spiritualizes as the altar of incense.

[4] 'Where the throne is always in sight the service must be perpetual' (H. B. Swete, *The Apocalypse of St. John* (1906), p. 297).

[5] Cf. Peterson, op. cit., pp. 5 f., 11 f., who, however, takes the twenty-four elders to mean earthly rulers.

releases the destroying angels at the four corners of the earth
(9. 13 f.). Similarly, the voice from the temple commands the
seven angels to pour their vials of wrath upon earth (15. 5–16. 1),
and when their judgements are executed those at the altar make
their response: 'Yea, Lord God the Almighty, true and just are
thy judgments' (16. 7). John's interest is primarily liturgical,
but it is not difficult to see that he is also giving his readers his
interpretation of history, viz. the belief that history is under the
direction of the heavenly world.

We pass now from the heavenly temple to the new Jerusalem.
In John's mind of course the two ideas would never appear
apart (cf. 3. 12): the description of the city in chapters 21–2
implies a temple, just as the description of the temple in chapters
4–20 implies a city. It would be wrong, however, to connect the
city of the final vision with the temple of the earlier section;
the two, as we shall see, stand for different things. Indeed for the
sake of clarity of interpretation there is much to be said for referring to the city of chapters 21–2 as the new or future Jerusalem
rather than the heavenly Jerusalem.

In a sense the Apocalypse is really a tale of two cities, the
heavenly and the earthly. The first part (chapters 4–20) which we
treated as a study of the heavenly temple could have been taken
as a study of the earthly city, for the section has a double theme.[1]
The city whose fortunes are traced, it may be noted, is not Jerusalem, despite the fact that it is at one point described as the place
'where their Lord was crucified' (11. 8; cf. 1. 7).[2] It is the earthly
city of sin and evil which symbolizes the world (cf. 17. 18). In
juxtaposition to this city is another city, that described in chapters 21–2. This city in turn symbolizes a world order, the new
world which will take the place of the present world. It is the
holy city, the new Jerusalem. The two cities are diametrical
opposites; one worships God, the other the beast. Consequently
the earthly city cannot have any place in the new world. It is in
fact marked out for judgement and destruction. Thus all the
while, in what is ostensibly an account of the heavenly temple,
the reader is being prepared for the revelation of the new

---

[1] For the earthly city of chapters 4–20 see 11. 8; 14. 8; 16. 19; 17. 5; 18. 10 ff.;
19. 2 f.
[2] The appellation 'where their Lord was crucified', like the title 'Sodom and
Egypt', is a description of the city's character. Cf. M. Kiddle, *The Revelation of St.
John* (1940), p. 199.

Jerusalem, until in the last chapters of the book the wretched and putrescent grandeur of 'Babylon' gives way to the transparent and eternal glory of the new Jerusalem.[1]

The first part of the vision of the new Jerusalem (21. 1–8) is best explained as an introduction and preview.[2] On the one hand, it establishes continuity with the preceding narrative (the account of the destruction of the existing city and world) by linking the advent of the new Jerusalem with the succession of eschatological events; on the other hand, it provides a cosmic background for the new city.

Then I saw a new (καινός) heaven and a new (καινή) earth; for the first heaven and the first earth had passed away, and the sea was no more.[3] And I saw the holy city, new (καινή) Jerusalem, coming down out of heaven from God, prepared as a bride adorned for her husband; and I heard a great voice from the throne saying, 'Behold, the dwelling of God (ἡ σκηνὴ τοῦ Θεοῦ) is with men. He will dwell (σκηνοῦν) with them, and they shall be his people, and God himself will be with them; he will wipe away every tear from their eyes, and death shall be no more, neither shall there be mourning nor crying nor pain any more, for the former things have passed away (21. 1–4).

The background of John's picture of the *civitas Dei* is Isa. 65. 17–19, where the prophet predicts the creation of a new heaven and a new earth and a new Jerusalem, an event which would be marked by the end of all sorrow and tears. The familiar figure of the city as a bride (Isa. 49. 18; 61. 10; cf. 52. 1), which was

---

[1] Cf. the parallels: the invitation from the angel (21. 9 = 17. 1); the woman (21. 9 = 17. 1); the translation of the seer (21. 10 = 17. 3); the vision (21. 10 ff. = 17. 3 ff.); the woman's attire (21. 11 = 17. 4; 18. 16); the kings of the earth (21. 24 = 17. 2, 18; 18. 3, 9). Cf. Comblin, op. cit., p. 8 n.

[2] We proceed on the assumption that the section (chapters 21–2) is a unitary whole. Charles (ii. 144–54) and others, most recently M. E. Boismard (' "L'Apocalypse" ou "les Apocalypses" de S. Jean', *RB*, 56 (1949), 507–46) find such difficulty in understanding certain parts (notably 22. 5) that they treat the section as an erroneous and misleading combination of elements that originally appeared quite separately. Thus according to Charles, 21. 1–4 (and 22. 3–5) is a vision of the new Jerusalem of the new world, whereas 21. 9–22. 2, 14–15 refers to the terrestrial Jerusalem of the millennium. The only merit in this unwarranted and unnecessary dissection of these chapters of the Apocalypse is that it explains the city mentioned in connection with the millennium (20. 9). But there is not nearly enough evidence for connecting the city of 20. 9 with that of 21. 9 ff. Indeed one cannot even say with any certainty that the 1000-year reign of Christ and the saints (20. 4–6) takes place from an earthly city at all. Cf. de Young, op. cit., pp. 151 f.

[3] Such a radical transformation of traditional cosmology is doubtless intended to prepare the reader for the novel character of what is to follow.

applied by Fourth Ezra[1] and Paul[2] to the heavenly Jerusalem, is now made the symbol of the new Jerusalem, the spouse not of God but of the Lamb. The image presents no great difficulty to the interpreter. At 19. 7 the bride is said to be ready for the wedding, here (21. 2) she is shown in her bridal attire, at 21. 9 f. she is described as the wife of the Lamb. One has only to ask who the Lamb's spouse can be for the imagery to become plain. The bride of Christ is the church. Therefore the new Jerusalem is no other than the new people of God.[3] John thus picks up the theme he introduced right at the outset:

He who conquers, I will make him a pillar in the temple (ναός) of my God; never shall he go out of it, and I will write on him the name of my God, and the name of the city of my God, the new (καινή) Jerusalem which comes down from my God out of heaven (3. 12).

He wishes us to know that this promise is fulfilled. The image is now expanded. Since Jerusalem always presupposes the temple, the representation of the church as the city of God naturally evokes the thought of God's presence (the other aspect of the nuptial figure), and we have the intimate picture of God tabernacling with his people, which is based on the Old Testament predictions concerning the new temple (Ezek. 37. 27; Lev. 26. 11 f.).[4] Thus under the images of the city and the sanctuary John gives his readers a glimpse of the ultimate stage or state in the relations of God and his people. What we see is a rough sketch (the detail will follow); even so it is enough to provide us with a key to understanding the remainder of the section.

Let us note the thoroughgoing nature of John's reinterpretation of the traditional hope of Israel. The vision is imparted to him only after the present world has passed out of existence. 'I saw a *new* heaven and a *new* earth;[5] for the first heaven and the first earth had passed away.' The city that John sees is thus part of the new creation. That is to say, it is a completely new phenomenon. It descends 'out of heaven', i.e. from the newly

---

[1] Above, pp. 33 f.   [2] Above, pp. 141 ff.
[3] Similar is the thought of 19. 8: the bride's attire is the good works of the faithful (cf. 6. 11; 7. 9, 13–14).
[4] Cf. also the language used at 21. 7.
[5] There is a new heaven as well as a new earth, since in ancient thinking heaven and earth are all of a piece (cf. Isa. 34. 4; 51. 6; Ps. 102. 25–6; Matt. 24. 35; 2 Pet. 3. 10; Rev. 20. 11).

created heavens. Such a novel idea, so far as one can ascertain from the texts available, was nowhere entertained by the Jews of the time. They habitually thought of the new creation and the new Jerusalem in terms of a rejuvenation and transformation of the old, and in the period after the New Testament, when eventually the rabbis believed the heavenly Jerusalem would descend to earth, what they envisaged was something quite different from what our author has in mind. The city expected by the rabbis was the heavenly prototypal city.[1] Such an idea has no place in John's new world. The prototypal city (like its ectype on earth) belongs to the old order of creation, 'the first heaven and the first earth', which in John's scheme of things has been destroyed. His city, like the world-order it symbolizes, is altogether new. It is not merely new in time ($\nu\acute{\epsilon}os$), but new in quality ($\kappa\alpha\iota\nu\acute{os}$). No hint is given as to its previous existence. All we know is that it descends 'out ($\acute{\epsilon}\kappa$) of heaven from ($\acute{\alpha}\pi\acute{o}$) God'.[2] What is John saying? Surely this: the new order issuing from the paschal victory of Christ is not part of the present order; it is not the fulfilment or *évolué* of the natural order or the historical process. It is rather the inbreaking of that which is outside and beyond history, the supersession and not the consummation of the old. Hence it is called new, or as certain other New Testament writers put it, not made by the hand of man.

One naturally wishes to know why the traditional images are used at all. The answer should not give any difficulty to those who understand the significance of the temple in the biblical tradition. It has to do with grace. For John, as for his mentors, the holy city (and its temple) is supremely the sign and symbol of God's gracious action on behalf of his creatures. It stands for the new covenant God has made with men. Thus, in the vision described in the passage we have just considered, no sooner has the seer had time to look at the new Jerusalem than a voice explains its meaning: 'Behold, the dwelling ($\sigma\kappa\eta\nu\acute{\eta}$) of God is with men. *He will dwell* ($\sigma\kappa\eta\nu\acute{\omega}\sigma\epsilon\iota$) *with them . . . God himself* ($\alpha\grave{\upsilon}\tau\acute{os}$) *will be with them*' (21. 3). The Greek is not immediately clear as to the subject of the verb ('dwell'), but the EVV are probably correct in making it refer to God. There is very likely

[1] Cf. above, pp. 34 ff.
[2] Cf. P. S. Minear, 'The Cosmology of the Apocalypse', *Current Issues in New Testament Interpretation*, ed. W. Klassen and F. Snyder (1962), pp. 23–37.

a play on the words 'dwelling' (σκηνή) and 'dwell' (σκηνώσει), whereby we are intended to pass from the conception of the tabernacle or temple to the subject of the verb (God). The 'dwelling of God' (ἡ σκηνὴ τοῦ Θεοῦ) is metonymic. As in the image of the city, it is referred to only in order to evoke the reality symbolized. No sooner does the image appear than it disappears and we behold God himself (αὐτὸς ὁ Θεὸς μετ' αὐτῶν ἔσται). Presently we shall be told that the temple is God (21. 22), which is really another way of saying the same thing.

The new Jerusalem then is spiritual. It is the community of the redeemed. 'He who conquers, I will make him a pillar in the temple of my God; never shall he go out of it, and I will write on him the name of my God, and the name of the city of my God, the new Jerusalem which comes down from my God out of heaven' (3. 12). Hence we find that there is after all continuity between the old and the new, though not the kind of continuity we expected. The new Jerusalem is fashioned from the material that once formed God's dwelling on earth (11. 1–2; 20. 9); it is built of living stones (cf. 1 Pet. 2. 5).

After John has had a glimpse of the new Jerusalem he is invited to ascend the sacred mount and view the city from closer quarters. The section that follows (21. 9–27) is a detailed description of the new Jerusalem. John has just had it explained to him that the city is the church, the place of God's dwelling. Such a city must therefore symbolize what the church is, and since it is where God Almighty dwells it must be the most magnificent city ever conceived by the mind of man.

'Come, I will show you the Bride, the wife of the Lamb.' And in the Spirit he (the angel) carried me away to a great, high mountain, and showed me the holy city Jerusalem coming down out of heaven from God, having the glory of God, its radiance like a most rare jewel, like a jasper, clear as crystal. It had a great, high wall, with twelve gates, and at the gates twelve angels, and on the gates the names of the twelve tribes of the sons of Israel were inscribed; on the east three gates, on the north three gates, on the south three gates, and on the west three gates. And the wall of the city had twelve foundations, and on them the twelve names of the twelve apostles of the Lamb.

And he who talked to me had a measuring rod of gold to measure the city and its gates and walls. The city lies foursquare, its length the same as its breadth; and he measured the city with his rod, twelve thousand stadia; its length and breadth and height are equal. He also measured its wall, a hundred and forty-four cubits by a man's measure, that is, an angel's. The wall was built of jasper, while the city was pure gold, clear as glass. The foundations of the wall of the city were adorned with every jewel; the first was jasper, the second sapphire, the third agate, the fourth emerald, the fifth onyx, the sixth carnelian, the seventh chrysolite, the eighth beryl, the ninth topaz, the tenth chrysoprase, the eleventh jacinth, the twelfth amethyst. And the twelve gates were twelve pearls, each of the gates made of a single pearl, and the street of the city was pure gold, transparent as glass (vv. 9–21).

The city is identified at the outset as the bride of the Lamb, i.e. the church, in order that the reader may be quite clear that it is spiritual realities which are in mind. The statement that John is taken to a great high mountain (here the sacred mountain of the new earth) is a further clue as to the interpretation of the vision (cf. Ezek. 40. 2 ff.). Ezekiel, it is true, saw a temple, whereas John sees a city. But this is a difference that should not be pressed; John's city is a temple. What are important are the numbers and measurements; these are symmetrical, like those of Ezekiel. The new Jerusalem has twelve gates, three to each of the four sides (21. 12 = Ezek. 48. 31–4), and twelve foundations (an idea not found in Ezekiel but in harmony with his symbolism).[1] The length, breadth, and height of the city are similarly reckoned in multiples of twelve, as are the measurements of its wall.[2] So to understand the meaning of the symmetry the natural thing to do is to ask what it meant for Ezekiel. The prophet, as will be recalled,[3] intended the symmetry of his city to symbolize Israel of the end-time restored and united for the service of God. Undoubtedly John intends it to mean the same. In fact, he tells us as much when he states that the gates of the city bear the names of the twelve tribes. For this immediately sends the reader back to what John said in an earlier part of his writing. The

---

[1] The twelve foundations mean not twelve foundations on top of one another (an idea as ludicrous to the ancients as to moderns) but twelve foundation-stones (θεμέλιοι), great oblong blocks such as the ancients used to begin their buildings (see below, p. 198). Normally these were placed end to end, but John thinks of them as punctuated by gates. Cf. Swete, op. cit., p. 283. For a helpful diagram see Farrer, *A Rebirth of Images*, p. 249.

[2] Ezekiel is content to specify the length and breadth of the city (48. 16). John's addition of height merely elaborates the image, though, as we shall see presently, it serves to convey another important insight.

[3] Cf. above, pp. 9 f.

twelve tribes are the 144,000 who were sealed against disaster at
7. 1–8 and subsequently gathered by the Messiah on Mount
Zion at 14. 1–5. The numbers and measurements in the plan of
the city correspond with the numbers of Israel of the new
covenant, the stones of which the city is built are living stones.[1]
But in case any uncertainty should remain in the minds of his
readers John obligingly repeats himself: the twelve foundation-
stones carry the names of the twelve apostles. To query how the
twelve apostles (v. 14) are to be equated with the twelve sons of
Israel (v. 12) would be to betray a singular lack of sympathy
with and understanding of John's way of thinking: both refer to
one and the same thing. The city of God is the people of God, in
their ultimate state—the church redeemed and united in the
eternal worship of God.[2]

It might seem that having presented the new Jerusalem as the
realization of Israel's most cherished hope John could safely
conclude. As it is, he has not finished all he wishes to tell us about
the glories that await the faithful. So he continues:

And I saw no temple ($\nu\alpha\delta\varsigma$) in the city, for its temple is the Lord
God the Almighty and the Lamb. And the city has no need of sun or
moon to shine upon it, for the glory ($\delta\delta\xi\alpha$) of God is its light, and its
lamp is the Lamb. By its light shall the nations walk; and the kings of
the earth shall bring their glory into it, and its gates shall never be
shut by day—and there shall be no night there; they shall bring into
it the glory and honour of the nations.[3] But nothing unclean shall
enter it, nor anyone who practises abomination or falsehood, but only
those who are written in the Lamb's book of life.

Then he showed me the river of the water of life, bright as crystal,
flowing from the throne of God and of the Lamb through the middle
of the city; also, on either side of the river, the tree of life[4] with its

[1] We shall arrive at the same conclusion if with Farrer we measure the twelve
edges of John's cubical city (*The Revelation of St. John the Divine*, p. 217). Twelve
times 12,000 makes the significant number of 144,000!

[2] The same fact will also be in mind if the representation of the foundations as
jewels (vv. 19–20) and the gates as pearls (v. 21) is inspired by the twelve precious
stones of Aaron's breastplate, which symbolized Israel (Exod. 28. 29).

[3] For vv. 23–6 compare Isa. 60. 1–20 and Zech. 14. 7 ff. John spiritualizes the
material elements of Isaiah's account of the eschatological pilgrimage. Instead of
animals, gold, and precious woods, the nations bring homage ($\delta\delta\xi\alpha$ $\kappa\alpha i$ $\tau\iota\mu\dot{\eta}$).

[4] The Greek is difficult to interpret. It is not clear whether one or several trees
are in mind or where they are located. If John is following Ezekiel (47. 7), as the
mention of the river suggests, $\xi\dot{\nu}\lambda o\nu$ $\zeta\omega\dot{\eta}\varsigma$ is a generic and he will have several trees
in mind ('. . . on this side of the river and that was the tree of life'). On the other
hand, if John is following Genesis (2. 9; 3. 22) (Rev. 22. 14) then he is thinking of

twelve kinds of fruit, yielding its fruit each month; and the leaves of
the tree were for the healing of the nations. There shall no more be
anything accursed, but the throne of God and of the Lamb shall be in
it, and his servants shall worship him; they shall see his face,[1] and his
name shall be on their foreheads. And night shall be no more; they
need no light of lamp or sun, for the Lord God will be their light, and
they shall reign for ever and ever (21. 22–22. 5).[2]

The vision changes before our eyes. The gates which we thought
were simply for symbolical effect swing open to admit the nations.
The city is no longer the self-contained box-like thing we took it
to be but a vast metropolis with crowds coming and going.
Those who enter the city are saved; those who do not are lost (21.
14). What has John done? What contradiction is this that peoples
the new world with the unconverted? Surely these perished along
with the old order. To many commentators it has seemed that
either John's imagination has got the better of him or that an
editor has hopelessly confused the vision. Neither in fact is the
case. Jewish eschatology, as we have repeatedly seen, made the
new Jerusalem the symbol of the unity not only of Israel but of
mankind, and John, who began by presenting his city as the new
world centre, apparently felt obliged to relate his vision to this
wider hope. The procedure he adopts makes for a certain am-
biguity on the part of minds that no longer work like his. He
prints over the image of the compact and clearly demarcated
Ezekielian city another image, the comprehensive image of
Isaiah, or, more correctly, since the images are not mutually
exclusive,[3] he concentrates on the Isaianic features of the city
already portrayed until these predominate to the exclusion of
everything else. The result is a picture of a great pilgrimage city,
the centre of the world, through whose ever-open gates stream

the single tree of life, as is common in the apocalyptic tradition (1 En. 24. 4;
25. 4–6), and the position of the tree is unclear. In either case, the new creation
is symbolized.

[1] The hope of every Jew (cf. Ps. 17. 15) and the object of all the pilgrimages (Pss.
42. 2; 84. 7)—to see the face of God—is realized in the city where no temple hides
the divine being. Hence John adds, 'his name shall be on their foreheads', i.e. they
are priests (cf. Exod. 28. 36–8; Lev. 8. 9).

[2] On the royal character of the faithful in the new age cf. 3. 21; 20. 6 and above
on 1. 6; 5. 10. Comblin unjustifiably holds that the idea of priesthood is no longer
present (op. cit., pp. 25 f. and n. 53). The language and imagery of 22. 4 clearly
imply their priestly office.

[3] Verses 9–21 contain elements from Deutero-Isaiah's eschatological city (cf.
vv. 11, 18–21), just as vv. 22–22. 5 contain features of Ezekiel's city (22. 1–2).

the nations and the great ones of the earth, offering their homage to God. Actually John has not done anything different from what he did in chapter 7, where alongside the clearly delineated 144,000 he places the vision of the great multitude which no man can number. The image of the circumscribed city and the image of the world-city are two ways of looking at one and the same thing. The new Jerusalem fulfils the traditional hope in both its priestly and prophetic expressions.

The picture of the pilgrims flocking into the new Jerusalem with their offerings impels the reader to inquire whether there is any particular festival that John has in mind. Comblin has shown that it is most likely to be Tabernacles.[1] Light and water, the chief characteristics of this feast, feature prominently in John's vision, and are given a new meaning. The light which now floods Jerusalem is not from the great candelabra ceremoniously lit at Tabernacles but from Christ who is himself the light of the world (21. 23; cf. above, John 8. 12). Similarly, the river of life, symbolized by the water-pouring at the feast, is now represented as flowing from the throne of God *and the Lamb* (22. 1; cf. 7. 17; 21. 6; John 4. 10, 14; 7. 37–8). John is thus seen to return to themes which he has used earlier in his work, thereby giving an intelligible structure to his book.[2] Fr. Comblin goes too far, however, when he suggests that under John's reinterpretation the image of the pilgrimage breaks down completely and we are left with the nations lodging permanently in Jerusalem. The nations pour in and out of the new Jerusalem doing homage to God, i.e. Jerusalem is now vindicated and exalted.

The most outstanding thing that John says about the new Jerusalem concerns its temple. 'I saw no temple in the city, for its temple is the Lord God the Almighty and the Lamb' (21. 22). This is a surprising statement;[3] yet on reflection it is not really surprising. It runs counter to the traditional hope, but at the same time is in a direct line of development with it. In the context of the Apocalypse it is the kind of conclusion one should expect; certainly the conclusion for which John has been preparing his readers. First, he says that the saints are before the

[1] Op. cit., pp. 28 ff.

[2] So interpreted, Revelation has interesting links with the fourth gospel. Cf. above on John 4. 10, 14; 7. 37–8; 8. 12; 19. 34.

[3] Strack and Billerbeck characteristically remark: 'Das zukünftige Jerusalem ohne Tempel—ein für die alte Synagoge unvollziehbarer Gedanke' (op. cit. iii.852).

throne of God, i.e. in his immediate presence (7. 9 ff.), then he states that the sanctuary in heaven is opened and its sacred contents laid bare for human eyes to see (11. 19). Later he drops the hint that the divine dwelling is none other than God himself (21. 3). Now he says quite simply that the temple is God and his Christ. The barriers separating God and men on earth have no place in the world to come, where nothing hides God from his people. 'His servants . . . shall see his face' (22. 4 f.).

Another way of saying the same thing is to interpret the vision to mean that the new Jerusalem is itself a temple. We recall that the city is cubiform, like the holy of holies in the temple of Jerusalem (1 Kgs. 6. 20; M. Midd. 4. 6). New Jerusalem and new temple are one and the same thing. Did John not tell us at the outset that the faithful would become pillars in the temple and bear the name of the new Jerusalem (3. 12)? If the new Jerusalem is one vast temple coextensive with the whole world, one can readily understand why John speaks of a new heaven and a new earth with no more sea and proceeds immediately to say that the new Jerusalem descends out of heaven (21. 1–2). The reason is that the new Jerusalem is the new heaven and the new earth. Both are one, for the sea that separated heaven and earth has been removed. Heaven and earth are of one piece, one great temple that is filled with the presence of God and the Lamb.

John's picture of God as a temple to the faithful and the faithful as a temple to God leads one to ask whether there is really any difference between what he is saying and what the other writers of the New Testament mean when they describe the church as God's temple. It is clear that we must say that there is a difference. The new Jerusalem is the new temple in its perfected and eternal existence; hence John is always careful to let his readers know that it is not simply the temple as such but the holy of holies, the most sacred part of the temple, that he is describing. John's new temple symbolizes the ultimate and final communion of God and his people. 'The dwelling of God is with men. He will dwell with them, and they shall be his people, and God himself shall be with them.'

This chapter has attempted to show how the ancient oriental and Jewish conception of the heavenly temple and city was taken over by the early church and put to Christian use. The reasons for its adoption as a Christian symbol may be summarized as follows:

(i) The conception offered a convenient way of demonstrating the superiority of Christianity over Judaism (Gal. and Heb.). Christianity, like the heavenly Jerusalem, is spiritual (Gal.). Its superiority to Judaism is like that of original to copy (Heb.).

(ii) It symbolized Christianity as the heir of the ancient promises concerning Israel of the end-time. Jewish hopes of the restoration of the material glories of Jerusalem were evidently regarded as having come to an end with the destruction of the city in A.D. 70. The new Jerusalem takes the place of the city which has been destroyed (Rev.).

(iii) It was a meaningful way of expressing the close relation of the faithful on earth with the faithful in heaven. The two form one temple, one dwelling-place of God, and offer one sacrifice, that which is offered through Jesus Christ (Heb. and Rev.).

(iv) It expressed well the conviction that the divine presence graciously imparted to the faithful in this life would not be withdrawn at death, but, on the contrary, enjoyed in a deeper and profounder way, and what the faithful were privileged to be on earth, namely, the dwelling of God, they would continue to be in the world to come.

(v) It symbolized the reward awaiting those who are faithful unto death. If one interprets the descent of the new Jerusalem as its permanent characteristic,[1] one must also do justice to the futuristic aspect which the symbol manifestly has for the author of Revelation. Becoming a pillar of the heavenly temple (3. 12) and enjoying the unmediated vision of God (21. 22; 22. 4) are eschatological rewards that await the faithful dead.

The shift of eschatological emphasis represented by the presence of the heavenly temple idea in the New Testament leads one to ask what is the relationship between the findings of this chapter and those of the preceding chapters. Can we after all regard the church militant as the fulfilment of the long-cherished

---

[1] Caird writes, 'Wherever a man lives by faith in Christ and bears witness to that faith without counting the cost, there is the holy city "coming down out of heaven from God"' (op. cit., p. 55; cf. p. 271).

hope concerning the new temple? This question raises issues of New Testament eschatology which go far beyond the limits of this book, and all that one can hope to do in the present circumstances is to give an answer without supporting it. One may say that the church on earth is and is not the fulfilment of the traditional hope. It is the fulfilment in so far as God dwells in it here and now; it is not in so far as his indwelling in this age is partial, incomplete, and hidden. The findings of this chapter are thus a necessary qualification to the conclusion of the preceding chapters, reminding us that the fulness of the divine presence and the unmediated vision of God, the perfection of communion, and the gathering together of the elect from the four corners of the earth still lie in the future. Affirmation of this futurist aspect of life in Christ is important. It reminds the church of its essential being as an institution unique among the institutions of the world. It also ensures that the tremendous claim which the church makes in calling itself the temple of God is tempered by the recognition, and the humility born of such a recognition, that it possesses only a part of all that it is destined to possess.

XI

CONCLUSION

THEOLOGY, like other sciences, has its categories or thought-forms; and biblical theology, no less than dogmatic or philosophical theology, has its own particular categories. Of necessity the biblical scholar is obliged to look for his categories in the scriptures. He is free to pick and choose, though his choice is of course naturally guided by his particular aim. The value of a particular category is determined by its utility as a principle of interpretation. The greater the data it accounts for, and the greater the degree to which it is able to correlate the data, the greater its value.

The study undertaken in this book has attempted to draw attention to one of the categories of the Bible and its importance for our understanding of the New Testament doctrine of the church.

The new temple is a central idea of biblical eschatology from the earliest times and is found in the most diverse backgrounds. It explains the priestly legislation and the priestly interpretation of history (both of which developed around the desire for a sanctuary worthy of God); it explains the great prophecies of the exile and post-exilic periods and the disappointment and enervation which the programme of Ezra and Nehemiah was designed to combat, just as it provides an important key to the meaning of apocalyptic. It is the common theme of such widely differing books as the strongly nationalistic Psalms of Solomon and the humanistic Sibylline Oracles on the one hand, and the idyllic tale of Tobit and the messianic parables of Enoch on the other hand, and it is the bond uniting both Palestinian and Hellenistic Judaism and orthodox and sectarian Judaism. The essence of biblical and post-biblical thinking on the eschatological age is the conviction that God will graciously condescend to dwell in the midst of his people in a new and unparalleled way and never again leave them. The divine presence was constitutive of Israel as the chosen people of God, and the temple was the guarantee of their existence as such. Only as God dwelt with Israel was Israel his people.

The New Testament declares that God has fulfilled his word of promise made by the prophets and erected a new and more glorious temple. The ministry of Jesus is the divine visitation in judgement and mercy. The people of God are judged, destroyed, and restored. The restoration, like previous ones in Israel's history, is marked by the restoration of God's dwelling-place. The new temple is not indeed the kind of temple men expected but it is the long-expected temple none the less. No one could question its authenticity, for it was not made by the hand of man, i.e. it was made by God himself. The age-old problem of reconciling the immanence and transcendence of God was thereby solved. The solution, while it came along lines already discernible in the old order, that is, the spiritualization of the temple and cult, was novel on account of its positive character. It issued from the resurrection of Jesus Christ and the gift of the Spirit. For this reason one must give due weight to the adjective when speaking of the new temple. The temple of the eschatological age both is and is not the temple of Old Testament and Jewish hope. It supersedes and not merely consummates the previous modes of the divine indwelling. God no longer dwells in a house with his people: he dwells in them; they are his temple.

As a metaphor of the church, the conception of the temple is perhaps most significant for our understanding of the New Testament doctrine of the church because of its theocentric character. Unlike the images of the body and the bride, which have to do with the church's relation to Christ, the temple image depicts the church's relation to God. The church is the temple of God, or God's Spirit; it is never the temple of Christ. The distinction admittedly is due largely to the traditional nuance of the temple idea, but it is significant that in all the New Testament texts, some of which subject traditional ideas to a good deal of reshaping, it is a distinction that is consistently maintained. While it is undoubtedly true that 'the conception of the indwelling Spirit is in Paul hardly separable from the conception of the living Christ',[1] it is significant that the apostle nowhere says that Christ dwells in the new temple. In the 'pure' temple texts there is no mention whatever of Christ, and where the image is fused with

---

[1] C. H. Dodd, *History and the Gospel* (1938), p. 56.

the images of the building and the body, Christ is placed alongside believers as a part of the temple, and the temple is still
God's. This nuance bears witness to an important aspect of the
New Testament doctrine of the church. The popular error of
substituting loyalty to Jesus for loyalty to God and reducing
theology to Christology has its counterpart in ecclesiology when
the church is viewed chiefly in terms of its relation to Christ. The
church's primary relation is to God; its ultimate loyalty is to
him. One of the greatest services biblical theology has rendered
to dogmatic theology in recent times is in helping it to view the
church as the people of God. The temple image has its own
particular contribution to make to this fundamental and meaningful way of looking at the church.

When the New Testament writers wish to describe Christ's
place in the church and the relation of Christians to him, they
either substitute the image of the building (οἰκοδομή) for the
temple image or else fuse the two images and represent Christ as
a part of the building. This fusion of images may indicate a conscious and deliberate attempt on the part of the writers to clarify
the position of Christ in regard to the church, or simply the
tendency of images to gravitate towards one another and form
new and composite images. At any rate, it enables the writers to
accord Christ his place in the church. This is depicted under the
figure of the cornerstone.

It is not difficult to see what the New Testament means by
designating Christ as cornerstone of the new temple. It refers, in
the first instance, to his pre-eminence, both in dignity and in
time. Only the choicest stones were used for cornerstones, and
pride of place was given to the one laid at the determinative
corner of the building, which was naturally the first one laid.
Christ is thus the beginning of the church; and in this respect the
figure of the cornerstone approximates in sense to the conception
of Christ as the first-born among many brethren and the first
fruits of the resurrection. Secondly, the designation also suggests
the close relationship between Christ and the church. Christians
are joined primarily to Christ and secondarily to one another.
'Come to *him*, to that living stone . . .' (1 Pet. 2. 4). There is also
the suggestion that Christ presupposes Christians as Christians
presuppose Christ. The two belong together and together form
the church. The closeness of the bond uniting them is indicated

by the description of Christ as a living stone to whom the faithful
are joined as living stones and by the statement that the temple
grows. This aspect of the temple image was well understood by the
early church fathers, who liked to describe the new temple as
a monolith (Hermas, *Sim.* ix. 9). There is no suggestion, however,
that the relationship between Christ and those joined to him is
so close that they are indistinguishable one from the other. As
cornerstone Christ's position is well defined and conspicuous.
Finally, the image serves to convey the dependence of the church
upon Christ. What the chief cornerstone was to an ancient
building, Christ is to his church. He supports it and determines
its 'lie', 'shape', unity, and growth. The foregoing ideas are
perhaps nowhere better expressed than in the Latin hymn from
the seventh century:

> Christ is made the sure foundation,
>   Christ the head and cornerstone,
> Chosen of the Lord and precious,
>   Binding all the church in one,
> Holy Zion's help for ever,
>   And her confidence alone.

   The temple image is particularly suggestive in what it has to
teach us concerning the life of the church. This is conveyed
under the image of building (construction), and is conceived of in
different ways. It is the responsibility of the apostles (2 Cor. 10.
8; 12. 19; 13. 10), each of whom has his own particular job
(1 Cor. 3. 10 f.; cf. Rom. 15. 20). It is also a duty enjoined upon
every believer (1 Cor. 14. 12; Rom. 15. 2). The gifts of the
ascended Lord are for this specific purpose (Eph. 4. 7 ff.), and
are worth while only if they contribute to this end (1 Cor. 14).
The church also possesses its own inherent powers of growth by
virtue of its union with Christ the living stone, and 'upbuilds
itself in love' (Eph. 4. 16).
   The conception of the church as a building under construction, with no suggestion of when the work will be completed, and
at the same time as a temple in which God is actually dwelling
and worship is being offered, looks like a contradiction. What
we have here, however, is a paradox which is basic to much
New Testament thinking, the paradox of present possession and
future hope. Like each of its members, the church is called to
become what it is, the dwelling-place of God in the Spirit.

Recognition of this fact preserves the church from the twin evils of complacency and despair.

The image of the church as God's temple conveys certain ideas concerning the church's life and task. Here one must proceed with caution. When the New Testament writers call the church God's temple or Christ's body they are not so much formulating a doctrine of the church as indicating how the faithful should live. In other words, the primary interest is ethical.[1]

The first mark of the church as God's temple is holiness. The temple is the temple *of God*, and is therefore holy. The Holy Spirit sanctifies the Christian community just as the divine presence sanctified the temple of Jerusalem. There is nothing mechanical or magical about the sanctification of the new temple. Holiness has now been transferred from a physical to an ethical basis, and is enjoined upon the church. Members are to glorify God in their bodies and put away every defilement of body and spirit, edifying (building up) one another in love and good works.

A further mark of the church as the temple is unity. To think of the church as God's dwelling is to think of its oneness. The principle of 'one God one temple' was as central to the minds of New Testament Christians as it was to their Jewish forbears. Temples in the plural is a characteristic of paganism and unthinkable. Hence we find Paul counteracting the divisive tendencies of the Corinthians by reminding them that they are God's temple. Ignatius similarly appeals to his readers: 'hasten all (of you) to come together as to one temple (ἕνα ναόν) of God' (Mg. 7. 2). The unity of the church is a unity which arises from God's indwelling his people, and it is to be guarded as zealously as one guards a holy place.

The temple image also points to the church's worship and service. This is the special feature of First Peter's treatment, where the *raison d'être* of the church is set forth as worship. Thus we pass into the realm of ideas expressed under the images of the priesthood and cult. If there was a new temple it followed that there was a new priesthood and sacrifice. The thought of Christians as priests is present in a number of New Testament texts and implied in others. 'You are . . . a royal priesthood' (1 Pet.

[1] Cf. F. W. Dillistone, *The Structure of the Divine Society* (1951), p. 69; Best, op. cit., p. 192 n.

2. 9; cf. v. 5). 'To him who loves us and has freed us from our
sins by his blood and made us a kingdom, priests to his God and
Father' (Rev. 1. 5 f.). 'Thou wast slain and by thy blood didst
ransom men for God . . . and hast made them a kingdom and
priests to our God' (5. 9 f.; cf. 20. 6). It is present by implication
in the various exhortations to believers to offer sacrifices to God
(Rom. 12. 1; 1 Pet. 2. 5; Heb. 13. 15 f.) and wherever worship
and witness are couched in sacrificial language (Heb. 4. 16; 7.
25; 10. 21 f.; Eph. 2. 18; also see below). The Christian community thus realizes the Old Testament ideal of the priesthood of
the whole people of God (Exod. 19. 6; Isa. 61. 6). Classic Pro-
testantism sought to recover this principle in its doctrine of the
'priesthood of all believers', but unfortunately this has more often
than not been taken to mean the individual Christian's privilege
of access to God in private prayer or, worse, his right to his own
interpretation of the scriptures. One way or the other, much
worship and witness is vitiated by a clericalism that obscures
the ministry of the whole congregation. The priesthood of
believers, as the New Testament understands it, is the priesthood of the body corporate. The church's responsibilities in this
regard are in no way fulfilled or lessened by its appointment of
particular individuals, ministers, priests, deacons, or others, since
these are for the purpose of building up the body (Eph. 4. 11 ff.)
so that it may the more effectively discharge its obligations. This
fundamental fact of New Testament thinking on the ministry will
be more readily grasped if we speak of the priesthood of the faithful rather than of the priesthood of the laity. All Christians are
priests, some are parsons (Luther).

Christian sacrifice takes different forms. First and foremost is
the sacrifice of praise and thanksgiving for the salvation pro-
cured by Christ's offering (Heb. 13. 15; Rev. 5. 8 ff., etc.). Since
it is at the eucharist that this sacrifice is most commonly offered
one may speak of the eucharistic sacrifice, though the expression
is not found in the New Testament. Next to praise and thanksgiving are good deeds and charity (Heb. 13. 16). The New
Testament's reference to material and monetary gifts as sacrifices
(Phil. 4. 18; cf. 2. 30; 2 Cor. 9. 12; Rom. 15. 27; Acts 24. 17)
warns us against thinking that the Christian cult is purely spiritual
in character, as worship 'in spirit and truth' (John 4. 23 f.) is
sometimes mistakenly taken to mean. The inclusive nature of the

new sacrifice is indicated by the exhortation to Christians to offer their bodies, i.e. their whole selves, as a sacrifice to God (Rom. 12. 1).[1]

Christians also have sacrifices to offer on behalf of others. This in fact is the whole point of the New Testament in calling Christians priests: a priesthood exists not for its own sake but for others. The sacrifice which one invariably thinks of in this connection is intercession; the faithful pray for others including those who do not pray for themselves. Actually the writers of the New Testament never call prayer a sacrifice, though they very likely thought of it as such. The aspect of the church's priestly service on behalf of the world that is most to the fore in the New Testament is its mission. Here once again we witness the church assuming the functions and responsibilities of Israel (cf. Exod. 19. 5 f.; Zech. 8. 20 ff.; Isa. 61. 5 f.). Thus First Peter says, 'You are . . . a royal priesthood . . . that you may declare the wonderful deeds of him who called you out of darkness into his marvellous light' (2. 9). Similarly, Paul states, 'My priestly service (ἱερουργεῖν) is the preaching of the gospel of God, and it falls to me to offer the Gentiles to him as an acceptable sacrifice (προσφορά) consecrated by the Holy Spirit' (Rom. 15. 16 NEB; cf. 11. 13). Those converted are the sacred first fruits (ἀπαρχή) (1 Cor. 16. 15; 2 Thess. 2. 13; cf. Rev. 14. 4 f.). In turn, the converts are themselves sacrifices, to which the missionary's life is added as a libation (Phil. 2. 17).

This line of thought suggests a meaningful way of understanding the church's calling in the world. It encourages one to regard every act of service and self-denial done for others in Christ's name and for his sake, every act of Christian witness, as a sacrifice acceptable to God and well-pleasing in his sight. It also helps us to think of the church not simply as those who meet together in certain buildings at certain times but also as those who are scattered in the world, and of worship not only as that which is offered to God on particular occasions but as that which is going on everywhere all the time.[2]

The ideas represented by the church as God's temple are thus

---

[1] The same will be in mind if, as seems likely, the *imitatio Christi* is viewed as a sacrifice (cf., above pp. 129 f. on 1 Pet., and A. Richardson, *An Introduction to the Theology of the New Testament* (1958), p. 296 on Eph. 5. 2).

[2] For priesthood as service in the world, see Eastwood, op. cit. pp. 232 ff.

of value not only for our understanding of the church's inner life and structure but also of its life and task in the world.[1]

In all this it is of paramount importance to remind ourselves that the priestly and sacrificial nature of the Christian life depends upon the sacrifice made by Jesus Christ. It is this above all that distinguishes the Christian priesthood from its Jewish and pagan counterparts. It is this that makes the church's offering not only acceptable to God but possible at all. In the same way as the death and resurrection of Christ resolved the age-old problem of mankind's providing a temple fit for God, so it enables mankind to offer acceptable worship to God. Christ is the priest *par excellence*, the 'great priest over the house of God' (Heb. 10. 21). The church's offering is taken up, sanctified, and incorporated (and thereby perfected) in his offering, and consequently made acceptable and pleasing to God. Hence we are exhorted 'to offer spiritual sacrifices acceptable to God *through Jesus Christ*' (1 Pet. 2. 5) . . . '*through him* let us continually offer up a sacrifice of praise to God' (Heb. 13. 15).

The fundamental New Testament conviction that the church's offering is dependent upon the offering of Christ leads naturally and directly to the conception that worship offered on earth is indissolubly joined with the worship offered in heaven, and that even now the faithful share in the worship of heaven; 'with angels and archangels, and with all the company of heaven, we laud and magnify thy glorious name'. Christians enjoy 'every spiritual blessing in the heavenly places' (Eph. 1. 3), they are 'fellow citizens with the saints and members of the household of God' (2. 19), they are 'surrounded by a great cloud of witnesses' (Heb. 12. 1), and 'have come to Mount Zion and to the city of the living God' (12. 22). Once again the temple image proved a useful symbol. How could the idea of access to God and nearness to him—the great feature of the new economy of salvation—be more expressively conveyed than under the images of the rent veil and the city whose temple is God and the Lamb? We touch here upon an aspect of New Testament teaching on the church which is important for present-day liturgical and ecclesiastical formulations. It is the conception that the faithful are eschatologically present in heaven and already sharing in the heavenly

---

[1] Cf. Best (op. cit., pp. 111, 142, 189), who believes that the body image has to do simply with the internal life of the church.

worship of the Lamb. The church that is called to serve men on earth is the church that serves God in heaven; the degree to which it is able to make its own particular contribution to the world's life depends upon the degree of its nearness to God.

The way is thus prepared for the use of the temple image as the symbol of the life of the faithful in the world to come. When the seer of the Apocalypse writes: 'I saw no temple in the city, for its temple is the Lord God the Almighty and the Lamb' (21. 22), he does not mean that the new Jerusalem does not have a temple. To be told that there is, after all, no new temple would be disconcerting, to say the least. What John means is that the temple of the new Jerusalem is God himself, who is directly and fully accessible to his people through his Son the Lamb. The intimacy predicted by Ezekiel for those who were without a temple in Babylon ('I will be to them a temple', 11. 16) is now experienced, but in an infinitely greater way. The same idea of full and uninterrupted communion with God is also suggested if John's words are interpreted to mean that the new Jerusalem has no temple because it is all temple. Not only is God a temple to the faithful; the faithful are a temple to him. 'If anyone loves me he will keep my word, and my Father will love him, and we will come to him and make our dwelling with him' (John 14. 23). The faithful in God and God in the faithful—this is the goal of salvation. Not in this world but in the world to come is the end and destiny of men to be sought.

APPENDIX A

The Foundation-Stone in Zion

THE conception of the foundation-stone in Zion at Isa. 28. 16 held great fascination for the rabbis. The following midrash conveys well the importance attached to the idea:

> The land of Israel lies in the middle of the world; Jerusalem lies in the middle of the land of Israel; the holy area lies in the middle of Jerusalem; the house of the temple lies in the middle of the holy area; the tabernacle lies in the middle of the temple house; and the foundation-stone (אבן שתיה)[1] lies in the front of the ark,[2] and from it the world issued. (Tanhuma, Qᵉdhôshîm, ed. Buber, p. 39a.)[3]

The statement that the foundation-stone lies in the holy of holies points to what is an ancient tradition. The Mishnah explains that after the disappearance of the ark from the temple a stone took its place (Yoma 5. 2), and in an old *baraitha* the idea is developed with scriptural passages in support of the theory that this stone was the embryo from which the whole of creation grew:

> A Tanna taught: (It was so called *shᵉthiyyāh*) because from it the world was founded. We were taught in accord with the view that the world was started (created) from Zion on. For it was taught: R. Eliezer (probably ben Hyrkanos, *c.* A.D. 100) says: The World was created from its centre, as it is said: *When the dust runneth into a mass, and the clouds keep fast together* (Job 38. 38). R. Joshua (b. Hananiah, *c.* 100) said: The world was created from its sides on, as it is said, *For He saith to the snow: 'Fall thou on the earth'; 'likewise to the shower of rain, and to the showers of His mighty rain* (Job 37. 6).[4] R. Isaac the Smith (*c.* 300) said, the Holy One, blessed be He, cast a stone into the ocean, from which the world was then founded, as it is said: *Whereupon were the foundations thereof fastened, or who laid the cornerstone thereof?* (Job 38. 6). But the Sages said: The world was (started) created from Zion, as it is said: *A Psalm of Asaph, God, God, the Lord (hath spoken)* (Ps. 50. 1), whereupon it reads on:

---

[1] The literal meaning of *shᵉthiyyāh* is 'foundation'. For convenience sake we use the term 'foundation-stone'. G. Friedlander suggests that *shᵉthiyyāh* means 'God has set (or fixed it' (*PRE*, p. 266)). Cf. D. Feuchtwang, 'Das Wasseropfer und die damit verbundenen Zeremonien', *MGWJ* 54 (1910), 720 ff.; J. Jeremias, 'Golgotha und der heilige Felsen', *Ang.* 2 (1926), 91 ff.

[2] i.e. in the holy of holies.

[3] S–B iii. 182 f.

[4] The dispute was part of the controversy concerning cosmological and cosmogonical topics which was carried on by these two rabbis. The opinion of R. Eliezer was most widely held.

Out of Zion, the perfection of the world (Ps. 50. 2), that means from Zion was the beauty of the world perfected (B. Yoma 54a, cf. Lev. R. 20. 4).

Many Midrashim enlarge upon the notion. The foundation-stone is regarded as the first solid thing created in the primeval morasses. In this connection the rabbis liked to draw an analogy from current physiological conceptions. As the body of an embryo grows in the mother's womb from its navel so the earth is formed concentrically around this stone:

> God created the world like an embryo. Just as the embryo proceeds from the navel onwards, so God began to create the world proceeding from its navel onwards and from there it was spread out in different directions. Where is the navel? It is Jerusalem. The navel itself is the altar. And why is it called *'ébhen sheˠthiyyāh*? Because the world was established from it (Bet ha-Midr. 5. 63. 1 ff.).[1]

The equation of the stone and the altar in this passage is highly significant and will have our attention below. For the present we have to understand how the stone in Zion came to be regarded as the highest point of the universe.

In oriental cosmogony the earth was thought of as a kind of hemispherical dome-shaped mountain which emerged out of the cosmic ocean (Ps. 104. 7 ff.). The mountain tops, since they were first to appear, were naturally regarded as the first things to be created, and the ancients always held that their temples were erected upon the primeval mountain. The Jews understandably made similar claims for their temple. Since Zion was the mountain *par excellence* the rock at its peak was regarded as the topmost part of the cosmos. The rabbis thus followed the prophets and psalmists of the Old Testament in thinking of Jerusalem as elevated high above the rest of the world (B. Ḳid. 69b; B. Zeb. 54b; Gen. R. 32. 10).

Now as the highest point of the world the sacred rock of Zion was easily regarded as the point of entry into heaven. In this connection the story of Jacob at Bethel provided most inspiration for the rabbis. Jacob's altar (understood by the rabbis as the *'ébhen sheˠthiyyāh*) is called the door to the upper world (Gen. R. 68. 12).[2] To be buried there is to be buried under the throne of God (B. Keth. 111a). The symbolism was developed still further. The place in the temple of

---

[1] The designation of the temple (or part of it) as the navel of the earth rests upon an ancient tradition (cf. Ezek. 5. 5 ff.; 38. 12; cf. Jub. 8. 12 ff.). Cf. A. J. Wensinck, 'The Ideas of the Western Semites Concerning the Navel of the Earth', *VAA* 17. i (1916), 1–65. The Greeks regarded the sanctuary of Apollo as the navel of the earth (Pl. *Rep.* iv. 427 c).

[2] Cf. Gen. 28. 17, where Jacob says of Bethel, 'How awesome is this place . . . this is the gate of heaven', and Deut. 4. 11, where Sinai is described as burning 'to the heart of heaven'.

Jerusalem marked by the stone is not only the entrance to the upper world; it in fact belongs to it. The heavens, no less than the earth, owe their existence to the foundation-stone (B. Yoma 54b; Nu. R. 12. 4). For the rock in the holy of holies is pre-existent and lay at Bethel long before Jacob found it.[1]

It is as the entrance to the lower world ($t^e h \hat{o} m$), however, that the sacred rock in Zion held greatest fascination for the rabbis. According to Semitic cosmology, the primeval waters were always liable to rise up and engulf the world again as had happened at the flood (Gen. 7. 11; 8. 2; cf. Job 7. 12). The foundation-stone therefore came to be invested with the important function of shutting off the exit from the mighty deep. The Talmud tells the story of how David on digging the foundations of the temple came upon a sherd. On his attempting to move the sherd the deep began to rise up and threatened to submerge the earth (B. Suk. 53ab; B. Mak. 11a). The Palestinian version of the legend suggests that the sherd was identified with the foundation-stone:

> The sherd said: 'You cannot lift me'. David said: 'Why?' The sherd replied: 'Because I am here to press down the deep'. David asked: 'And since when are you here?' The sherd answered: 'From the hour when God let his word be heard on Mount Sinai, saying, 'I am the Lord thy God'. At that time the earth trembled and sank, and I was put here to press down the deep' (P. Sanh. 29a).[2]

In other words, the rock which God has placed in Zion maintains the well-being of the universe by keeping the flood waters of the unruly abyss at bay.

Access to the deep was nevertheless regarded as desirable and necessary, since the deep supplied the earth with water. Israel had always valued the 'blessings of the deep that couches beneath' (Gen. 49. 25; cf. Deut. 33. 13; Ps. 33. 7), and, as might be expected, the stone in Zion was said to mark the spot where the resources of the powerful subterranean ocean were tapped for the well-being of man and beast. Hence the stone came to be known as the 'stone of quench-ing' (P. Yoma 42c). As such, the stone in Zion, connected as it was with the altar in the temple, contributed greatly to the mythology associated with the rain-making ceremonies of the Feast of Taber-nacles.[3] At Tabernacles water and wine were ceremoniously poured

---

[1] Jeremias, *Ang.* 2 (1926), 93.

[2] Cf. R. Patai, *Man and Temple in Ancient Jewish Myth and Ritual* (1947) p. 57. For similar notions in Babylonian literature see A. Parrot, *Babylon and the Old Testament* (1958), p. 49 n.

[3] S–B iii. 182; Jeremias, 'Golgotha', op. cit., p. 96; cf. Feuchtwang, op. cit., pp. 722 f.; Patai, op. cit., pp. 24 ff.

into funnels at the sides of the altar and flowed, as it was believed, into the abyss (B. Suk. 49a). The intention of this piece of ritual was to induce the sympathetic co-operation of the great deep in order that there should be an adequate supply of water for the ensuing season.[1]

Still more interesting in this connection is the eschatological orientation of the tradition. R. Eliezer ben Jacob (c. 90), commenting upon the water as the priest poured it into the holes at the sides of the altar, said, 'Hereafter they (the waters) will issue out from under the threshold of the House' (M. Shek. 6. 3). At what point the connection between the water-pouring ceremony of Tabernacles and Ezekiel's river from the new temple was made we have no means of knowing, but that Zech. 14. 16–19 contributed to it seems indisputable. Zech. 14 was in fact one of the *haphtaroth* or readings used at Tabernacles (B. Meg 31a).[2] Moreover, the gift of water, which it was hoped the rite would secure, came to be regarded as a symbol of the outpouring of the Holy Spirit in the messianic times (P. Suk. 55a; Gen. R. 70. 8).[3] All these conceptions owe something to the idea of the temple, or more precisely the sacred rock in the temple, as the navel of the earth.

Now the deep in ancient thinking is the habitat of the spirits of the dead. Accordingly it is at the navel of the earth that Enoch sees the 'accursed valley', i.e. Gehenna (26–7), and Jerusalem is regarded as one of the entrances to Gehenna (B. 'Er. 19a; cf. Gen. R. 44. 21). But also in the underworld are Sheol and Paradise, and the altar-stone thus marks the entrance to the place of the righteous departed. Already in the Pseudepigrapha it is stated that Adam is buried 'in the land of his creation' (Jub. 4. 29), and according to *Vita Adae et Evae*, 45, Adam requested to be laid to rest 'towards the sunrising in the field of yonder dwelling', i.e. the sanctuary (cf. Jub. 8. 19; *PRE* 20). The Apocalypse of Moses states that Adam and Abel were buried in the spot where God found the dust to make Adam (40), i.e. at the altar-stone (cf. Gen. R. 14. 8).[4] There Adam's remains rest safely beyond the reach of the destructive flood waters of the deep (*PRE* 20). There too under the altar Melchizedek lies.[5] Since the altar-stone was also believed to be the entrance to heaven, it followed that the souls under the altar were considered to be close to God. 'Everyone who is

[1] Cf. B. Ta'an 2ab; 25b; P. Suk. 54b; P. R.H. 57b.
[2] H. St. J. Thackeray, *The Septuagint and Jewish Worship* (1921), pp. 64 ff.
[3] S–B ii. 434 f.
[4] On the Syriac legends on Adam's burial in 'the cave of treasures' also see Wensinck, op. cit., pp. 27 ff.; and generally Jeremias, 'Wo lag Golgotha und das Heilige Grab?', op. cit., pp. 141–73.
[5] *The Book of the Secrets of Enoch*. Appendix, ed. W. H. Morfill and R. H. Charles (1896), p. 91.

buried under the altar is as though he were buried under the throne of God' (Aboth of R. Nathan 26).[1]

This survey shows how the foundation-stone of Isa. 28. 16 was developed into an all-embracing tradition. The stone in Zion is the foundation not only of the temple but of the universe. It is as much a physiological and theological as a geographical phenomenon. From this stone creation grows and draws its life. Here the destinies of the living and the dead are fixed. Here too the new world will emerge.

[1] Cf. R. Eliezer (c. 90) : 'The souls of the righteous are hidden under the Throne of Glory' (B. Shab. 152b). Also B. Keth. 111a; Rev. 6. 9.

APPENDIX B

Upon this Rock

How one should interpret our Lord's designation of Peter as the rock upon which he will build his church at Matt. 16. 18 is not at all clear. The substantive 'rock' (πέτρα, Aramaic כיפא) in the New Testament refers to rocky ground (Luke 8. 6), such as one might use for laying the foundation of a building upon (Luke 6. 48), or to a piece of rock, i.e. a stone (λίθος), which one might use for the foundation or other part of a building (Rom. 9. 33; 1 Pet. 2. 7 f.).

Scholars are divided as to which of these meanings πέτρα has at Matt. 16. 18. Selwyn thinks that it means the ground upon which the foundation is laid,[1] Schlatter thinks that it denotes a stone,[2] while Lindars goes further and identifies it as the cornerstone.[3]

The thought of the text resembles that of Matt. 7. 24 par.,[4] and the fact that a definite connection between Matt. 16. 18 and Matt. 7. 24 is made in the long recension of Ignatius' epistle to the Philadelphians ('God established his church upon the rock . . . against which the floods and winds have beaten but have not been able to overcome it')[5] suggests that πέτρα in Matt. 16. 18 stands for the ground upon which the foundation is laid. Support for this interpretation may be found in 1 QH 6. 26 f., 'Thou wilt set the foundation (of the community) upon rock (על סלע סוד)' (cf. 7. 8–9).[6] On the other hand, if the rock in mind is the foundation-stone of Isa. 28. 16 and the *'ébhen sheᵉthiyyāh* of the rabbis,[7] as the reference to the underworld ('gates of Hades') suggests,[8] then the evidence tips in favour of the rock being a stone. Jeremias thus identifies the rock of our text with the historic rock in Zion which at once held down the powers of the deep and acted as the foundation of the temple of Jerusalem.[9] Drawing upon the rabbinic habit of personalizing the rock as Abraham, this scholar writes:

---

[1] E. G. Selwyn, *The First Epistle of St. Peter* (1946), p. 163.

[2] A. Schlatter, *Der Evangelist Matthäus* (1929), p. 507.

[3] Lindars, op. cit., p. 182.

[4] J. A. Bengel, *Gnomon of the New Testament* (1857), i. 324.

[5] O. J. F. Seitz, 'Upon this Rock: A Critical Re-examination of Matt. 16. 17–19', *JBL* 69 (1950), 329–40.

[6] Dupont-Sommer, op. cit., p. 220. Cf. Betz, op. cit., pp. 76 ff.; above, p. 52.

[7] On which see Appendix A.

[8] In the Old Testament the deep is represented as having gates, which threaten to enclose mortals (Pss. 9. 13; 107. 18; Job 38. 17; Jonah 2. 6; cf. Wisd. 16. 13).

[9] *Jesus als Weltvollender*, pp. 62 f.

Just as Abraham was the rock upon which the temple of the old covenant was built, so Peter, as the recipient of the divine revelation, is the rock upon which the new temple of the messianic community is built.[1]

The parallel is interesting, but the identification of the building erected upon the rock as a temple has no support in the text.

The most that one can say with any degree of confidence is that the founding of the church is depicted under the general image of the erection of a building upon an impregnable foundation. The builder is Christ, who is thought of as performing a role attributed to God in Jewish writings (1 QH. 6. 26 f.; 7. 8 f.; cf. 1 Sam. 2. 35; 2 Sam. 7. 11, etc.). The reference is to the future, in the first instance presumably to the death and resurrection of Jesus Christ, which will mark the beginning of the new people of God. What relation Peter has to the church is unclear. He may form a part of the building (cf. Eph. 2. 20), or he may not. Yet even if we should not think of the apostle as forming an actual part of the edifice the relationship between him and those who do form the church will be so close that we may think of him in a general sense as the *fundamentum ecclesiae*. Peter who has the divine revelation imparted to him and responds believingly is a type of those living stones who comprise God's house. But too much attention should not be paid to the superstructure which is erected upon the rock, for clearly this is not the point of the image. The emphasis is rather on the foundation and its impregnable character.

[1] Ibid., p. 63. Cf. R. N. Flew, *Jesus and his Church* (1938), p. 93; O. Cullmann, *Peter: Disciple, Apostle, Martyr* (1953), pp. 201 f.; J. Lowe, *Saint Peter* (1956), p. 57.

APPENDIX C

Christ the Cornerstone[1]

THAT the author of the Epistle to the Ephesians intends to attribute special importance to the position in the church occupied by Christ is obvious from the designation cornerstone. The church, he writes, is built upon the foundation (ἐποικοδομηθέντες ἐπὶ τῷ θεμελίῳ) of the apostles and prophets, Christ Jesus himself being the chief cornerstone (ὄντος ἀκρογωνιαίου), in whom the whole structure is joined together (ἐν ᾧ πᾶσα οἰκοδομὴ συναρμολογουμένη) and grows into a holy temple in the Lord (αὔξει εἰς ναὸν ἅγιον ἐν Κυρίῳ) in whom you also are built into it (ἐν ᾧ καὶ ὑμεῖς συνοικοδομεῖσθε) for a dwelling place (εἰς κατοικητήριον) of God in the Spirit (2. 20–2).

It is clear that the cornerstone is conceived of as unifying the new temple. The precise location of the stone is less clear.

Traditionally commentators have held that the stone is at the foot of the building, at one of the corners.[2] On the face of it, this appears to be the natural sense, especially if one is to be guided by Isa. 28. 16, the sole LXX text in which the rare word ἀκρογωνιαῖος occurs. But this interpretation was so energetically contested by Jeremias some years ago that it has few supporters today. Jeremias argued that the stone in question is connected not with the lower part of the building

---

[1] Based on an article by the author in *NTS* 8 (1962), 352–9.

[2] So Eusebius of Caesarea (*PG* 24. 291); Marius Victorinus (*PL* 8. 1261); Ambrosiaster (*PL* 17. 402); Jerome (*PL* 24. 333 f.); Chrysostom (*PG* 62. 44); Augustine (*PL* 37. 1101 f.); Pelagius (*Pelagius's Expositions on Thirteen Epistles of St. Paul*, ed. A. Souter (1926), ii. 356); Cyril of Alexandria (*PG* 72. 880 f.); Theodoret (*PG* 82. 525); Cassiodorus (*PL* 70. 832); Bede (*PL* 92. 252, 577); Theophylact (*PG* 124. 1065); Calvin (*Inst.* 4. 6, 5; *Serm.* 15, col. 430); J. A. Bengel (*Gnomon of the New Testament* (1863), iii. 80); W. W. Lloyd (*CRev.*, 3 (1889), 419), T. K. Abbott (*The Epistles to the Ephesians and to the Colossians* (1897), p. 70); J. A. Robinson (*St. Paul's Epistle to the Ephesians* (1903), p. 164), *EGT* (1903), iii. 299); G. H. Whitaker ('The Chief Corner Stone', *Exp.* 22 (8th ser. 1921), 471); J. H. Moulton and G. Milligan (*VGT* (1930), p. 19); E. F. Scott (*The Epistles of Paul to the Colossians, to Philemon and to the Ephesians* (1930), p. 178). The only ancient authority that I know of who interpreted the cornerstone differently was Tertullian. He took it to be a top-stone (*Adv. Marc.* 3. 7). Augustine (*PL* 37. 110 ff.) and Pelagius (ed. Souter, op. cit., p. 356) can, however, think of Christ as both corner- and top-stones of the building. It may be added that the stone at the head of the corner (κεφαλὴ γωνίας) of Ps. 117 (118). 22 is understood by Origen (*In Matt.* 21. 24, ed. E. Klostermann (1899), pp. 615 f.), Hilary of Poitiers (*PL* 9. 1942), and Ammonius of Alexandria (*PL* 85. 1385) as a top-stone.

but with the top (the pinnacle or πτερύγιον of Matt. 4. 5 par.). It is
a copestone, an *Abschlussstein* and not a *Grundstein*.[1] In support of this
interpretation, Jeremias cited a number of texts, the most important
of which was the apocryphal first-century (A.D.) Jewish Testament of
Solomon.[2] The passage in question, which describes how at the erection of the temple of Jerusalem Solomon had a cornerstone put at the
top of the building, reads as follows:

> 22. 7 And Jerusalem had been built and the temple was in process of
> completion (συνεπληροῦτο). And there was a great cornerstone (λίθος
> ἀκρογωνιαῖος) which I wished to put at the head of the corner crown-
> ing the temple of God (εἰς κεφαλὴν γωνίας τῆς πληρώσεως τοῦ ναοῦ
> 8 τοῦ Θεοῦ). And all the tradesmen and all the spirits who laboured on it
> came together to bring the stone and set it on the pinnacle of the
> 9 temple (εἰς τὸ πτερύγιον τοῦ ναοῦ) but they could not shift it. [Solomon
> then recounts how he despatched a servant to Arabia with instruc-
> tions to capture a powerful spirit. The creature is duly brought to the
> 23. 1 king, who addresses it.] I said to him, 'What can you do?' He said,
> 'I have power both to move mountains and to lay low the palaces of
> 2 kings.' I replied to him, 'Then, if you are able, lift this stone and set it
> at the point of the corner of the temple (εἰς τὴν ἀρχὴν τῆς γωνίας τοῦ
> 3 ναοῦ). [The Spirit] obeyed, crawled under the stone, lifted it, and
> went up the steps, carrying the stone, and placed it at the summit of
> the entrance to the temple (εἰς τὴν ἄκραν τῆς εἰσόδου τοῦ ναοῦ).
> 4 And I Solomon rejoiced and said, 'Truly, the scripture is now fulfilled
> which said: The stone which the builders rejected is become the head
> of the corner (κεφαλὴν γωνίας).'[3]

The new interpretation gained additional support from the attractive correspondence it suggested between the position of Christ in the
building (οἰκοδομή) as the top-stone and his position in the body
(σῶμα) as the head. Thus we find one commentator writing, 'As
Christ is the κεφαλή of the σῶμα, he is the ἀκρογωνιαῖος of the οἰκοδομή'.[4]
Hence most exegetes follow Jeremias,[5] and some go further and understand ἀκρογωνιαῖος as a keystone (*clef de voûte*), which, placed in the

---

[1] J. Jeremias, 'Der Eckstein', *Ang.* 1 (1925) 65–70. The interpretation was
subsequently supported on a number of occasions: 'Κεφαλὴ γωνίας—ἀκρογωνιαῖος',
ZNW 29 (1930), 264–80; *Jesus als Weltvollender* (1930), p. 80; 'Eckstein–Schluss-
stein', *ZNW* 36 (1937), 154–7; *TDNT* i. 792 f.; *TWNT* iv. 277–83.

[2] The other authorities used by Jeremias are 2 Kgs. 25. 17 (Symmachus), which
translates כתרת ('chapiter', RV, 'capital', RSV) by *akrogōniaios*, Isa. 28. 16
(Peshitta), which renders cornerstone as 'head of the wall', and Aphraates,
Hom. 1. 6 f.

[3] Translation by C. C. McCown, *The Testament of Solomon* (1922), pp. 66–70.

[4] Hanson, *The Unity of the Church in the New Testament*, p. 131.

[5] Dibelius, *An die Kolosser, Epheser, an Philemon*, pp. 54 f.; Schlier, *Christus und die
Kirche im Epheserbrief*, p. 49; F. Jeremias, 'Das orientalische Heiligtum', *Ang.* 4
(1932), 64 f.; Cadbury, *The Beginnings of Christianity*, v. 374; Michel, *TWNT* iv.

centre of the archway which, it is assumed, spanned the entrance, is said to have acted as a locking stone for the whole building.[1] The traditional interpretation has some modern supporters, however, and Jeremias's argument has been contested on several occasions.[2] The matter calls for further consideration.

Before we examine the new interpretation we include for the sake of completeness another piece of evidence which shows that corner-stones were used at the top of the temple of Jerusalem. It is from one of the recently discovered apocalypses of James.[3] This adds to our knowledge of the particulars of James's martyrdom from the memoirs of Hegesippus (which state that James was testifying to his Lord from the pinnacle of the temple (ἐπὶ τὸ πτερύγιον τοῦ ναοῦ) when the scribes and Pharisees hurled him down to the Kidron valley)[4] by informing us that James stood on a cornerstone:

> They found him [James] standing on the battlement of the temple, on the solid cornerstone (ⲕⲟⲟϩ). They consented to cast him down from the height and they cast him down . . ., and [since he was not killed outright] they seized him and dragged him, stretching him out on the ground and throwing a stone on his stomach (61. 20 ff.)[5]

The Coptic word ⲕⲟⲟϩ means 'corner' or 'angle' (γωνία, γωνιαῖος), and it is used at 1 Pet. 2. 6 in the sahidic and boharic versions to translate ἀκρογωνιαῖος. But although the main idea connoted is ex-tremity there is no doubt whatever that the stone in mind in the present text occupied an elevated position.

This text and those quoted by Jeremias show that cornerstones were used at the top of buildings. This point is not in dispute; the question is whether the cornerstone of Eph. 2. 20 is at the top or bottom of the building.

Before we consider whether the cornerstone of Eph. 2. 20 can justifiably be regarded as the top-most cornerstone a preliminary point is clear. There is little, if any, justification for taking the corner-stone at the top of the building as the keystone of the arch, which, it is

892; Vielhauer, op. cit., p. 127; A. K. Coomaraswamy, 'Ekstein', *Speculum*, 14 (1939), 66 ff.; Hanson, op. cit., p. 131; E. E. E. Le Bas, 'Was the Corner-Stone of Scripture a Pyramidion?', *PEQ* 82 (1946), 103–15.

[1] Wenschkewitz, op. cit., p. 178; Cerfaux, *The Church in the Theology of St. Paul*, p. 346; Best, op. cit., p. 166. Cf. the footnote to Eph. 2. 20 in the NEB.

[2] G. B. Ladner, 'The Symbolism of the Biblical Corner Stone in the Medieval West', *MS* 4 (1942) 43–60; E. Percy, *Die Probleme der Kolosser- und Epheserbriefe* (1946), pp. 329 ff., 485 f.; S. Lyonnet, 'De Christo summo angulari lapide secundum Eph. 2. 20', *VD* 27 (1949), 74 ff.; Mussner, op. cit., pp. 108 f.

[3] The text is published by A. Böhlig and P. Labib in *Koptisch-gnostische Apokalypsen aus Codex V von Nag Hammadi* (1963).

[4] Eusebius, *HE* 2. 23. 3–18.

[5] A. Böhlig, 'Zum Martyrium des Jakobus', *NT* 5 (1962), 210.

held, spanned the entrance to the temple. Here Jeremias was more careful than his followers.[1] In the first place, the keystone interpretation loses the whole thrust of γωνιαῖος in ἀκρογωνιαῖος. The stone ceases to be a stone *at the corner*. Even if in New Testament times γωνιαῖος had lost its force and ἄκρος had come to reflect the dominant sense of the word, the texts quoted above indicate beyond question that the stone occupied a corner or angle. But there are more serious objections to the keystone idea. Apart from the fact that arches do not appear to have been a common feature of Semitic architecture,[2] in none of the texts in which the term ἀκρογωνιαῖος appears is there anything which comes anywhere near to suggesting that a keystone is in mind. Isaiah 28. 16 has, of course, to be ignored. 2 Kgs. 25. 17 at best indicates that the stone occupied an elevated position. Test. Sol. 22. 7 ff. is more specific but the most it proves is that the stone was at a corner of the building. It is said in the context (22. 3) that the stone was placed at the summit of the entrance to the temple (εἰς τὴν ἄκραν τῆς εἰσόδου), but this cannot safely be taken to indicate more than the side or gable-end of the temple in which the door was situated. The keystone interpretation must therefore be rejected as a piece of fanciful exegesis.

We proceed to examine the general top-stone theory.

Our first consideration is building practice in the ancient Near East. Ancient buildings, like those of the present day, had many corner-stones (quoins), the only difference apparently being that they, or at least the ones in the first course, tended to be of considerable size and cost.[3] Unlike modern architecture, which places the first cornerstone on the top of the foundation, which is dug and filled with mortar, ancient architecture began by laying the cornerstone. It was often placed near ground level, and, together with the other stones that were placed next to it, served as the foundation (1 Kgs. 5. 17; 7. 10; Isa. 28. 16; Jer. 51. 26; Job 38. 6). Whether the stones were placed end to end in a line, as was normally the case, or side by side in platform fashion, it was the practice to begin at one corner with the cornerstone. Since this stone was the one that gave the line of the building it was carefully selected, dressed, squared, and tested (cf. Isa. 28. 16).[4] One is not surprised therefore to find it described as

[1] He excluded the possibility of a keystone in *Ang.* 1 (1925), 69; *ZNW* 29 (1930), 277.

[2] But not as uncommon as Lyonnet supposes (op. cit., p. 81). Cf. Yalcut Gen. 102 to Gen. 28. 22; Pirke R. Eliezer 35 (ed. Friedlander, p. 266). Lintels were used in the temple of Herod (M. Mid. 2. 3; F. J. Hollis, *The Archaeology of Herod's Temple* (1934), p. 266).

[3] Sir Charles Warren uncovered one such stone in the temple of Herod which measured 38 feet and 9 inches in length (C. W. Wilson and C. Warren, *The Recovery of Jerusalem* (1871), p. 121).

[4] Stone blocks have been found in ancient Roman quarries bearing the un-

costly (Isa. 28. 16; 1 Kgs. 5. 17). Thus of the many cornerstones in the building the one laid first was naturally regarded as the most important, and its laying the occasion for celebration (Job 38. 6; Ezra 3. 10–11). The rendering 'chief cornerstone' which has come down to us in the Authorized Version and Revised Version from the Vulgate (*summus angularis lapis*),[1] although it has no philological basis in either the Greek or the Hebrew, serves to identify the particular cornerstone in mind.

I do not know of any comparable significance that was attached to the last cornerstone to be laid. Jeremias refers to Ps. 118 (117). 22 ('the stone which the builders rejected has become the head of the corner (רֹאשׁ פִּנָּה, εἰς κεφαλὴν γωνίας)') and Zech. 4. 7 ('Zerubbabel ... shall bring forward the top stone (הָאֶבֶן הָרֹאשָׁה, λίθον τῆς κληρονομίας)').[2] It is true that Symmachus renders רֹאשׁ פנה of Ps. 118. 22 as ἀκρογωνιαῖος, and the author of the Testament of Solomon referred the text to the stone at the top of the temple, but it is by no means certain that the Psalmist had the upper part of the building in mind. The stone may have been used in a new building.[3] Alternatively, the stone of Zech. 4. 7, although it is clearly a stone at the top of the building, is not necessarily a cornerstone. The kind of response expected from the onlookers at the laying of the stone ('Zerubbabel ... shall bring forward the top stone amid shouts of "Grace, grace to it!"', lit. 'how beautiful') and the parallel implied in v. 9 (just as Zerubbabel laid the first stone of the temple so he will lay the last), suggests that a crowning (? apex) stone with a sculptured face is in mind. The weakness of Jeremias's treatment of these texts is due in large part to the assumption with which he begins. Working from the indubitable fact that פנה means 'corner' and is often used for the corners of the walls of Jerusalem (2 Kgs. 14. 13; 2 Chr. 25. 23; Neh. 3. 24, 31 f.), he takes the term to mean battlement.[4] But, as Ladner points out,[5] this is to beg the question since the corners of the city were not necessarily battlements. *Pinnāh* can refer to a corner at any level of the building; in Jer. 51. 26 and Job 38. 6 it is connected (as the parallelism clearly indicates) with the foot of the building. *Rō'sh* intensifies the idea implied in *pinnāh*: it is the stone at the extremity of the angle. But as the term *rō'sh* is frequently used in the sense of first in a series (1 Chr.

favourable verdict REPR (*obatum*) (Sir Wm. Ramsay, *Pauline Studies* (1906), p. 253; *Exp.* 9 (5th series, 1899), pp. 35 f.). Cf. Ps. 118. 22.

[1] Cf. the JB, which reads 'main cornerstone'.

[2] *Ang.* 1 (1925), 67.

[3] If, as is suggested by the use of Ps. 118. 22 in Mark 12. 10 pars. and Acts. 4. 11, the remnant idea is in mind, it does not seem likely that the stone would be used in the same building.

[4] *Ang.* 1 (1925), 65 f.   [5] Op. cit., p. 45.

12. 9 f.; Exod. 12. 2; Num. 10. 10; 28. 11) *rō'sh pinnāh* could refer to the first or chief cornerstone to be laid in the building.

We come now to the keyword ἀκρογωνιαῖος. It is the Koine equivalent of the Attic γωνιαῖος. The fact that it is used in the LXX to translate *pinnāh* at Isa. 28. 16 and by Symmachus to translate *rō'sh-pinnāh* at Ps. 117 (118). 22 shows that it refers to a stone at the corner of the building and that the emphasis is on extremity rather than height. J. Armitage Robinson comments, 'Ἀκρογωνιαῖος stands to γωνιαῖος as ἐπ' ἄκρας γωνίας stands to ἐπὶ γωνίας: the first part of the compound merely heightens the second.'[1] *Akros*, it is true, is chosen by the LXX to represent *rō'sh* and means 'top' (Exod. 34. 2; Isa. 28. 4; Ps. 71 (72). 16; cf. Luke 16. 24), but it frequently stands for קצה, 'end', 'extremity', particularly when the point connoted is viewed in relation to its opposite. For example, the cherubim at either end of the lid of the ark are described thus, 'one cherub on the one end (ἐπὶ τὸ ἄκρον) and one cherub on the other end (ἐπὶ τὸ ἄκρον τὸ δεύτερον)' (Exod. 38 (37). 7). We find the same thing in classical and New Testament Greek. Aristotle in describing the different classes of society speaks of the rich and the poor, the two extremes, as οἱ ἄκροι (*Polit.* IV. x. 4). In the gospel of Mark, the Son of Man is said to gather his elect ἀπ' ἄκρου γῆς ἕως ἄκρου οὐρανοῦ (13. 27).[2] In the compound ἀκρογωνιαῖος, ἄκρος therefore considerably strengthens the force of γωνιαῖος and accentuates the fact that the term refers to a stone at one or other corner of the building.

Now ἄκρος also has the sense of 'first' in time, dignity, order, or position in biblical and classical Greek. This nuance may well be preserved in ἀκρογωνιαῖος; compare ἀκροθίνιον (Hdt. i. 86; viii. 121; Thucyd. i. 132. 2; Heb. 7. 4). The reference would thus be to the first or determinative cornerstone in the building, the one which the builder used to determine the 'lie' and line of the building (πᾶσα (ἡ) οἰκοδομή, Eph. 2. 21).[3] In this case the Latin rendering *summus angularis lapis* and the translation 'chief cornerstone' of the Authorized and Revised Versions may be less widely off the mark than commentators generally hold. However, this is a question in which philology alone will not help us. Much will depend upon the context in which the word is used.

As far as philological considerations are concerned, then, there does not appear to be any strong reason for abandoning the traditional interpretation of ἀκρογωνιαῖος in Eph. 2. 20.

[1] Op. cit., p. 164.
[2] Cf. Deut. 4. 32; 13. 8; 30. 4; Ps. 18. 7 (19. 6); Jer. 12. 12; Matt. 24. 31.
[3] Cf. Whitaker, op. cit., p. 471. The JB renders the text thus, 'As every (the entire) structure is aligned on him, all grow into one holy temple in the Lord'.

The next question to be considered is usage. The texts produced by Jeremias showed that the term ἀκρογωνιαῖος could and did refer to a stone at the top of the edifice. But there are other texts which prove equally conclusively that it indicated a stone at the bottom. We refer to Isa. 28. 16 and the texts based upon it. It will not do to suggest, as Jeremias does, that Isa. 28. 16 is not in mind at Eph. 2. 20. This Old Testament text is directly quoted at Rom. 9. 33 and it would be *a priori* surprising if it (the one LXX passage where ἀκρογωνιαῖος appears) was not in mind in Ephesians (cf. 1 Pet. 2. 6–8). Eph. 2. 20 belongs, as we shall see, to a cluster of 'stone' texts which has as its scriptural proof Isa. 28. 16.[1] In any event, a different sense for ἀκρογωνιαῖος should be sought only if the context itself forces one to look for it.[2] As it is, ἀκρογωνιαῖος stands in the same close relation to θεμέλιος in Eph. 2. 20 as it does in Isa. 28. 16, and the context, as we shall see, makes sense only when a *Grundstein* is in mind.

The context of Isa. 28. 16 warns the apostate rulers of Jerusalem that their vaunted alliance with the powers of the underworld will be destroyed by the upsurging waters, for they have rebelled against Yahweh, the one who in fact controls access to the deep.

Behold, I am laying (ἐμβάλλω) in Zion for a foundation (εἰς τὰ θεμέλια) a stone, a tested stone, a precious cornerstone (ἀκρογωνιαῖον), of a sure foundation (θεμέλια): He who believes (ὁ πιστεύων ἐπ᾽ αὐτῷ[3]) will not be in haste.[4]

The juxtaposition of ἀκρογωνιαῖος and θεμέλιον and the duplicated εἰς τὰ θεμέλια show beyond all doubt that it is the base of the building that is in mind. The wording 'I am laying . . . for (εἰς) a foundation . . . a cornerstone, of a (εἰς) sure foundation' reflects what we have seen was current building practice: the laying of the cornerstone marked the beginning of the foundation (cf. Jer. 51. 26; Job 38. 6).

Jewish exegesis faithfully observed this meaning. The Jews of Qumran, who quoted Isa. 28. 16 in support of their doctrine of the community as a spiritual temple, understood the stone of this text to be a *Grundstein*:

---

[1] Cf. Michel, *TWNT* iv. 892.

[2] Lyonnet, op. cit., p. 80.

[3] The messianic interpretation is already hinted at by the words 'in him', which are not in the Hebrew. The Targum carries the suggestion further: 'Behold, I will appoint in Zion a King, a strong King . . .' (J. F. Stenning, *The Targum of Isaiah* (1949), pp. 88 f.). Cf. E. J. Kissane. *The Book of Isaiah* (1941), i. 318. See below on the use of the text in the Qumran literature.

[4] For a discussion on what the prophet meant by the cornerstone see S. H. Hooke, 'The Corner-Stone in Scripture', *The Siege Perilous* (1956), pp. 235 ff. Hooke believes that the prophet is alluding to the righteous remnant. On the interpretation of the stone in the writings of Qumran see above p. 47 and below p. 202.

They shall lay a foundation (מוסד) of truth for Israel (1 QS 5. 6).[1]

It is the tried wall, the precious corner-stone (פנת יקר); its foundations shall not tremble nor flee from their place. It is the Dwelling of infinite holiness (קודש קודשים) for Aaron . . . the House (בית) of perfection and truth in Israel to establish the Covenant according to the everlasting precepts (8. 7 ff.).[2]

Similarly the rabbis, as we have seen, took the stone in Zion, i.e. the cornerstone of Isa. 28. 16, as a 'foundation' stone. In point of fact, their favourite designation for this stone is '*ébhen sheᵉthiyyāh*, which means literally 'foundation-stone'. The stone was believed to perform the important function of shutting the exit from the great deep and thereby providing a foundation, so to say, upon which God could build the cosmos.[3]

When we come to those New Testament texts in which the term ἀκρογωνιαῖος appears it is plain that a stone at the foot of the building is denoted. First we have Rom. 9. 33 and 1 Pet. 2. 6 ff. By combining the stone of stumbling and the rock of offence (λίθος προσκόμματος καὶ πέτρα σκανδάλου) of Isa. 8. 14 with the cornerstone of Isa. 28. 16 the writers make it clear that they understood the latter as a stone near ground level. The Mishnah states that the rock in the holy of holies stood three finger-breadths above the ground (Yoma 5. 2), and the New Testament writers would easily think of the ἀκρογωνιαῖος as a stone on which one might trip and fall. How this could possibly apply to a stone at the top of the building is not at all clear. As far as Eph. 2. 20 itself is concerned the words ἀκρογωνιαῖος and θεμέλιος stand in too close proximity for the author not to be thinking of the lower part of the building. The passage may best be translated: 'built upon the foundation of the apostles and prophets of which (genitive absol. ὄντος) Christ Jesus himself is the (foremost) cornerstone'.[4] The context (2. 11 ff.) is concerned with the unity of the church, and vv. 19–22 form the conclusion. Christ, 'who has made us both one' (v. 14), is depicted as the cornerstone 'in whom (ἐν ᾧ) the whole structure is joined together (συναρμολογουμένη) and grows into a holy temple in the Lord' (v. 21). The same idea is present at 4. 16, where a physiological image is fused with the architectural image. If, however, we follow Jeremias's suggestion the crucial unifying function attributed to Christ is jettisoned completely, for the stone mentioned in 2 Kgs. 25. 17 and apparently also Test. Sol. 22. 7 ff. was placed on the top of the two pillars (Jachin and Boaz) at the entrance to the

---

[1] Wernberg-Møller, op. cit., p. 28.

[2] Dupont-Sommer, op cit., p. 91.

[3] Cf. Appendix A.

[4] H. von Soden, *Die Briefe an die Kolosser, Epheser, Philemon, die Pastoralbriefe* (1893), p. 126; E. Haupt, *Der Epheserbrief* (1897), p. 95.

temple (1 Kgs. 7. 15–22; 2 Kgs. 25. 13–17; 2 Chr. 3. 15–17; 4. 12–13; Jer. 52. 17–23) for purely decorative purposes.[1]

A further point of importance which militates against interpreting the cornerstone of Eph. 2. 20 as a top-stone is the fact that it echoes many of the ideas attributed by the rabbis to the *'ébhen sheˀthiyyāh* or foundation-stone. The designation *'ébhen sheˀthiyyāh*, as we noted above, derived from the belief that it sealed off the waters of the mythical subterranean ocean and so formed the point from which the world was created. It is to the latter organic role of the foundation-stone we would call attention.

As we saw earlier, a common expression for the *'ébhen sheˀthiyyāh* was the 'navel of the earth' (סבור הארץ).[2] 'Just as the embryo proceeds from the navel onwards, so God began to create the world from its navel onwards and from there it was spread out in different directions' (Bet ha-Midr. 5. 63. 1 ff.). What the navel in current physiological thinking means to the developing embryo, the foundation-stone means to creation: it is the source of life and sustenance. By a very natural extension of thought the stone was regarded as the bond uniting earth and heaven, the human and the divine (B. Yoma 54b; Gen. R. 4. 2; Nu. R. 13. 4).

It seems to us that there are valuable clues here for understanding the meaning of the term cornerstone in Eph. 2. 20.

The theme of the section Eph. 2. 11–22 is salvation and unity in Christ. Jesus the Messiah, by virtue of his death, reconciled Jews and Gentiles (vv. 13–18) and, by virtue of his resurrection, is the determinative cornerstone in the spiritual temple which unites the races (vv. 20–2). The thought is essentially dynamic: the whole construction grows (αὔξει): αὔξει in v. 21 looks back to ἀκρογωνιαῖος, which, as the navel, is the vital principle of life. Since the ἀκρογωνιαῖος is a living stone (λίθος ζῶν),[3] full weight must be accorded to the dynamic and organic overtones of the related terms οἰκοδομή and συνοικοδομεῖν. At 4. 16 we have the conception of the body (σῶμα) growing into a building: τὴν αὔξησιν τοῦ σώματος ποιεῖται εἰς οἰκοδομὴν ἑαυτοῦ. On the one hand, the building grows from Christ the cornerstone (ἐν ᾧ), and, on the other, it grows (according to current biological ideas) from Christ the head (ἐξ οὗ). The physiological image determined the apostle's thought no less than the architectural image (cf. 4. 16), and failure to take account of this has been partly responsible for contributing to the current misinterpretation of ἀκρογωνιαῖος.

---

[1] The stone of Zech. 4. 7 also seems to have had a chiefly artistic function.
[2] Appendix A.
[3] Cf. 1 Pet. 2. 4 ff., where Christ the living stone (v. 4) is equated with the cornerstone.

The idea of a building rising up to some aerially suspended stone would have been as unintelligible to the ancients as the idea of a body growing up to the head. Not only does the interpretation pose the architecturally impossible notion of an unfinished building with the top stone already in position,[1] but also, by its very definition, sets a limit to the whole conception of building[2] and destroys the essential dynamism of the image. The figure of the foundation-stone, on the other hand, is especially suited to the discussion in hand. The writer wishes us to know that what the historic stone in the temple of Jerusalem meant to creation, Christ the cornerstone in the temple of the Spirit means to the new creation (that is, the καινὸς ἄνθρωπος of v.15). He creates it, sustains it, imparts harmony and unity to it, just as he determines its 'shape' and growth.

We may conclude then that the traditional understanding of the cornerstone of Eph. 2. 20 as a stone connected with the foundation of the building is to be preferred.

[1] As advocates of the top-stone view are obliged to admit (Vielhauer, op. cit., p. 125; Knox, *St. Paul and the Church of the Gentiles*, p. 189; Best, op. cit., pp. 166 f.).
[2] Lyonnet, op. cit., p. 82.

APPENDIX D

The True Sanctuary of Hebrews
and
The Heavenly City of Plato

THE language used by the epistle to the Hebrews to describe the sanctuary in which Christ officiates as high priest reminds one of Plato's 'heavenly' city (Rep. ix. 592 ab).[1] Christ is called 'a minister in the sanctuary and the true tent (τῶν ἁγίων λειτουργὸς καὶ τῆς σκηνῆς τῆς ἀληθινῆς)' (8. 2). 'Then through the greater and more perfect tent (διὰ τῆς μείζονος καὶ τελειοτέρας σκηνῆς) (not made with hands, that is, not of this creation) he entered once for all into the Holy Place' (9. 11 f.). Again, 'for Christ has entered, not into a sanctuary made with hands, a copy of the true one (ἀντίτυπα τῶν ἀληθινῶν), but into heaven itself, now to appear in the presence of God on our behalf' (9. 24). The earthly sanctuary is 'a copy and shadow (ὑποδείγματι καὶ σκιᾷ) of the heavenly sanctuary (ἐπουρανίων)' (8. 5). The heavenly sanctuary is true (ἀληθινή) (8. 2).

But when a closer look is taken at the subject it will be seen that there are important differences between Hebrews and Plato.

In the first place, whereas Plato's city is wholly removed from this earth, the true sanctuary of Hebrews is firmly rooted in history. The work of Christ has pierced the 'veil' between the earthly and the heavenly, so that the true sanctuary embraces earth as well as heaven. Christ ascends from earth to heaven and enters the true tent.[2] Christians, similarly, have access to the heavenly world (4. 16; 6. 19 f.; 7. 25; 9. 24; 10. 19; cf. 12. 22).

Secondly, Plato undoubtably thought of his city, as he thought of his archetypes generally, as immutable. Hebrews, on the other hand, thinks of the archetypal tent as profoundly affected by the work of Christ (9. 23). Christ has become 'a minister in the sanctuary and the true tent' (8. 2; cf. 9. 11 f., 23). To put the difference in other words, the interest of Hebrews is not metaphysical or cosmological but historical and eschatological.[3]

---

[1] Quoted above p. 38. Plato's doctrine of the 'heavenly' city is influenced by his doctrine of ideas, but is not to be confused with it.

[2] Cf. R. Williamson, 'Platonism and Hebrews', *SJT* 16 (1963), 423.

[3] Cf. C. K. Barrett, 'The Eschatology of the Epistle to the Hebrews', *The*

Thirdly, Plato's archetypal city is in the last resort purely contingent. It is for him 'who wishes to contemplate it' and 'it makes no difference whether it exists now or ever will come into being' (Rep. ix. 592b). What Hebrews has in mind admits of no such contingency. 'We have this as a sure and steadfast anchor of the soul, a hope that enters into the inner shrine behind the curtain, where Jesus has gone as a forerunner on our behalf' (6. 19 f.).

It is manifest that there is nothing like a thoroughgoing Platonism in Hebrews or even a deliberate borrowing of key concepts. But it seems incorrect to say, as Barrett does, that 'the heavenly tabernacle in Hebrews is not the product of Platonic idealism but the eschatological temple of apocalyptic Judaism.[1] It is no doubt true that the background of the author is Jewish rather than Greek, but that is not to say that he is unaffected by Platonic ideas. We shall probably be closest to the facts if we conclude that he, like Philo and others, was more or less unconsciously drawing upon the general stock-in-trade of the eclectic philosophical milieu in which he grew up.

Background of the New Testament and its Eschatology, ed. W. D. Davies and D. Daube, (1956), pp. 385, 388 f.

[1] Op. cit., p. 389.

SELECT BIBLIOGRAPHY

(For Commentaries see text and footnotes)

AALEN, S., ' "Reign" and "House" in the Kingdom in the Gospels', *NTS* 8 (1962) 215–40.

ABELSON, J., *The Immanence of God in Rabbinic Literature* (London, Macmillan & Co., 1912).

ALLEGRO, J., 'Fragments of a Qumran Scroll of Eschatological Midrāšim', *JBL* 77 (1958), 350–4.

ARNDT, W. F., and GINGRICH, F. W., See Bauer.

BAILLET, M., 'Fragments araméens de Qumrân 2: Description de la Jérusalem Nouvelle', *RB* 62 (1955), 222–45.

BALTZER, K., 'The Meaning of the Temple in the Lukan Writings', *HTR* 58 (1965), 263–77.

BARCLAY, W., 'Hellenistic Thought in New Testament Times', *ET* 72 (1961), 258–61.

BARRETT, C. K., 'Paul and the "Pillar" Apostles', *Studia Paulina*, ed. J. N. Sevenester and V. C. van Unnik (Haarlem, De Erven F. Bohn N.V., 1953).

—— 'The Eschatology of the Epistle to the Hebrews', *The Background of the New Testament and its Eschatology*, ed. W. D. Davies and D. Daube (Cambridge University Press, 1956), 363–92.

BARTH, M., *The Broken Wall: A Study of the Epistle to the Ephesians* (London, Collins, 1960).

BARTHÉLEMY, D., and MILIK, J. T. (ed.), *Discoveries in the Judaean Desert*, vol. i (Oxford, Clarendon Press, 1955).

BAUER, W., *A Greek–English Lexicon of the New Testament and Other Early Christian Literature*, tr. by W. F. Arndt and F. W. Gingrich (Cambridge University Press, 1957).

BAUMGARTEN, J. M., 'Sacrifice and Worship Among the Jewish Sectarians of the Dead Sea (Qumrân) Scrolls', *HTR* 46 (1953), 141–59.

BEHM, J., θύω, etc., *TDNT* iii. 180–90.

BEITENHARD, H., *Die himmlische Welt im Urchristentum und Spätjudentum* (Tübingen, J. C. B. Mohr, 1951).

BEST, E., *One Body in Christ: A Study in the Relationship of the Church to Christ in the Epistles of the Apostle Paul* (London, S.P.C.K., 1955).

BETZ, O., 'Felsenmann und Felsengemeinde (eine Parallele zu Mt. 16. 17–19 in den Qumranpsalmen)', *ZNW* 48 (1957), 49–77.

BLASS, F., and DEBRUNNER, A., *A Greek Grammar of the New Testament and Other Early Christian Literature*, tr. and ed. by R. W. Funk (Cambridge University Press, 1961).

BLAUW, J., *The Missionary Nature of the Church: A Survey of the Biblical Theology of Mission* (London, Lutterworth, 1962).

BLENKINSOPP, J., 'The Oracle of Judah and the Messianic Entry', *JBL* 80 (1961), 55–64.

BÖHLIG, A., 'Zum Martyrium des Jakobus', *NT* 5 (1962), 207–13.

—— and LABIB, P., *Koptisch-gnostische Apokalypsen aus Codex V von Nag Hammadi, Wissenschaftliche Zeitschrift der Martin Luther Universität Halle.* Sonderband (Wittenberg, 1963).

BONNARD, P., *Jésus-Christ édifiant son Église* (Neuchâtel and Paris, Delachaux et Niestlé, 1948).

BONSIRVEN, J., *Le Judaïsme palestinien au Temps de Jésus-Christ* abr. edn. (Paris, Beauchesne, 1950).

—— *Textes rabbiniques des deux premiers siècles chrétiens* (Rome, Pontificio Instituto Biblico, 1955).

BOUSSET, W., *Die Religion des Judentums im späthellenistischen Zeitalter*, 3rd. ed. ed. by H. Gressmann (Tübingen, J. C. B. Mohr, 1926).

BRINKER, R., *The Influence of Sanctuaries in Early Israel* (Manchester University Press, 1946).

BROWN, F., DRIVER, S. R., and BRIGGS, C. A., *A Hebrew and English Lexicon of the Old Testament*, based on the Lexicon of W. Gesenius (Oxford, Clarendon Press, 1953).

BROWN, J. R., *Temple and Sacrifice in Rabbinic Judaism* (Evanston, 1963).

BULTMANN, R., *The History of the Synoptic Tradition* (Oxford, Blackwell, 1963).

BURCH, V., *Anthropology and the Apocalypse* (London, Macmillan, 1939).

BURKITT, F. C., 'Notes and Studies, Hosanna', *JTS* 17 (1916), 142–5.

—— 'The Cleansing of the Temple', *JTS* 25 (1923–4) 386–90.

BURROWS, E., 'Some Cosmological Patterns in Babylonian Religion', *The Labyrinth*, ed. S. H. Hooke (London, S.P.C.K. 1935), 45–70.

BUSE, I., 'The Cleansing of the Temple in the Synoptics and John', *ET* 70 (1958), 22–4.

CALDECOTT, A., 'The Significance of the "Cleansing of the Temple"', *JTS* 24 (1923), 382–6.

CAUSSE, A., 'La vision de l'humanité dans la prophétie deutéro-ésaïque', *RHPR* 2 (1922), 465–98.

—— 'Du groupe ethnique à la communauté religieuse: le problème sociologique du judaïsme', *RHPR* 14 (1934), 285–335.

—— 'Le mythe de la nouvelle Jérusalem du Deutéro-Esaïa à la IIIᵉ Sibylle', *RHPR* 18 (1938), 377–414.

—— 'De la Jérusalem terrestre à la Jérusalem céleste', *RHPR* 27 (1947), 12–36.

CERFAUX, L., 'Regale Sacerdotium', *RSPT* 28 (1939), 5–39, reprinted in *Recueil Lucien Cerfaux*, ii (Gembloux, 1954), 283–315.

—— *The Church in the Theology of St. Paul* (New York, Herder and Herder; London, Thos. Nelson & Sons Ltd., 1959).

CHARLES, R. H., (ed.), *The Apocrypha and Pseudepigrapha of the Old Testament*, 2 vols. (Oxford, Clarendon Press, 1913).

CLEMENTS, R. E., *God and Temple* (Oxford, Blackwell, 1965).

CODY, A., *Heavenly Sanctuary and Liturgy in the Epistle to the Hebrews: The Achievement of Salvation in the Epistle's Perspectives* (St. Meinrad, Grail Publications, 1960).

COLE, A., *The New Temple. A Study in the Origins of the Catechetical 'Form' of the Church in the New Testament* (London, Tyndale Press, 1950).

COMBLIN, J., 'La Liturgie de la Nouvelle Jérusalem (Apoc. xxi. 1–xxii. 5)', *ETL* 29 (1953), 5–40.

CONGAR, Y. M. J., *The Mystery of the Temple* (London, Burns Oates, 1962).

CONZELMANN, H., *The Theology of Saint Luke* (London, Faber and Faber, 1960).

COOMARASWAMY, A. K., 'Eckstein', *Speculum*, 14 (1939), 66–9.

CORRELL, A., *Consummatum Est* (London, S.P.C.K., 1958).

CROSS, F. M., Jr., 'The Priestly Tabernacle', *BA* 10 (1947), 44–68 (= *The Biblical Archaeologist Reader* (New York, Doubleday and Co., 1961), 201–28).

CULLMANN, O., πέτρα, *TWNT* vi. 94–9.

—— *Early Christian Worship* (London, S.C.M. Press, 1953).

—— 'The Significance of the Qumran Texts for Research into the Beginnings of Christianity', *JBL* 74 (1955), 213–26.

—— 'A New Approach to the Interpretation of the Fourth Gospel', *ET* 71 (1959), 39–43.

DAHL, N. A., *Das Volk Gottes. Eine Untersuchung zum Kirchenbewusstsein de Urchristentums* (Oslo, 1941).

DANBY, H., *The Mishnah* (Oxford, Clarendon Press, 1933).

DODD, C. H., 'The Fall of Jerusalem and the "Abomination of Desolation"', *JRS* 37 (1947), 47–54.

—— *According to the Scriptures* (London, Nisbet, 1952).

—— *Interpretation of the Fourth Gospel* (Cambridge University Press, 1953).

—— *Historical Tradition in the Fourth Gospel* (Cambridge University Press, 1963).

DOEVE, J. W., 'Purification du Temple et Desséchement du Figuier', *NTS* 1 (1955), 297–308.

DUPONT-SOMMER, A., *The Essene Writings from Qumran* (Oxford, Blackwell, 1961).

EASTWOOD, C., *The Royal Priesthood of the Faithful* (London, The Epworth Press, 1963).

EICHRODT, W., *The Theology of the Old Testament*, vol. i (London, S.C.M. Press, 1961).

ELLIS, E. E., *Paul's Use of the Old Testament* (Edinburgh, Oliver & Boyd, 1957).

—— 'II Corinthians 5. 1–10 in Pauline Eschatology', *NTS* 6 (1960), 211–24, reprinted in *Paul and His Recent Interpreters* (Grand Rapids, Wm. B. Eerdsmans, 1961, 35–48).

EPSTEIN, I. (ed.), *The Babylonian Talmud Translated into English*, 34 vols. and index (London: Soncino Press, 1935–52).

FARRER, A. M., *The Glass of Vision* (London, Dacre Press, 1948).

—— *A Rebirth of Images* (London, Dacre Press, 1949).

FEUCHTWANG, D., 'Das Wasseropfer und die damit verbundenen Zeremonien', *MGWJ* 54 (1910), 720 ff.

FEUILLET, A., *Destinée des chrétiens et fondements de l'eschatologie paulinienne*, Institut Catholique de Paris, no date given, reprinted in *RSR* xliv (1956), 161–93, 360–402.

FITZMYER, J. A., 'Qumrân and the Interpolated Paragraph in II Cor. vi. 14–vii. 1', *CBQ* 23 (1961) 271–80.

FLUSSER, D., 'The Dead Sea Sect and Pre-Pauline Christianity', *SH* 4 (1958), 215–66.

FORD, J. M., 'The Jewel of Discernment': A Study of Stone Symbolism, *BZ* 11 (1967), 109–16.

FRAEYMAN, M., 'La spiritualisation de l'idée du Temple dans épîtres pauliniennes', *ETL* 23 (1947), 378–412.

FRANKFORT, H., *Kingship and the Gods* (Chicago University Press, 1948).

—— (ed.), *Before Philosophy: The Intellectual Adventure of Ancient Man* (London, Penguin Books, 1949).

FREED, E. D., 'The Entry into Jerusalem in the Gospel of John', *JBL* 80 (1961), 329–38.

FREEDMAN, H., and SIMON, M. (ed.), *Midrash Rabbah*, 10 vols. (London, Soncino Press, 1939).

FRIDRICHSEN, A., 'Themelios, 1 Kor. 3. 11', *TZ* 2 (1946), 316.

FRIEDLANDER, G., *Pirkê de Rabbi Eliezer* (London, Kegan Paul & Co., 1916).

FUNK, R. W., See Blass.

GAECHTER, P., 'The Hatred of the House of Annas', *TS* 8 (1947), 3–34.

GÄRTNER, B., *The Temple and the Community in Qumran and the New Testament* (Cambridge University Press, 1965).

Goguel, M., *The Life of Jesus* (London, Allen and Unwin, 1933).

Gray, G. B., 'The Sacrificial Worship in Heaven', *in Sacrifice in the Old Testament* (Oxford, Clarendon Press, 1925), 148–78.

Hannay, T., 'The Temple', *SJT* 3 (1950), 278–87.

Hanson, S., *The Unity of the Church in the New Testament, Colossians and Ephesians* (Uppsala, Almquist & Wiksells Boktryckeri, 1946).

Hastings, J. (ed.), *A Dictionary of the Bible*, 4 vols. (Edinburgh, T. & T. Clark, 1898–1904).

—— (ed.), *A Dictionary of Christ and the Gospels*, 2 vols. (Edinburgh, T. & T. Clark, 1906–8).

Hatch, E., and Redpath, H. A., *A Concordance to the Septuagint* (Oxford, Clarendon Press, 1892–1906).

Hettlinger, R. F., '2 Cor. 5. 1–10', *SJT* 10 (1957), 174–94.

Hooke, S. H. (ed.), *The Labyrinth* (London, S.P.C.K., 1935).

—— 'The Corner-Stone in Scripture', *The Siege Perilous* (London, S.P.C.K., 1956), 235–49.

Jeremias, F., 'Das orientalische Heiligtum', *Ang.* 4 (1932), 56–69.

Jeremias, J., 'Der Eckstein', *Ang.* 1 (1925), 65–70.

—— 'Wo lag Golgotha und das Heilige Grab?', *Ang.* 1 (1925), 141–73.

—— 'Golgotha und der Heilige Felsen', *Ang.* 2 (1926), 75–128.

—— 'Die Berufung des Nathanaël', *Ang.* 3 (1928), 2–5.

—— *Jesus als Weltvollender* (Gütersloh, C. Bertelsmann, 1930).

—— 'Κεφαλὴ γωνίας—ἀκρογωνιαῖος', *ZNW* 29 (1930), 264–80.

—— 'Eckstein — Schlusstein', *ZNW* 36 (1937), 154–7.

—— ''Ακρογωνιαῖος', *TDNT* i. 792–3.

—— 'λίθος', *TWNT* iv. 277–83.

—— 'The Gentile World in the Thought of Jesus', *BSNTS* 3 (1952), 18–28.

—— *The Eucharistic Words of Jesus* (London, S.C.M. Press, 1963).

—— *Jesus' Promise to the Nations* (London, S.C.M. Press, 1958).

Joüon, P., 'Les mots employés pour désigner "le temple" dans l'ancien testament, le Nouveau Testament et Josèphe', *JRSR* 25 (1935), 329–43.

Käsemann, E., *Das wandernde Gottesvolk* (Göttingen, Vandenhoeck und Ruprecht, 1938).

Kennard, S., *Jesus in the Temple* (diss Strasbourg 1935).

Kennedy, A. R. S., 'Tabernacle', *HDB* iv. 653–68.

Kittel, G., and Friedrich, G. (ed.), *Theologisches Wörterbuch zum Neuen Testament* (Stuttgart, W. Kohlhammer, 1932–).

Klausner, J., *The Messianic Idea in Israel, from its Beginning to the Completion of the Mishnah* (London, Allen and Unwin, 1956).

KLIJN, A. F. J., 'Stephen's Speech—Acts vii. 2–53', *NTS* 4 (1957) 25–31.

KNOX, W. L., *St. Paul and the Church of Jerusalem* (Cambridge University Press, 1925).

—— *St. Paul and the Church of the Gentiles* (Cambridge University Press, 1939).

KUHN, K. G., 'Les rouleaux de cuivre de Qumrân', *RB* 61 (1954), 193–202.

LADNER, G. B., 'The Symbolism of the Biblical Corner Stone in the Medieval West', *MS* 4 (1942), 43–60.

LE BAS, E. E. E., 'Was the Corner-Stone of Scripture a Pyramidion?', *PEQ* 82 (1946), 103–15.

LIDDELL, H. G., and SCOTT, R., *A Greek–English Lexicon* (Oxford, Clarendon Press, 1940), revised by H. S. Jones.

LIGHTFOOT, R. H., *History and Interpretation in the Gospels* (London, Hodder and Stoughton, 1935).

—— *The Gospel Message of St. Mark* (Oxford, Clarendon Press, 1950).

LINDARS, B., *New Testament Apologetic* (London, S.C.M. Press, 1961).

LINDESKOG, G., 'The Veil of the Temple', *CN* 11 (1947), 132–7.

LOHMEYER, E., *Lord of the Temple* (Edinburgh, Oliver and Boyd, 1961).

LUCK, U., 'Himmlisches und irdisches Geschehen im Hebräerbrief', *NT* 6 (1963), 192–215.

LUCKENBILL, D. D., 'The Temples of Babylonia and Assyria', *AJSL* 24 (1907/8), 291–322.

LYONNET, S., 'De Christo summo angulari lapide secundum Eph. 2. 20', *VD* 27 (1949), 74–83.

MANDELKERN, S., *Veteris Testamenti Concordantiae Hebraicae atque Chaldaicae* (Graz, 1955).

MANSON, T. W., 'The Cleansing of the Temple', *BJRL* 33 (1951), 271–82.

MAY, H. G., 'The Ark—a Miniature Temple', *AJSL* 52 (1936), 215–34.

McCOWN, C. C., *The Testament of Solomon* (Leipzig; J. C. Hinrichs, 1922).

McKELVEY, R. J., 'Christ the Cornerstone', *NTS* 8 (1962), 352–9.

MENDER, S., 'Die Tempelreinigung', *ZNW* 47 (1956), 93–112.

MICHEL, O., ναός, οἰκοδομή, οἶκος, *TWNT* iv–v.

MIGNE, J. P. (ed.), *Patrologia Latina*, ed., Paris, 1844–64.

—— (ed.), *Patrologia Graeca*, ed., Paris, 1857–66.

MILIK, J. T., See Barthélemy.

MINEAR, P. S., *Images of the Church in the New Testament* (Philadelphia, Westminster Press, 1960).

—— 'The Cosmology of the Apocalypse', *Current Issues in New Testament Interpretation*, ed. W. Klassen and F. Snyder (New York, Harper and Bros., 1962), pp. 23–37.

MONTEFIORE, C. G., and LOEWE, H., *A Rabbinic Anthology* (London, Macmillan & Co., 1938).

MOORE, G. F., 'Intermediaries in Jewish Theology', *HTR* 15 (1922), 41–85.

—— *Judaism in the First Centuries of the Christian Era*, 3 vols. (Cambridge, Mass., 1927–30).

MORGENSTERN, J., *The Ark, the Ephod and the 'Tent of Meeting'* (Cincinnati, Union of American Hebrew Congregations, 1945).

MOULE, C. F. D., 'Sanctuary and Sacrifice in the New Testament', *JTS* (N.S.), 1 (1950), 29–41.

—— *An Idiom Book of New Testament Greek* (Cambridge University Press, 1953).

MOULTON, J. H., and G. MILLIGAN, *The Vocabulary of the Greek Testament* (London, Hodder and Stoughton, 1930).

MUNCK, J., 'Israel and the Gentiles in the New Testament', *BSNTS* i–iii (1950), 26–38.

—— *Paul and the Salvation of Mankind* (London, S.C.M. Press, 1959).

—— *Petros und Paulus in der Offenbarung Johannis* (Copenhagen, 1950).

MUSSNER, F., *Christus, das All und die Kirche, Studien zur Theologie des Epheserbriefe* (Trèves, 1955).

NOTH, M., *Das System der zwölf Stämme Israels* (Stuttgart, 1930).

—— 'Jerusalem und die israelitische Tradition', *OS* 8 (1950), 28–46 (= 'Jerusalem and the Israelite Tradition', *The Laws in the Pentateuch and other Studies* (Edinburgh, Oliver and Boyd, 1966), 132–44).

OESTERLEY, W. O. E., 'The Temple', *DCG* 2 (1908), 208–13.

O'NEILL, J. C., *The Theology of Acts* (London, S.P.C.K., 1961).

PATAI, R., *Man and Temple in Ancient Jewish Myth and Ritual* (London, Nelson, 1947).

PEDERSEN, J., *Israel: Its Life and Culture*, 2 vols. (Copenhagen, 1940).

PETERSON, E., *The Angels and the Liturgy* (London, Darton, Longman and Todd, 1964).

PFAMMATTER, J., *Die Kirche als Bau. Eine exegetisch-theologische Studie zur Ekklesiologie der Paulusbriefe* (Rome, 1961).

PHYTHIAN-ADAMS, W. J. T. P., *The People and the Presence: A Study of the At-one-ment* (London, Oxford University Press, 1942).

PORTEOUS, N. W., 'Jerusalem–Zion: The Growth of a Symbol', *Verbannung und Heimkehr*, ed. A. Kuschke (Tübingen, J. C. B. Mohr, 1961) 235–52.

RAD, G. VON, 'Zelt und Lade', *NKZ* 42 (1931), 476–98.

—— *Old Testament Theology*, vol. i (Edinburgh, Oliver and Boyd, 1962).

RAMSEY, A. M., *The Glory of God and the Transfiguration of Christ* (London, Longmans, 1949).

REICKE, B., 'The Constitution of the Primitive Church in the Light of Jewish Documents', *The Scrolls and the New Testament*, ed. K. Stendahl (London, S.C.M. Press, 1958).

RIESENFELD, H., *Jésus Transfiguré: l'arrière-plan du récit évangélique de la Transfiguration de Notre-Seigneur* (Copenhagen, 1947).

ROBINSON, J. A. T., *The Body: A Study in Pauline Theology* (London, S.C.M. Press, 1952).

—— 'Elijah, John and Jesus', *NTS* 4 (1958), 263–81 (= *Twelve New Testament Studies* (London, S.C.M. Press, 1962), 28–52).

—— 'The Destination and Purpose of St. John's Gospel', *NTS* 6 (1960), 56–65 (= *Twelve New Testament Studies*, 107–25).

ROBINSON, T. H., 'The Den of Thieves', *Exp.* 9 (8th series) (1915), 459–67.

ROTH, C., 'The Cleansing of the Temple and Zechariah 14. 21', *NT* 4 (1960), 174–81.

SCHECHTER, S., *Some Aspects of Rabbinic Theology* (London, A. and C. Black, 1909).

SCHLIER, H., *Christus und die Kirche im Epheserbrief* (Tübingen, J. C. B. Mohr, 1930).

SCHMIDT, M., *Prophet und Tempel. Eine Studie zum Problem der Gottesnähe im Alten Testament* (Zollikon-Zürich, Evangelischer Verlag AG, 1948).

SCHMOLLER, A., *Handkonkordanz zum Griechischen Neuen Testament* (Stuttgart, Bible Society, 1953).

SCHRENK, G., ἱερόν, *TDNT* iii. 230–47.

SCOTT, E. F., *The Crisis in the Life of Jesus* (New York, Chas. Scribners' Sons, 1952).

SEITZ, O. J. F., 'Upon this Rock: A Critical Re-examination of Matt. 16. 17–19', *JBL* 69 (1950), 329–40.

SIMON, M., 'Le discours de Jésus sur la ruine du Temple', *RB* 56 (1949), 70–5.

—— 'Retour du Christ et reconstruction du Temple dans la pensée chrétienne primitive', *Aux sources de la tradition chrétienne, Mélanges M. Goguel* (Neuchâtel, Delachaux et Nestlé, 1950), 247–57.

—— 'Saint Stephen and the Jerusalem Temple', *JEH* 2 (1951), 127–42.

—— *St. Stephen and the Hellenists in the Primitive Church* (London and New York, Longmans, Green & Co., 1958).

SINGER, S. (ed.), *The Authorized Daily Prayer Book of the United Hebrew Congregation of the British Empire* 26th edn. (London, Eyre and Spottiswoode, 1960).

SMITH, C. W. F., 'No Time for Figs', *JBL* 79 (1960), 315–27.

—— 'Tabernacles in the Fourth Gospel and Mark', *NTS* 9 (1963), 130–46.

SPICQ, C., 'Le philonisme de l'Épître aux Hébreux', *RB* 56 (1949), 542–72; 57 (1950), 212–42.

Spörri, T., *Der Gemeindegedanke im ersten Petrusbrief* (Gütersloh, C. Bertelsmann, 1925).

Stählin, G., ξένος κτλ. *TWNT* v. 1–31.

Stendahl, K. (ed.), *The Scrolls and the New Testament* (London, S.C.M. Press, 1958).

Strugnell, J., 'The Angelic Liturgy at Qumrân—*4Q serek šîrôt 'ôlat haššabat*', *VT Suppl.* 7 (1960), 318–45.

Sundkler, B., 'Jésus et les païens', *RHPR* 16 (1936), 462–99.

Strack, H. L., and Billerbeck, P., *Kommentar zum Neuen Testament aus Talmud und Midrash*, 5 vols. (Munich, C. H. Beck, 1922–61).

Swetnam, J., 'The Greater and More Perfect Tent. A contribution to the Discussion of Hebrews ix. 11', *Biblica*, 47 (1966), 91–106.

Thackeray, H. St. J., *The Septuagint and Jewish Worship* (London, H. Milford, 1921).

Thornton, L. S., *The Common Life in the Body of Christ* (London, Dacre Press, 1941).

Torrance, T. F., *Royal Priesthood* (Edinburgh, Oliver and Boyd, 1955).

Townsend, J. T., *The Jerusalem Temple in New Testament Thought* (diss. Harvard, 1958).

Vaux, R. de, *Ancient Israel: Its Life and Institutions* (London, Darton, Longman and Todd, 1961).

Vermes, G., *The Dead Sea Scrolls in English* (London, Penguin Books, 1962).

Vielhauer, P., *Oikodome. Das Bild vom Bau in der christlichen Literatur vom Neuen Testament bis Clemens Alexandrinus* (diss. Heidelberg, 1939).

Volz, P., *Die Eschatologie der jüdischen Gemeinde im neutestamentlichen Zeitalter* (Tübingen, J. C. B. Mohr, 1934).

Wallace, D. H., 'The Essenes and Temple Sacrifice', *TZ* 13 (1957), 335–8.

Weber, F., *Jüdische Theologie auf Grund des Talmud und verwandter Schriften, gemeinfasslich dargestellt*, 2nd edn. (Leipzig, Dörfling-Franke, 1897).

Wenschkewitz, H., 'Die Spiritualisierung der Kultusbegriffe Tempel, Priester und Opfer im Neuen Testament', *Ang.* 4 (1932), 77–230.

Wensinck, A. J., 'The Ideas of the Western Semites Concerning the Navel of the Earth', *VAA* 17 (1916), 1–64.

Wernberg-Møller, P., *The Manual of Discipline, Translated and Annotated with an Introduction* (Leiden, E. J. Brill, 1957).

Werner, E., ' "Hosanna" in the Gospels', *JBL* 65 (1946), 97–122.

Whitaker, G. H., 'The Chief Corner Stone', *Exp.* 22 (8th series) (1921), pp. 430–2.

—— 'The Building and the Body (Eph. ii. 21 f.; iv. 16; Col. ii. 19)', *Theology*, 13 (1926), 335–6.

WHITELEY, D. E. H., *The Theology of St. Paul* (Oxford, Blackwell, 1964).

WILLIAMSON, R., 'Platonism and Hebrews', *SJT* 16 (1963), 415–24.

WOLFSON, H. A., *Philo: Foundations of Religious Philosophy in Judaism, Christianity and Islam*, 2 vols., rev. ed. (Cambridge, Mass., Harvard University Press, 1948).

WRIGHT, G. E., 'The Significance of the Temple in the Ancient Near East', *BA* 7 (1944), 41–88, in three parts:

    I. H. H. Nelson, 'The Egyptian Temple', 44–54.
    II. A. Leo Oppenheim, 'The Mesopotamian Temple', 54–63.
    III. G. E. Wright, 'The Temple in Palestine–Syria', 65–88.

YATES, J. E., *The Spirit and the Kingdom* (London, S.P.C.K., 1963).

YOUNG, J. C. DE, *Jerusalem in the New Testament. The Significance of the City in the History of Redemption and in Eschatology* (Kampen, J. H. Kok, 1960).

INDEX OF TEXTS

OLD TESTAMENT

Genesis
1. 7	157
7. 11	190
8. 2	190
21	45
28. 10 ff.	54 f., 140
16	77
17	189
49. 11	59
25	190

Exodus
12. 46	83
19. 5 f.	130, 159, 184 f.
6	129, 164, 184
23. 22	129
25. 9	25
25. 40	25
10–22	11
26. 31–5	11, 72
27. 1–8	10
9–19	10
16	72
28. 29	173
29. 45 f.	121
33. 7–11	3
8	3
10	3
36. 35–8	11
37. 1–9	11
38. 1–7	10
7	200
9 ff.	10
40. 34 ff.	76

Leviticus
17. 11	44
26. 12	94 f., 97, 120, 169

Numbers
2	11
3. 25	72
9. 12	83
10. 33–6	3
35 f.	3
12. 7	134

14. 14	3
44	3
16. 3	101
20. 10–11	136
21. 16–18	136
24. 2	11

Deuteronomy
4. 11	189
5. 4	26
6. 20–5	5
12	4
12. 8 f.	112
21. 3	60
26. 5–11	5
33. 2	26
13	190

Joshua
18. 1	3
24. 2–13	5

Judges
5. 4 f.	26
6. 25 f.	60
18. 31	3

1 Samuel
1. 3	3
2. 35	194
4. 21 f.	7
6. 7	60
26. 19	5

2 Samuel
7	17, 134 f.
7. 10–14	50
11	194
12–16	6
13	96, 135
14	96, 135
15. 25	3

1 Kings
5. 17	198 f.
6. 20	176
7. 10	198
15–22	203

1 Kings (cont.)	
23 ff.	156 f.
8. 10 f.	76
27	26
30	26
39	26
41 ff.	64
43	26
15. 9 ff.	60
22. 19 ff.	25

2 Kings	
9. 13	60
11	60
14. 13	199
18. 1 ff.	60
3–6	4
20. 20	81
22. 2–23. 25	4
25. 1 ff.	6
13–17	203
17	202

1–2 Chronicles	
1–2 Chr.	13
1 Chr. 22. 18	112
2 Chr. 25. 23	199

Ezra	
3. 10–11	199
12–13	12, 23
6. 15	13

Job	
7. 12	190
38. 6	198 f., 201

Psalms	
11. 4	26
29. 10	6
33. 7	190
34. 20	83
40. 4 ff.	43
42. 1 ff.	5
2	5
43. 3 f.	5
46. 1 ff.	6
4 f.	81
47. 8	6
48. 12–14	5
50	43
50. 23	43
51. 11	105

15–17	43
18 f.	43
63. 2	5
65. 1 f.	5
68. 7 f.	26
17 f.	26
69. 9	43, 78
30 f.	43
78. 69	6
82	6
84. 1–2	5
10	5
93. 1 ff.	6
2 ff.	6
99. 1 f.	6
103. 19	26
104. 7 ff.	189
105. 41	136
118. 22	49, 127, 132, 195, 199 ff.
25	58, 163
122. 1 ff.	5
3–9	5
123. 1	26
125. 1	6
132. 11–14	6, 96
137. 1–6	7
4	5
4–6	7
6	5
139. 7–12	26
141. 2	43

Isaiah	
1. 11–17	43
2. 2	6, 17
2–4	6, 9, 65, 112, 130
6. 1 ff.	25 f., 76
8. 6	81
14	121, 127, 131 f., 202
11. 11 ff.	9
19. 13	49
27. 13	9
28. 16	47 f., 48 f., 52, 114 f., 121, 127, 131 f., 188, 192 f., 195 ff.
30. 29	5
33. 20	5
35. 10	5
40. 5	76
11	11
27	7
41. 17 ff.	11
43. 5 f.	11

Isaiah (*cont.*)

49. 6	14
14	7
19 ff.	11
51. 9–11	157
52. 11	95, 97
53. 5	14
12	76
54. 1–3	11
6–8	7
11–12	11, 51
56. 6–8	12
7	11, 21, 62, 112
57. 19	111, 113
59. 20	123
60. 1–20	173
4–5	12
7	12
13–18	11
61. 5 f.	185
6	184
62. 11	60
63. 9	105
65. 17–19	168
19	5
66. 1	26
1–2	43
18–21	12
21	165

Jeremiah

3. 17 f.	9, 22
6. 20	43
7	65
7. 11	62 f.
21–2	43
14. 19	7
17. 12	25
23. 5 f.	9
25. 30	26
31. 6 ff.	9
33	95
39. 1–8	6
51. 26	198, 201
52. 4 ff.	6

Lamentations

1–2	7

Ezekiel

5. 5 ff.	189
8. 8–17	94
9. 3	7

6	133
10. 4–5	7
11. 15	5
16	26, 187
23	7
20. 34	96
40 ff.	9
34. 11 ff.	9
37. 27	94 f., 97, 120 f., 169
38. 12	189
40–8	viii, 9 ff., 37
40. 1 ff.	25
2 ff.	172
41. 3–4	10
13–14	10
42. 15–20	10
43. 1 ff.	10
45. 3–4	10
47. 1 ff.	81
7	173
48. 1 ff.	10
15 ff.	10
16	172
21–2	10
30–5	10
31–4	10, 172

Daniel

3. 38–40	44
7. 9 ff.	26
25	158
9. 27	94
11. 31	94
12. 7	158

Hosea

1. 10	123
6. 6	43
14. 2	43

Amos

1. 2 ff.	6, 26
5. 21–7	43
9. 11	89 f.

Jonah

2. 4	5

Micah

4. 1	6, 17, 65
4. 1–3	6, 9, 112
6. 6–8	43

Habakkuk
2. 20 — 26
3. 3 — 26

Haggai
2. 9 — 12, 112

Zechariah
1. 16 — 13
2. 5 — 158
3. 1–7 — 25
4 — 159
4. 7 — 199, 203
9 — 13
11–14 — 13
6. 12 — 13
15 — 13
8. 3–8 — 13
19 — 5
20–3 — 13, 185
9. 9 — 59 ff., 82
10 — 113
10. 8 ff. — 13
14 — 81, 191
14. 4 — 59
7 ff. — 173
8 — 81, 163
10 — 13, 17
16 f. — 6, 13, 163
16–19 — 164, 191
21 — 66, 77

Malachi
1. 6–2. 9 — 13
3. 1–4 — 13, 66, 130
4 — 24
14 — 13

APOCRYPHA

1 Esdras
5. 63–5 — 12, 23

Tobit
1. 4 — 16
12. 15 — 160, 165
13. 5 — 16
11 — 16
14. 4 ff. — 16
5 — 16, 24

Judith
16. 16 — 44

Wisdom
9. 8 — 25

Ecclesiasticus
35. 1 — 45
36. 11–14 — 16
48. 10 — 16
50 — 15 f.
50. 22–4 — 16

1 Maccabees
1. 54 — 94
13. 51 — 59

2 Maccabees
1–2 — 5
1. 24–9 — 16
2. 4–8 — 16, 160
7 — 16
18 — 16
7. 37 f. — 46
10. 6 f. — 59

PSEUDEPIGRAPHA

Jubilees
1. 17 — 95
2. 22 — 45
4. 29 — 191
6. 18 — 32
8. 12 ff. — 189
19 — 191

Aristeas
19 — 44
37 — 44
83–104 — 15
139 — 109
170 — 44
234 — 44

Vita Adae et Evae
45 — 191

Apocalypse of Moses
33. 1 ff. — 32
40 — 191

1 Enoch
14. 8 ff. — 156
16 ff. — 28
25. 3 — 28

1 Enoch (cont.)
25. 4 f. — 29
26. 1 f. — 28
26–7 — 191
45. 3 — 141
46. 8 — 31
53. 6 — 31
57. 1 f. — 31
71. 5–7 — 31
89. 50 — 29
    51–90. 5 — 29
    73 — 23
90. 28 f. — 23, 30
    29 — 24
    29–34 — 112, 118
    33 ff. — 30
    36 — 30
91. 13 — 30

2 Enoch
20–1 — 31
45. 3 — 44
61. 2 — 141

Testaments of the XII Patriarchs
Levi
2. 7 — 157
3. 4–6 — 31 f.
    7 — 165
5. 1–2 — 32 f.

Benjamin
9. 2 — 24

Sibylline Oracles
iii. 98 ff. — 19
    105–7 — 19
    702 ff. — 18 f.
    710 f. — 18
    716–18 — 18
    755 f. — 19, 112
    755–76 — 118
    773 ff. — 18
v. 424 ff. — 19

2 Baruch
4. 2 — 40 f.
2–4 — 24, 32 f.
6. 5–10 — 160
8. 1 f. — 72
32. 2 ff. — 23, 33
80. 2 — 160

4 Baruch
3. 18 — 160

4 Ezra
9. 24 — 34
    26–10. 57 — 33
10. 7 — 33 f.
    44 ff. — 33
    54 — 34
13. 36 — 34

Psalms of Solomon
8. 36 — 17
17. 24 — 17
    28 f. — 17
    30 f. — 66
    32 ff. — 17, 130
    33 ff. — 17, 60

4 Maccabees
6. 27 ff. — 46
17. 22 — 46

Testament of Solomon
22. 7–23. 4 — 196, 198, 202

JOSEPHUS
Antiquities
8. 79–87 — 156
11. 80–1 — 23
15. 417 — 64
20. 169–72 — 59

Wars
2. 261–3 — 59
5. 194 — 64
    211–14 — 72
    219 — 72
6. 288–300 — 72

Apion
2. 103–9 — 64
    193 — 19

PHILO
De Migratione Abrahami
9 — 55

Legum Allegoriae
i. 108 — 55
iii. 102 — 40

De Cherubim
100 — 54

PHILO (*cont.*)
De Ebrietate
101   55

Quod Deus immutabilis sit
150   55

De Specialibus Legibus
i. 66   40
67   19

De Vita Mosis
i. 158   39
ii. 74–6   39

De Opificio Mundi
15 ff.   39
137   55
145 f.   54

De Sobrietate
62   54

De Somniis
i. 21–34   54
34   39
66   40
146–8   55
149   54
215   40, 54
ii. 188 f.   40
251   54

De Virtutibus
188   54

Quaestiones in Exodum
ii. 52   39
82   39

Quis Rerum Divinarum Heres
205–6   40

TARGUMS
Hag. 1. 8   23
Isa.
28. 16   201
53. 5   14

DEAD SEA SCROLLS
CD
1. 7   47

3. 19   90
4. 1 ff.   53 f.
7. 4   52
16   89 f.

1 QH
3. 21 f.   37
4. 24 f.   37
6. 12 f.   37
15 ff.   47
25 f.   49
25–7   52
26   47 f.
26 f.   193 f.
7. 4   52
8 f.   49, 52, 193 f.

1 QM
2. 1 ff.   53
12. 12 ff.   53
19. 5 ff.   53

1 QS
5. 5   133
5–6   46 f., 49 f., 202
6   120
8. 4 f.   98
4 ff.   52
4–10   46 ff.
5   101
7   49
7 ff.   47, 202
9   101
9. 3 ff.   45 f., 47 f., 49 ff., 133
5b–7   48 f.
6   49
11. 7 f.   37
8   47, 98
1 QSb 4. 25 ff.   37 f.

4 QFlor.
1. 4   38
6 f.   45, 47, 51
11–13   89 f.

4 QpIsa^d   51

4 QSl 40. 2–18   36 f.

RABBIS
Sh^emoneh 'Esrēh
10   20 f.

Rabbis (cont.)

| 14 | 20 |
| 17 | 20 |

Mishnah
  Aboth

| 3. 2 | 46 |
| 6 | 46 |

| Berakhoth 9. 5 | 64 |

| Kelim 1. 8 f. | 64 |

Middoth

2. 3	198
6	21
4. 6	176

| Pesaḥim 10. 6 | 20 |

| Sanhedrin 10. 3 | 21 |

| Shekalim 6. 3 | 21, 191 |

Sukkah

3	163
4. 5	163
5. 3	81

Yoma

3. 6	165
5. 1	72
2	188, 202
7. 4	165

| Ta'annith 4. 2 | 5 |

Talmud: Babylonian

  Baba Bathra

| 75b | 36 |
| 122a | 21 |

| Berakhoth 26b | 5 |

| 'Erubin 19a | 191 |

| Hagigah 12b | 31, 35, 165 |

| Kethuboth 111a | 189, 192 |

| Kiddushin 69b | 189 |

| Makkoth 11a | 190 |

Megillah

| 17b–18a | 21 |
| 31a | 191 |

| Menaḥoth 110a | 45, 165 |

Pesaḥim

| 5a | 21 |
| 57a | 23 |

Sanhedrin

| 98a | 61 |
| 110b | 21 |

| Shabbath 152b | 192 |

Sukkah

| 49a | 191 |
| 53ab | 190 |

Ta'annith

| 2ab | 191 |
| 5a | 27, 35 |

Yoma

9b	23
53b	23
54b	188 f.
54b	190, 203

Zebaḥim

| 54b | 189 |
| 62a | 165 |

Talmud: Palestinian

| Berakhoth 4. i. 7b | 5 |

| Sanhedrin 29a | 190 |

Sukkah

| 54b | 191 |
| 55a | 191 |

Ta'annith

2ab	191
25b	191
65a	23

| Yoma 42c | 190 |

Extra-Canonical Tractates

Aboth of R. Nathan

Aboth of R. Natham (*Cont.*)
26   192
35   22

Pirkê de R. Eliezer
20   191
35   198

MEKILTA
Exod. 15. 17   35

TOSEFTA
Sukkah
3. 3   21
11 f.   136

MIDRASHIM
Gen. Rabbah
4. 2   203
14. 8   191
32. 10   189
44. 21   191
55. 7   35
68. 12   77, 189
69. 7   35, 77, 140
70. 8   191

Deut. Rabbah
6. 11   136

Lev. Rabbah
20. 4   189

Num. Rabbah
8. 4   111
12. 4   190
7   35
13. 4   203
18. 22   137

Bet ha Midrash
i. 55, 23   35
iii. 67, 29   35
v. 63, 1 ff.   189, 203

TANHUMA
Q^edhôshîm, ed. Buber, p. 39a   188

YALCUT
Gen. 102   198

CLASSICAL WRITERS
Aristotle
Politics
iv. x. 4   200

Cicero
De Natura Deorum ii. 71   53

Epictetus
Discourses
I. xiii   55
xiv. 13 f.   54
II. viii. 11 f.   54

Euripides
Fragments 329   53

Herodotus
i. 86   200
viii. 121   200

Isocrates
Orations 2. 20   53

Marcus Aurelius iii. 5   54

Plato
Cratylus 400c   55
Gorgias 493a   55
Leges iv. 716d   53
Politics 300d   38
Republic
iv. 427c   189
vii. 514 ff.   39
515 a, c   38
516a   38
517d   38
ix. 592ab   38, 205
Timaeus
28a–9a   38, 39 f.
29b   38
48e–9a   38
52a   38
52bc   39

Seneca
Epistles
xxxi. 11   55
xli. 1   54
2   54
lxxiii. 16   53
xcii. 10   55

Seneca (*cont.*)

xcv. 50	53
cxx. 14	55
De Consolatione ad Helviam	
xi. 7	53, 55
De Consolatione ad Marciam	
xxiv. 5	55
De Otio v. 5 f.	55

Thucydides I. 132. 2	200

Xenophon

Anabasis v. vii. 32	53
Memorabilia Socratis I. iii. 3	53

NEW TESTAMENT

Matthew

2. 3	60
4. 5	196
7. 24	193
10. 5 f.	85
11. 20–4	61
12. 6	68
16. 18	113, 193–4
18. 2 f.	59
20. 21	59
21. 5	60
10	60
14 ff.	63
23. 17	103
19	103
37	58
38	68
38 f.	85
24. 2	68
26. 61	68, 87
27. 5	73
51 ff.	72

Mark

1. 10 f.	74
14 f.	61
8. 31	69 ff., 71
9. 7	74
33 ff.	59
10. 32	59
37	59
45	59, 67
11. 11	61 f.
16	65
17	62, 64, 112
18	64 f.

20 ff.	63
23	65
27–33	63, 67
28	78
12. 1–11	66
10	127, 132, 199
35	58
13	68
13. 1 f.	68
2	69 f., 71 f., 85
14	94, 158
26	85
27	67, 200
28	65
14. 22–5	67
49	58
58	67–72, 79, 86 f., 145, 147, 149
61	68
63	68
15. 29–30	69 f.
37–9	72
38	71

Luke

2. 27 ff.	63, 85
41 ff	85
6. 48	193
8. 6	193
13. 34	58
19. 11	59
44	61, 86
47 f.	58, 63, 85
20. 1	63, 85
21. 5 f.	86
20	91
24	159
37	58
22. 28–30	67
53	58
24. 53	85

John

1. 9	81
14	75 f., 78, 163
29	76 f.
35–42	76
36	76
51	77, 140
2. 13	76
13–22	63, 66, 77 ff.
15 f.	77 ff.
16	77 ff., 78, 141
18	78

John (*cont.*)

19	69 ff., 69, 78 f.	36	76
19 ff.	69	36 f.	83
19–21	79, 83	20. 22	80 f.
20	71		
21	68, 76, 78	Acts	
23	78	1. 4 ff.	63
3. 5	81	6–8	105
4. 9	88	8	84 f., 90
10	80, 175	2. 16 ff.	105
13 f.	75, 83	46	85
14	80, 83, 175	3. 1 ff.	85
20–6	79	4. 11	127, 132, 199
20 ff.	88	5. 12	85
21 ff.	77, 79 f.	20	63, 85
23	78 ff., 184	42	85
42	80	6. 11	86
6. 4	76	13 f.	86 f.
31 ff.	137	14	69
35	80	7	87 ff.
55	83	7. 48	149
63	81	8. 1	144
7. 2	58	4	144
37 f.	75, 79, 80 f., 83, 137, 175	4–8	87 f.
38	80, 83	13. 46	87
39	80 f., 83	15. 13–18	89 f.
40	137	2 ff.	89
8. 12	81, 175	17. 24	149
9. 1–12	81	18. 6	87
10. 16	82	19. 21	90
22	58	21. 28	86
40	58	28 f.	64
11. 52 f.	82	24. 17	184
54	58	28. 28	87, 90
55	76		
12. 1	58, 76	Romans	
12 ff.	60	1. 16	85
12. 13	59	3. 25	150
15	82	5. 2	107
20 ff.	82	9. 4	121 f.
23	82	26	123 f.
27–33	82	33	121, 131, 193, 201 f.
13. 1 ff.	76	11. 13	185
14. 2–3	140 f.	26	85, 123 f.
6	77, 140	12. 1	129, 130, 184 f.
23	187	1 f.	107
18. 28	76	15. 2	182
39	76	16	185
19. 14	76	20	99, 182
29	76	27	184
31–34	83		
34	75, 79 f., 81, 175	1 Corinthians	
35	83	3	112, 117 f., 146
		3. 10 f.	106, 182

1 Corinthians (*cont.*)
   11   99, 114, 118, 120
   16   94, 100, 102 f., 105 f., 122,
      146
   16–17   93, 98–102, 106 f.
   18   105
5. 7   83
6. 19   93, 100 f., 106 f., 122, 146
   19–20   102–4, 107
10. 4   136 f.
12. 13   101, 104
14. 12   182
15. 44   145
16. 15   185

2 Corinthians
  2. 15   107
  3. 18   105
  4. 6   105
  5. 1–5   93, 120, 144–7
    2 ff.   122
    8–9   104
    17   110
    14–16   93 f.
  6. 16–7. 1   93–8, 102, 105, 131
    16   93, 94 f., 100, 120
    16 ff.   122
  7. 1   96
  9. 11 f.   107
    12   184
  10. 8   182
  12. 19   182

Galatians
  2. 9   135
    11 ff.   89, 142 f.
    3. 28   110
    4. 21–7   142 f.
    26   34, 120, 141–4

Ephesians
  1. 3   119, 186
  2. 4–6   119
    6   119
    11 ff.   108 ff., 202 f.
    15   110, 204
    18   107, 110, 111, 119, 184
    19   119, 186
    19 ff.   47, 112 ff., 195 ff.
    20   99, 127 f., 194, 195 ff.
    20–2   93, 106, 108–120, 146,
      195–204
    21   98, 101, 200

3. 5   131
  12   107
  17   98, 116
4. 7 ff.   182
  11   113
  11 ff.   119, 184
  15 f.   115
  16   115 f., 119, 182, 202 f.
5. 2   185

Philippians
  2. 17   107, 185
    30   184
  3. 20   143 f.
  4. 18   107, 184

Colossians
  1. 22   107
  2. 7   98, 116
    19   116, 119

1 Thessalonians
  1. 9   94

2 Thessalonians
  2. 3–4   124, 135 f.
    13   185

1 Timothy
  3. 4   133
    5   133
    12   133
    15   132 f., 135

2 Timothy
  1. 16   133
  2. 19   133

Titus
  1. 11   133

Hebrews
  1. 5   135
    14   148
  2. 5   148
  3. 1–6   132, 134 f.
  4. 1 ff.   152
    14   149
    16   153, 184
  5. 7   150
  6. 5   148, 154
    19–20   109, 148 f., 206
    20   152

Hebrews (cont.)
7. 4 ... 200
17 ... 150
25 ... 153, 184
26 ... 149
27 ... 151
8. 1 f. ... 149 f.
2 ... 149, 150, 205
3 ... 151
5 ... 149, 205
9 ... 159
9. 1-5 ... 147
6-10 ... 147 f.
8 ... 148 f.
11 ... 149, 150
11-12 ... 148, 150, 205
23 ... 149
24 ... 149, 151, 205
25 f. ... 151
28 ... 151
10. 1 ... 153
5 ... 150
11-14 ... 151
12 ... 151
19 ... 148 ff.
19-20 ... 109, 149 f.
20 ... 73, 150
21 ... 135, 184, 186
22 ... 153
11. 6 ... 153
10 ... 152
13-16 ... 151 f.
12. 1 ... 186
2 ... 152 f.
18 ... 153
18-24 ... 142
22 ... 148, 152, 186, 205
22-4 ... 152-4
13. 10 ... 151
14 ... 142, 148, 152
15 ... 130, 184, 186
15 f. ... 151, 184
16 ... 184

James
1. 1 ... 144

1 Peter
1. 1 ... 144
3 ... 127
23 ... 127
2. 2 ... 129
4 ff. 48, 114 f., 119, 125-32,

181, 203
5 ... 106, 117, 127, 133, 171, 184, 186
6 ... 197
6-8 ... 121, 201
6 ff. ... 131, 202
7 f. ... 193
9 ... 125, 130, 164, 183 f., 185
25 ... 126
4. 17 ... 132 f.
5. 2 f. ... 126

Revelation
1. 5 f. ... 164, 184
6 ... 159, 165, 174
12-13 ... 160
13 ... 165
3. 12 ... 135, 161, 167, 169, 171, 176 f.
21 ... 165, 174
4 ff. ... 26
4-20 ... 155, 161, 167
4. 1 f. ... 156
2 ff. ... 156, 160 f.
4 ff. ... 160
6 ... 156 f.
5. 8 ... 165 f., 184
9 ... 164 f., 184
10 ... 159, 164 f., 174
6. 9 ... 156, 161, 166, 192
7 ... 161-6, 175
7. 1-8 ... 159, 173
9 ... 161, 164 f., 165
9 ff. ... 163 f., 176
9-17 ... 161 f.
11 ... 160 f., 165
14-15 ... 164 f.
15 ... 157, 160 f., 163 ff., 166
17 ... 163
8. 2 ff. ... 160 f.
3 ff. ... 161, 165 f.
5 ff. ... 166
9. 13 ... 161, 166 f.
11. 1 f. ... 171
1-3 ... 158 ff.
3-13 ... 159 f.
4 ... 159
8 ... 159, 167
19 ... 160, 176
13. 6 ... 136, 160 f.
14. 1 ... 156 f.
1 ff. ... 161
1-5 ... 162, 173

Revelation (*cont.*)

4	164, 185
15	160
18	161, 166
15. 2 ff.	156 f.
4	164
5	160, 165
16. 7	161, 166 f.
17	160
17. 14	158
19. 7	169
8	169
20. 4–6	168
6	159, 165 f., 174, 184
9	160, 168, 171
14	113
21–2	155, 161, 167–76
21. 1–2	176
1–4	168 ff.
1–8	168
21. 3	121, 160, 163 f., 170, 176
9–21	168 f., 171 ff.
10	156 f.
12	172
22	171, 175, 177, 187
22–22. 5	173 ff.
23	81, 175
22. 1	80, 83, 157, 163, 175
3–4	165 f.
4 ff.	174, 176, 177
5	165
17	80, 83

APOSTOLIC FATHERS

Barnabas

3. 6	110
4. 11	103
5. 7	110
6. 15	103
7. 5	110

1 Clement

2. 6	102
5. 2	135

Hermas
Similitudes

ix. 3. 4 f.	128
ix. 9	117, 182
9. 7	115
Vision iii. 2. 6	115

Ignatius

Ephesians 9. 1	128
Magnesians 7. 2	183

APOCALYPSES

James 61. 20 ff.	197

INDEX OF SUBJECTS

Ἀκρογωνιαῖος, 112, 114–16, 126 f., 195–204; see also Cornerstone, Stone.
Ἄκρος, 198, 200.
Ἀληθής, 38, 149, 205.
Altar, 20, 23, 80 f., 191 ff.
  in heaven, 151, 157, 178 ff., 161, 166.
Amphictyony, 3.
Angels, of the presence, 31 f., 36 ff., 40, 160 f., 165 f.
Ἀπόσπασμα, 54.
Anthropology:
  of Stoics, 55.
  of Paul, 104.
Apostles:
  foundation of church, 112 f.
  foundation of new Jerusalem, 113, 172 f.
Archetype, 6, 25, 33, 38 ff., 87, 147, 153, 205 f.; see also Ἰδέα, μίμημα, παράδειγμα, σκία, ὑπόδειγμα.
Ark, of the covenant, 3 f.
  missing from the second temple, 23, 160.
  in heaven, 160.
Ἀχειροποίητος, 67, 70, 87, 148.

Bethel, 77, 189.
Body:
  not the temple in Greek thought, 53 ff.
  of the individual the temple of God, 103 f.
  the prison of the soul, 55.
  glorified body of Christ the new temple, 68 f., 76, 78 f., 79.
  church as body of Christ, vii, 79, 92, 101, 119, 138, 145 f., 180; see also σῶμα.
Building, 108, 112–20, 180 ff., 193 f., 195–204.
  heavenly, 119, 144–7.
  See also οἰκοδομή, οἶκος, οἰκία, Temple.

Centrifugal movement of salvation in New Testament, 84 ff., 90.
Centripetal movement of salvation in Old Testament, 4 f., 80, 84; see also Pilgrimage.

Church:
  as new temple, vii f., 74, 79, 87, 92–107, 108–20, 125–32, 133, 138 177; see also community, heavenly temple.
  connection of early church with Jerusalem, 84 f.
  expansion of, 87 f.
  theocentric character of church, 106, 118, 180 f.
  holiness, see Holiness.
  relation to Jesus Christ, 98, 106, 118 ff., 127 f., 180 f., 195 ff.; see also Cornerstone, Foundation.
  relation to traditional hope, 138 f., 180.
  organic character, 99, 115 f., 118 f.
  celestial character, 119 f., 142 f., 186 f.
  worship, see Cult; see also Heavenly temple.
  ministry, 183, 185 f., see Priesthood.
  mission, 87 f.
  service in the world, 185 f.
City, see Jerusalem.
  heavenly city of Plato, 38, 205 f.
  in New Testament, 152 ff.
Cleansing of temple, see Temple.
Colt, used by Jesus, 59 f.
Community, as temple, see Temple.
Cornerstone:
  in Qumran literature, 48 f.
  in gospels, 66.
  in Eph. 2. 20–2, 112–16, 120, 195–204.
  in 1 Pet. 2. 6, 127 f.
  in Rabbis, 201.
  Christ, 66, 114–16, 181 f., 195–204.
  not a stone at top of building, 114, 195–204.
  See also Ἀκρογωνιαῖος, Rock, Stone, Foundation.
Correspondence, between earthly and heavenly, 25, 27, 30, 35, 157.
Cosmology, 2, 26, 80 f., 115, 120, 156 f., 189 ff., 203.
Council of Yahweh, 25 f.
Court, of temple, 71 f.

cleansed by Jesus, 62–7, 77–9.
not to be included in measurement of temple, 158 f.
Covenant, 3 f., 5, 67, 152 f., 170, 194.
Cross, 73, 110 f., 164, *see* Jesus Christ, death.
Cult:
  in ancient society, 1–2.
  in Israel, 2, 44 f.
  God's gift, 2, 44, 170.
  of temple of Jerusalem, 4 f., 64 f., 153 f.
  centralization of, 4 f.
  criticism of, 42 f., 46 f., 86.
  reform of cult, 4, 53, 61–7, 77 f.
  equivalents, 42–6, 53, 55 f.
  dilemma of, 44 f., 56 f.
  in post-exilic period, 13, 23.
  in eschatological age, 12, 20 f., 23 f., 64, 130, 175; *see also* Temple, eschatological.
  heavenly cult, 31 f., 35 ff., 152 ff., 161 ff., 165 f.
  union of earthly and heavenly, 36 ff., 153 f., 166 f., 186 f.
  spiritualization of cult, *see* Spiritualization.
  abrogation of traditional cult by death of Christ, 67 ff., 71 ff.
  Christian cult, 85, 107, 129 f., 138, 152–4, 175, 177, 183–6; offered through Jesus Christ, 130, 149 ff., 164, 186.
Cursing of fig-tree, 62–7.

Δαίμων, 54.
David, Davidic leader, 4, 6, 13 ff., 17 f., 21, 50, 59 f.; *see also* Messiah.
Death of Christ, *see* Jesus Christ.
Deep, the great, 157, 163, 189 ff., 193, 201, 203.
Deuteronomist interpretation of divine indwelling, 19, 26 f., 76.
Deuteronomist reform, 4.
Disciples, the eschatological people of God, 60, 67; *see also* Apostles.
Dispersion, 5, 7, 20 f., 44, 55 f., 154; *see also* Exile.
  New Testament reinterpretation, 144, 153 f.
Δόξα, 75, 105 f., 121 f., 173.
Dwelling, *see* Temple, οἰκοδομή, οἶκος, Presence of God.

'Ébhen sheʿthiyyāh, *see* Rock.
Εἰκών, 38; *see also* Archetype.
Election, of Jerusalem, 6.
Elijah, 16.
Entry of Jesus into Jerusalem:
  in the Synoptics, 59–61.
  in Fourth Gospel, 82.
Ethics, 42, 53, 56, 93 f., 97, 102 ff., 183.
Exile, 7, 21, 26 f.; *see also* Dispersion.
  New Testament reinterpretation, 144 153 f.

False witnesses, 67–70, 86.
Festivals:
  at Jerusalem, 4 ff., 13, 20 f., 153 f.
  in the Fourth Gospel, 80 ff.
  in Hebrews, 152 f.
  in book of Revelation, 163 ff., 174 ff.
Fig-tree, *see* Cursing.
Foundation:
  in Old Testament, 198 ff.
  in Qumran literature, 47 ff., 52.
  in ancient building practice, 198 f.
  Christ the, 98 f., 106, 118, 120, 127 f., 182.
  Peter, 193 f.
  apostles and prophets, 112 f.
  of the new Jerusalem, 172 f.
  See also θεμέλιος, Rock in Zion, Cornerstone.

Gentiles:
  converted at eschatological temple, 12 f., 15 f., 17 f., 18 f., 22, 30, 85, 118 f.
  court of, 64 ff.
  salvation of, in Christian era, 82, 84, 89 ff.
  mission to, 88 ff.
  admission to church, 88 ff., 95.
  fellow heirs, 108 ff.
  united with Jews in new temple, 112 ff.
  but not like two walls, 115.
  share in worship, 111 f., 165, 175.
  See also Pilgrimage.
Gerizim, 79, 88.
Glory, *see* Presence of God.
Gnostics, 109, 112, 119.
Γωνία, 196 f.
Γωνιαῖος, 197 f., 200.
Greek influence in New Testament, *see* Platonic Idealism, Stoics.

Heaven, 27, 28 f., 109, 119, 143, 146, 149, 157, 176, 177 f., 205; *see also* Temple, Heavenly building, Heavenly.

High Priest, 35, 37 f., 40, 165, 173, *see also* Jesus Christ.

Holiness, and temple, 1, 36, 97, 101 f., 117, 183.

Holy of Holies:
  in temple of Jerusalem, 10 f., 72 f., 77, 160, 165, 176, 188.
  in tabernacle, 11.
  in spiritual temple of Qumran, 49.
  in heavenly temple, 28 31 f., 148–51, 160, 165.
  Hosanna, 58, 60.

'Ιδέα, 38 f.; *see also* Archetype.

Images, of the church, vii, 179.
  in the Fourth Gospel, 75.
  in Paul, 92, 107, 117, 146, 180 f.
  in 1 Peter, 125.
  in Revelation, 155 f., 160 f., 170, 174 f.
  fusion of, 73, 92, 120, 174, 180 f.

Imitation of Christ, *see* Jesus Christ.

Individual, as temple, *see* Temple.

Indwelling of God, *see* Presence of God.

Jerusalem:
  centre of world, 15, 84, 188 f.; *see also* Temple.
  choice by David, 4.
  divine election, 6.
  centralization of worship at, 3 ff.
  destruction of, 6 f., 32 f., 90 f., 143, 177.
  entry of Jesus into, 58 ff., 82.
  in eschatology, 10 ff., 11 f., 15, 37 f., 53, 123 f., 143, 158 f., 167–76.
  heavenly, 32 ff., 40 f., 141 ff.
  new, 155, 161, 167–76, 177, 187.
  descent of, 34 ff., 176 f.
  council of, 89.
  Paul's attitude towards, 90, 123 f.
  See also Zion, Temple, Festivals.

Jesus Christ:
  and the Kingdom of God, 59, 61, 66.
  entry into Jerusalem, 59–62, 77–9.
  and the temple, 58, 61–74, 75–84, 87.
  and the disciples, 59, 67, 74.
  and Israel, 61, 63, 66 ff., 70 f., 72.
  trial, 67–72.
  death, 67, 71–3, 76, 78, 81–4; as a sacrifice, 67, 76, 83; affects status of Gentiles, 108 ff.; destroys 'middle wall of partition', 109 f.; gathers together the people of God, 67, 82 f.; and the heavenly sanctuary, 148–51; basis of priesthood of the faithful, 164 f., 186.
  resurrection, 67 ff., 72, 78 f., 81 ff., 84, 89 f., 138 f., 146 f., 181, 186.
  the Lamb, 157, 162, 166, 186 f.
  Lamb of God, 76 f.
  displaces the temple of Jerusalem, 75–84.
  the new temple, 75 ff., 78 f., 81.
  foundation of new temple, 98 f., 112–20, 127 f., 195 ff.
  the rock, 81, 136 f.
  the cornerstone, 66, 114–16, 181 f., 195–204.
  the living Stone, 126 ff., 132, 181 f., 203.
  head of the corner, 127.
  High priest, 130, 148 f., 164 f.
  imitation of, 129.
  See also Messiah.

Judgement, 7, 9, 26, 29, 65, 87.

κατασκευάζειν, 134.

Κατοικητήριον, 112, 116, 146.

Keystone, 115, 197 f.

King, *see* David, Messiah.

Kingdom of God, 59, 61, 66.

Κόσμος νοητός, 39.

Lamb, *see* Jesus Christ.

Last Supper, 67.

Law, 44–6, 50, 55 ff., 88 f., 93, 109 f., 121, 141 f.
  and the cult, 44 f., 50, 56 f.; as a sacrifice, 45 f., 50.

Λίθος, 126 f., 193, 199, 202.

Liturgy, *see* Cult.

Λόγοι, 54.

Λόγος, 40.

Man, as temple, *see* Temple.

Mêmrâ, 27; *see also* Presence of God.

Messiah, viii, 16 f., 21 f., 48, 59 ff., 68, 74, 76, 82, 114, 201.
  and new temple, 17 f., 20 f., 31, 66, 85.
  builder of temple, 14 f., 17 f., 72, 118.
  and the cult, 17 f., 65 ff., 77 ff.
  gathers together people of God, 14, 17, 67, 82, 161, 172 f.

See also David, Jesus Christ.
Μίμημα, 24, 38; *see also* Archetype.
Ministry, 98, 183 ff., *see* Priesthood.
Mission, 87 f., 130.
Monolith, 115, 117, 182.
Mount of Olives, 65.
Mount Zion, *see* Zion, Mountain.
Mountain, 21, 28 f., 65, 79, 156 f., 160, *see* Zion.

Name, of God, dwells in temple, 26, 76, 139.
Ναός, 73, 78, 92 ff., 98 f., 101, 108, 112, 117, 135, 158, 160, 164, 173; *see also* Temple.
Nations, *see* Gentiles.
Navel, temple as, *see* Temple.
Neopythagoreanism, 25.

Οἰκητήριον, 144, 146.
Οἰκία, 144 f.
Οἰκοδομή, 92, 98 f., 108, 112, 114, 116 f., 119, 131, 144–7, 181, 196, 200, 203.
Οἶκος, 125, 128, 133 f., 141.

Organic character of church, *see* Church.

Palace, 160; *see also* Temple.
πανήγυρις, 152.
Παράδειγμα, 38; *see also* Archetype.
Parousia, 85, 124.
Passover, 20, 59, 65, 76, 83; *see also* Temple, Festivals.
Pattern, 25; *see also* Archetype.
Paul:
    background, 120 ff.
    work of, 98 f.
    missionary strategy, viii, 90, 123 f.
Pentecost, 85.
Πέτρα, 136, 193 f.; *see also* Rock.
Pilgrimage:
    to Jerusalem, 4 ff., 12 f., 15, 18, 22, 82; *see also* Gentiles.
    motif in New Testament, 82, 147, 151 ff., 162 f., 174 f.
Pillar, 135, 171, 177.
Platonic idealism, 27 f., 38, 40, 149, 154, 205 f.
Πόλις, 38, *see also* City.
Πολιτεία, 109, 111.
Πολίτευμα, 143.

Prayer, as sacrifice, 43 f., 46, 166. *See also* spiritualization.
Presence of God:
    in the temple, 1–8, 26 f., 97.
    in the ark, 3.
    in the tabernacle, 3, 97.
    sanctuaries of Palestine, 3 f., 26.
    on earth, 27 f.
    symbolized by the temple, 1, 3, 183.
    constitutive of people of God, 179 f.
    in heaven, 27–38, 148 f., 154.
    in man, 53–5, 102–4.
    result of grace, 2, 170.
    source of holiness, 1, 183.
    creates unity, *see* Temple.
    restated by Deuteronomist and Priestly writers, 26 f., 76.
    transcendentalized, 25 ff., 40 f., 56 f.
    loss of, 6 ff., 23 f.
    experienced in the exile, 26 f.
    missing from second temple, 23 f.
    promised in the eschatological age, 10 f., 13 f., 20 f., 74, 75, 77, 84 f., 94 f., 96 f., 100, 105 f., 121, 153, 176, 179.
    realized in Christ, 75 f., 77, 85.
    in the church, 74, 95, 100 f., 105 f., 123, 138 f., 177 f., 179 f., 182.
    symbolized by the heavenly sanctuary of Hebrews, 148 f.
    represented in Christian era by the Spirit, 84 f., 101, 105 f.
    different from old dispensation, 95, 100, 180.
    paradox, 182 f.
    See also Temple, Jerusalem.
Priesthood:
    ancient, 1 f.
    at Jerusalem, 23, 64, 68.
    at Qumran, 46, 49–53.
    of Christ, 130, 160.
    of the faithful, 52, 129 f., 158, 161, 164 f., 174, 183–6.
    in heaven, 31 f., 35 ff., 39 f.
    See also Jesus Christ.
Priestly writers, 10 f., 27, 101.
Prophets, 9, 26.
    criticism of sacrifice, 43.
    foundation of church, 113.

Qumran, 15, 36–8, 45–53, 70, 86, 96 f., 100, 102, 113, 117, 120, 122, 128 ff., 137 f., 152, 154, 201 f.

Remnant, 9, 66.
Resurrection, 70 ff., 78 f., 81, 145 f., 181; *see also* Jesus Christ.
Reunion, of people of God, 9, 12 ff., 16 f., 18, 20 f., 67, 74, 82, 126 f., 161, 172 f., 178; *see also* Ingathering, Unity.
River, from the temple, River (water) of life, 2, 80 f., 83, 136 f., 157, 163, 173, 175, 191.
Rock:
  foundation of new community, 52, 193–4.
  sacred rock in Zion, 6, 77, 157, 188–92, 201–3.
  Christ, 136 f.
  Peter, 135 f., 193–4.
  See also Foundation, Cornerstone.
Royalty:
  and divine presence, 14.
  Church's royal character, 159, 164 f., 174.

Sacrifice, *see* Cult.
Sacrificial character of Christian Life, *see* Cult.
Samaritans, 79 f., 87 f.
Sanctuaries of Palestine, 3 f., 26.
  unifying role, 1, 3 f.
  central sanctuary, 1 f., 4 f.
Sanctuary, *see* Temple.
  in heaven, 147–51.
Sea, *see* Deep.
  sea of glass, 156 f.
Semina divina, 53.
Servant of the Lord, 14.
Sheᵏhînāh, 27, 46, 76, 139; *see also* Presence of God.
Shiloh, 3; *see also* Sanctuaries.
Σκηνή, 89, 147 ff., 160, 168, 170 f.; *see also* Tent, Tabernacle.
Σκηνόω, 75.
Σκία, 38, 149, 205; *see also* Archetype.
Soul as temple, *see* Temple.
Σῶμα, 55, 78, 92, 102–4, 106; *see also* Body.
Σῶμα-σῆμα, 55.
Spirit, Holy, 76, 80 f., 83, 84 f., 87, 91, 92, 100 f., 105 f., 117, 122, 138 f., 180, 183, 191.
Spiritual temple, *see* Temple.

Spiritualization:
  in Greek and Jewish literature, 42 f., 53–7; *see also* Stoic.
  inhibited by hope of restoration of material temple, 53, 56.
  in New Testament, 122, 131, 180.
  motives for, 56, 180.
Stoic conception of spiritual temple, 39, 42 f., 53 ff., 104, 122, 146.
Stone:
  Christ the Stone, 132; *see also* Rock, Cornerstone, Foundation.
  Christ the living Stone, 127 ff., 181 f., 203.
  Christians living stones, 116, 128, 181 f.
  of stumbling, 127, 202.
  at Corner, *see* Cornerstone, γωνία, γωνιαῖος.
  keystone, 115, 197 f.
Synagogue, 5, 7, 31, 154, 160 f., 164.

Tabernacle, 3 f., 6, 10 f., 23, 147.
  heavenly, 25, 36, 76, 148 ff., 205 f.
  See also σκηνή, Tent.
Tabernacles, Feast of, 13, 58, 75 f., 81 f., 137, 163 f., 190 f.
Temple:
  significance in Ancient Near East, viii, 1–2, 26.
  dwelling-place of deity, 1–6, 26.
  theocentric character of temple image, 106, 118, 180 f.
  focal-point of community, 1 ff., 11.
  unifying role, 1–8, 10 f., 19, 22, 82, 120, 182.
  centre of universe, 2, 15, 28, 81, 188 f.
  cosmological associations, 2, 6, 26, 80 f., 115, 120, 156 ff., 188 ff., 203.
  navel of earth, 2, 28, 188 f., 203.
  bond of heaven and earth, 2, 77.
  source of blessing, 2, 28, 81, 190.
  source of holiness, 1, 183; *see also* Holiness.
  of Jerusalem, 3–8, 9–24, 47, 53, 58, 61–74, 75–84, 84 ff., 123–4, 140 ff., 158 f., 164, 167 f., 174; altar, *see* Altar; balustrade, 64, 109 f.; foundation, *see* Foundation; pinnacle, 196 f.; veil, *see* Veil; festivals, *see* Festivals; descration of, 23, 73, 103, 158; destruction of, 6–7, 29 f., 32, 46, 65 f., 67–73, 77–80, 86 f.,

143, 159; restoration of, see Temple, eschatological; second temple not satisfactory, 12–14, 17, 22–4, 36; and Jesus, 58, 61 ff., 75 ff., 87; cleansed by Jesus, 58, 61–7, 77–80, 82; attachment of early church to, 84 ff.; displaced by Jesus and the church, 65 f., 75–91.

eschatological temple, vii, 6, 7 f., 9–24, 51, 82, 179 f.; see also New temple, Heavenly temple, Spiritual temple; built by Messiah, 14 f., 72.

man as temple, in Stoics and Philo, 53–5; in Paul, 102–4, 106, 116.

soul as temple, 53–5.

community as temple, in Qumran, 46–53, 55 f., 201 f.; in New Testament, 92–102, 105 ff., 154.

church universal as temple, 106, 108–23, 125 ff.

heavenly temple, in Jewish thought, 25–38, 54, 56 f.; in Paul, 93, 119, 144–7; in Hebrews, 147–54, 205 f.; in Fourth Gospel, 140 f.; in Revelation, 155, 157, 158 ff.; descent to earth, 29 ff., 34 ff., 40, 177.

no temple in New Jerusalem, 171, 175 ff.

new temple, passion; see also eschatological temple, spiritual temple, heavenly temple; relation of new temple to traditional hope, 138 f., 180.

spiritual temple, see man as temple; see Soul as temple; see community as temple; see church universal as temple; see also new temple, heavenly temple.

Tent (of Meeting), 3 f., 160; see also Tabernacle.

heavenly tent, 150, 160; see also heavenly temple.

Testimonia, 94 f., 97 f., 107, 120 f., 127, 131 f., 137 f.

Thanksgiving as sacrifice, 43 f.; see also Spiritualization.

Θεμέλιος, 98 f., 112 ff., 133, 172, 201 f.; see also Foundation.

Throne of God (and the Lamb), 28 f., 157, 160, 163, 165 f.

Tower, temple as, 19, 29.

Transcendentalization, 25 ff., 40, 56 f.

Trial of Jesus, 67–72, 77, 86 f.

Twelve:
tribes, symbolized by sanctuary of Ezekiel and priestly writers, 3, 11.
return of twelve tribes, 21.
council of twelve in Qumran, 48.
gates and foundations of new Jerusalem 172.
disciples, 67.
apostles, 172 f.
twelvefold people of God, 161, 172 f.; see Unity.

Unity:
of community symbolized by temple, 1, 3 f., 5, 7 f., 11 f., 82, 120.
of mankind symbolized by temple, 18 f., 22, 29 ff.
symbolized by new temple, 118, 183, 202, 203 f.
in the church, 98, 101 f., 106, 108, 109 ff., 114 f., 118, 120.
of heavenly and earthly worship, 36 ff., 154, 166 f., 177, 186; see also Twelve.

Ὑπόδειγμα, 149, 205; see also Archetype.

Veil:
of tabernacle, 11, 149 f.
of temple, rent by Christ, 72–73, 109, 149 f., 205.

Wall of partition, 64, 109 f.

Water, see River.

Worship, see Cult.

Χειροποίητος, 67, 87, 148.

Zion, 11, 18, 29, 51, 65, 67, 82, 91, 112, 123 f., 189.
synonym for Jerusalem, 11.
heavenly, 29, 33 f., 151–4, 157, 161 f., 173, 186.

INDEX OF AUTHORS

Aalen, S., 134 f.
Abbot, T. K., 109, 112 f., 115, 195.
Abelson, J., 27.
Allegro, J., 51.
Aphraates, 196.
Aristides, 110.
Arnold, W. R., 3.
Ambrosiaster, 195.
Ammonius, 195.
Athanasius, 115.
Augustine, 79, 115, 195.

Baillet, M., 37.
Barclay, W., 53.
Barrett, C. K., 135, 153, 205 f.
Barth, K., 93, 150.
Barth, M., 109.
Barthélemy, D., 37 f.
Baumgarten, J. M., 49.
Beare, F. W., 127 f., 131, 133.
Bede, 115, 195.
Beer, G., 31.
Behm, J., 44, 53.
Bengel, J. A., 193, 195.
Best, E., 99, 110, 144, 146, 183, 186, 197, 204.
Betz, O., 52, 193.
Bigg, C., 128, 132.
Blauw, J., 84, 130.
Blenkinsopp, J., 59.
Boer, H. R., 85.
Böhlig, A., 197.
Boismard, M. E., 168.
Bonnard, P., vii, 93, 99.
Bonsirven, J., 21, 35.
Bousset, W., 18, 30, 160.
Box, G. H., 34.
Brandon, S. G. F., 91.
Brown, J. R., 46.
Bruce, F. F., 87.
Bultmann, R., 70.
Burch, V., 163.
Burkitt, F. C., 66, 85.
Burrows, E., 2.

Cadbury, H. J., 132, 196.
Caird, G. B., 159, 177.
Calvin, J., 91, 115, 195.

Carrington, P., 58.
Cassiodorus, 195.
Causse, A., vii, 12, 15.
Cerfaux, L., 95, 104, 111, 119, 129, 197.
Charles, R. H., 16 f., 25, 30, 31, 34, 157, 165, 168, 191.
Chrysostom, 195.
Cicero, 53.
Clement, 1, 102, 135.
Clements, R. E., 3, 27.
Cody, A., 147 ff.
Cole, A., 69, 87, 90.
Comblin, J., 156, 163, 168, 174 f.
Congar, Y. M. J., vii, 5, 100, 116, 122, 129.
Conzelmann, H., 63, 85.
Coomaraswamy, A. K., 197.
Corell, A., 80.
Cranfield, C. E. B., 61, 70, 128.
Cross, F. M., 3.
Cullmann, O., 79, 86, 137, 194.
Cyril of Alexandria, 115, 195.

Dahl, N. A., 87, 144.
Daube, D., 22, 205.
Davey, F. N., 78 f.
Davies, W. D., 205.
Deissmann, A., 104.
Dibelius, M., 72, 111, 143, 196.
Dillistone, F. W., 183.
Dobschütz, E. von, 136.
Dodd, C. H., 65, 72 f., 78, 83, 91, 131 f., 180.
Doeve, J. W., 63.
Dupont-Sommer, A., 37, 47, 51 f., 193, 202.

Eastwood, C., 129, 185.
Eichrodt, W., 44.
Eliade, M., 25.
Elliott-Binns, L. E., 85.
Ellis, E. E., 124, 145 f.
Epictetus, 54 f.
Euripides, 53.
Eusebius, 195, 197.
Ewald, P., 117.

Farrer, A. M., 65, 156, 161, 172 f.

Feuchtwang, D., 158, 190.
Feuillet, A., 145.
Findlay, G. G., 103.
Fitzmyer, J. A., 95, 97.
Flew, R. N., 66, 194.
Flusser, D., 138.
Fraeyman, M., 56, 95, 119, 121 f.
Frankfort, H., 1 f.
Freed, E. D., 59.
Freedman, D. N., 1.
Fridrichsen, A., 99, 115.
Friedlander, G., 188, 198.

Gaechter, P., 64.
Gärtner, B., vii, 37, 46 f., 49 ff., 96 f., 100, 133, 138, 152.
Gaster, T. H., 3, 48, 50.
Goguel, M., 58, 68, 70, 72.
Gray, G. B., 25, 32.
Gressmann, H., 18, 19.
Gunkel, H., 26.

Hannay, T., 13.
Hanson, R. P. C., 147.
Hanson, S., 101, 108, 111, 117, 196 f.
Harless, G. C. A., 116.
Harris, J. R., 132.
Hastings, A., 84.
Haupt, E., 114, 202.
Headlam, A. C., 123 f., 132.
Heinrici, C. F. G., 94.
Héring, J., 101.
Hermas, 115, 117, 182.
Hettlinger, R. F., 145.
Hilary of Poitiers, 195.
Hollis, F. J., 198.
Hooke, S. H., 2, 47, 201.
Hort, F. J. A., 131.
Hoskyns, E. C., 78 f.

Isocrates, 53.

James, M. R., 17, 72.
Jeremias, A., 25.
Jeremias, F., 2, 196.
Jeremias, J., vii, 60, 77, 137, 188, 190 f. 193 f., 196 ff.
Jerome, 72, 195.
Jonge, M. de, 32.
Josephus, 19, 59, 64, 72, 134, 156.

Käsemann, E., 119.
Kautzsch, E., 31.

Kennard, S., 68.
Kiddle, M., 167.
Klijn, A. F. J., 86.
Knox, W. L., 88, 204.
Kraus, H. J., 3.
Kühl, E., 131.
Kuhn, K. G., 95, 97.
Kümmel, W. G., 61.
Kuschke, A., 6.

Labib, P., 197.
Ladner, G. E., 197, 199.
Le Bas, E. E. E., 197.
Lightfoot, R. H., 65, 72, 78, 83.
Lindars, B., 60, 65, 70 f., 78, 124, 132, 193.
Lindeskog, G., 73, 150.
Lloyd, W. W., 195.
Lohmeyer, E., 62 f., 70, 85.
Lowe, J., 194.
Luck, U., 149.
Lyonnet, S., 197 f., 201, 204.

May H. G., 3.
Manson, T. W., 58.
Manson, W., 65.
Marius Victorinus, 195.
McCown, C. C., 196.
McNeile, A. H., 68.
Meier, J., 134.
Meinertz, M., 116.
Meissner, B., 25.
Michel, O., 133, 135, 146, 196, 201.
Milik, T. J., 37 f., 46 f.
Milligan, G., 153, 195.
Minear, P., vii, 92, 170.
Moffatt, J., 102 f., 148, 152.
Moore, G. F., 5, 27, 46, 61.
Morfill, W. H., 191.
Morris, L., 76.
Montefiore, H. W., 150.
Moule, C. F. D., 70, 103, 115.
Moulton, J. H., 153, 195.
Mowinckel, S., 16.
Munck, J., vii, 85, 88, 123 f., 135.
Mussner, F., 111 f., 117, 119, 197.

Noth, M., 3 f., 44.
Nygren, A., 150.

O'Neill, J. C., 87.
Origin, 195.

Parrot, A., 190.
Patai, R., 190.
Peake, A. S., 148.
Pedersen, J., 6, 156.
Pelagius, 195.
Percy, E., 197.
Peterson, E., 152, 165f.
Pfammatter, J., vii, 93.
Philo, 19, 39 f., 54 f., 104, 206.
Plato, 38 f., 55, 189.
Plummer, A., 94, 97, 104.
Plumtre, E. H., 133.
Porteous, N. W., 6.

Rad, G. von, 10.
Ramsey, A. M., 76.
Ramsey, W., 199.
Rawlinson, A. E. J., 61 f.
Reicke, B., 49.
Richardson, A., 185.
Robertson, A., 104.
Robinson, J. A., 99, 109 f., 115, 117, 195, 200.
Robinson, J. A. T., 82, 144 f.
Roth, C., 66.
Rudolf, W., 13.

Salmon, S. D. F., 114.
Sanday, W., 123 f., 132.
Schlatter, A., 193.
Schlier, H., 109, 112, 119, 196.
Schmidt, M., 10.
Schrink, G., 66, 73.
Scott, E. F., 62, 66, 195.
Seitz, O. J. F., 193.
Selwyn, E. G., 126, 128 f., 132 f., 145, 193.
Seneca, 53 ff.
Sevenester, J. N., 135.
Simon, M., 70, 86 ff.
Singer, S., 20, 22.
Skinner, J., 19.
Smith, C. W. F., 58.
Soden, H. von, 114, 202.
Spicq, C., 152 f.
Spörri, T., 126, 133.
Stählin, G., 111.
Stendahl, K., 49.
Stenning, J. F., 201.

Stewart, R. A., 46.
Strack, H., and Billerbeck, P., 14, 21 f., 27, 30, 35, 46, 61, 64, 136, 159, 175, 188, 191.
Strugnell, J., 36 f.
Sundkler, B., vii, 15, 67.
Swete, H. B., 166, 172.

Tasker, R. V. G., 97.
Taylor, V., 60 f., 66, 68, 70.
Tertullian, 195.
Thackeray, H. St. J., 191.
Theodoret, 115, 195.
Theophylact, 195.
Thornton, L. S., 93.
Torrence, T. F., 129.
Townsend, J. T., 123.

Unnik, V. C. van, 135.

Vermes, G., 45 f., 51.
Vielhauer, P., vii, 92, 106, 109, 112, 119, 146, 197, 204.
Volkmar, H., 132.
Volz, P., 21, 60.

Wagenführer, M. A., 116.
Warren, C., 198.
Weber, F., 22, 35.
Weiss, J., 99, 104.
Wenschkewitz, H., 30, 32, 40, 42, 44, 46, 53, 56, 104, 106, 122, 197.
Wensinck, A. J., 189, 191.
Wernberg-Møller, P., 47 f., 50, 202.
Werner, E., 60 f.
Westcott, B. F., 148, 150.
Whitaker, G. H., 116, 195, 200.
Whiteley, D. E. H., 146.
Williamson, R., 205.
Wilson, C. W., 198.
Windisch, H., 95, 128.
Wolfson, H. A., 39.
Wright, G. E., 1.

Xenophon, 53.

Yates, J. E., 73.
Young, J. C. de, 141 ff., 168.

PRINTED IN GREAT BRITAIN
AT THE UNIVERSITY PRESS, OXFORD
BY VIVIAN RIDLER
PRINTER TO THE UNIVERSITY